To ... d
I h... s
boo...
ta...
side!
Have a super christmas
Love + huggs
Amy Amy xx

ESCAPE
TO THE
POLE

ESCAPE TO THE POLE

TWO KIWI GUYS DODGE CREVASSES,
STARVATION AND MARRIAGE

KEVIN BIGGAR

RANDOM HOUSE
NEW ZEALAND

A RANDOM HOUSE BOOK published by Random House New Zealand
18 Poland Road, Glenfield, Auckland, New Zealand

For more information about our titles go to www.randomhouse.co.nz

A catalogue record for this book is available from the National Library of New Zealand

Random House New Zealand is part of the Random House Group
New York   London   Sydney   Auckland   Delhi   Johannesburg

First published 2010

© 2010 Kevin Biggar

The moral rights of the author have been asserted

ISBN 978 1 86979 399 9

Design: Carla Sy
Cover design: Laura Forlong
Maps: Janet Hunt

FSC
Mixed Sources
Product group from well-managed
forests and other controlled sources
Cert no. SCS-COC-001217
www.fsc.org
©1996 Forest Stewardship Council

Printed in New Zealand by Printlink

To Magda and Kate
for putting up with us

CONTENTS

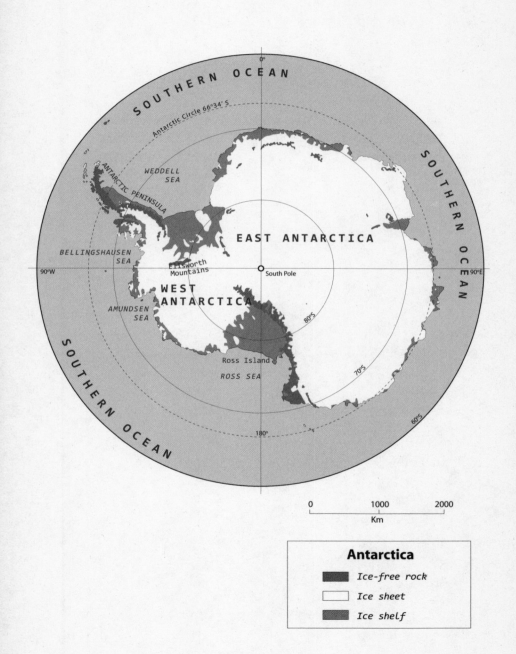

SOUTHERN OCEAN

Antarctic Circle 66°34' S

WEDDELL
SEA

ANTARCTIC PENINSULA

SOUTHERN OCEAN

BELLINGSHAUSEN
SEA

EAST ANTARCTICA

90°W

Ellsworth
Mountains

South Pole

90°E

WEST
ANTARCTICA

AMUNDSEN
SEA

80°S

Ross Island

70°S

ROSS SEA

60°S

SOUTHERN OCEAN

180°

0   1000   2000
Km

Antarctica

Ice-free rock

Ice sheet

Ice shelf

PROLOGUE

A few years ago, during my OE in England, I found myself sitting in a darkened lecture theatre while a tall, well-dressed man with a distinguished voice showed slide after gruesome slide on a screen.

Now an image of toes, bulbous and black as plums. Now a face, horribly gaunt and distorted, with a gash for a mouth, and framed by a straggly beard and crazed hair. There is a collective gasp as the audience realises that it is the man in front of us, but ravaged by unimaginable hardship.

'Sometimes it got so cold in the tent at night that my lips would freeze together and I had to cut them apart with a knife,' he explains.

He is Ranulph Fiennes, one of a new generation of adventurers who have been going back to Antarctica to recreate the exploits of the original explorers: Scott, Shackleton and Amundsen.

Just a year earlier, Fiennes and Dr Mike Stroud had attempted to pull sleds unsupported coast to coast across the entire Antarctic continent. It was much too far, their sleds were too heavy, yet they very nearly pulled it off. Three hundred miles short of their goal, emaciated and nearly out of food and fuel, they had become so weak that they began literally falling over in their tracks. Were it not for their radio contact with the outside world, they would have paid the same ultimate price as Captain Scott.

Fortunately they were both rescued — well, most of them. Judging from the photos, Fiennes wouldn't ever have to pay full price for a pedicure again.

I stare open-mouthed. Transfixed. My stomach churning. I ache to jump into the photos and take my place in the harness, to leap across the crevasses and push on to the horizon. When the presentation is over I stand self-consciously in line to buy his book, more than a little in awe, wanting to somehow create a connection. Wanting Fiennes to look down the line and bark, 'You there! You look like you've got what it takes, young man. We need a helicopter pilot for my next expedition to Mount Erebus. No, no don't worry, all training supplied!'

He doesn't of course. I shuffle to the front and mumble a few embarrassed words as I buy my book. Outside, I put on my op-shop coat, throw my army-surplus boot over my old second-hand bike and squeak out into the night.

And that *really* should have been that.

1. KEVIN OF HOWICK

Lord! Give me chastity and continence — but not yet.

— St Augustine

MY GIRLFRIEND IS LOVELY, charming and delicious. When I come to visit, she runs down the stairs and staggers me back with a two-footed jump into my arms, peppering my face with kisses.

She races me into the surf at Mount Maunganui, turning to laugh at the leadenness of my still-recovering legs. She is always first in the water so she can turn and splash me.

Now we have just run off a mountainside in Turkey and are hanging under two whispering parapentes, high above the perfect white crescent sand of Oludeniz. She laughs and squeals as she flies by, kicking her dangling feet as we float down to the turquoise Adriatic twinkling below.

Now we are walking along the cliffs at Makara Beach, near Wellington, in the afternoon sunshine. We press a blanket into the long grass and lie down out of the breeze listening to the waves suck and grumble below. We snack on pieces of fresh bread spread with tangy blue cheese and capped with a slice of warm, red tomato.

She lies back like fairytale royalty, blonde hair tumbling down over her shoulders, and a drop of rosé on her lips. Drowsied by the wine and the sun, she falls asleep, her hand light and cool in mine. Time obligingly stops and life stretches out, a timeless, sunny, agenda-less dream.

Or is it?

At first the signs are subtle. She is reading a magazine article about a celebrity wedding and I watch as she trails her fingers down the photos as if feeling the taffeta and lace of a fussy bridal frock. Then there is the certain purposeful just-making-sure-you-know-I'm-here snuggling during a movie wedding scene. Now there is a cooing as we pass a trophy toddler in a teddy bear suit being pushed by a glamorous mother.

As I am apparently deaf to these murmurings the volume is turned up. Now there is an accusing glance as she reaches for a tissue during those movie nuptials. Now there is noticeably more elbow in the snuggling. Now the overpackaged babies being pointed out are even further away.

An eyebrow has been raised, an unseen egg timer has been upturned. At some point no answer would be the answer to the question that hasn't been asked.

Mum is not so tactful. 'She's not going to wait around forever, Kevin,' she says, stroking the white ball of fluff sitting on her lap.

Chantelle the Evil Cat smirks through half-closed eyes, and gives a long, low, rumbling chuckle.

This should be an easy decision — I'm with a wonderful woman, why am I hesitating? Why is it so hard to get over the line?

Is it because I'm worried that if I get married and mortgaged I'll lose the restless, driving, thrusting energy of the single man, and instead find myself falling into the abyss of emasculation, at the bottom of which is cardigans, pipes and slippers? Am I worried that instead of estimating the power-to-weight ratios of my hover car, or the decompression stops required to ascend from my undersea base, I'll be sitting on the sofa watching home-makeover shows, lobotomised by oxytocins and spending my weekends choosing between puce and mauve-coloured drapes and matching the doilies for the coasters for the glasses?

Yes. A bit.

Is it because I'm worried that I'll lose that feeling of just being a short plane ride away from unleashing my whip-cracking fedora-wearing bad-arseness on the tomb robbers of the Central Asian Plateau, followed by steamy nights in the moody recesses of a felt yurt palace with grateful, nubile (and commitment-free) Mongoliana princesses? Is it because I know if I get married then these ridiculous fantasies that will, in all likelihood, never happen, will *in fact* never happen? Instead, will the wonderful menagerie of bizarre exoticness that populates my many potential futures be swept away and replaced with crushing ordinariness?

Well, actually . . . maybe. Okay . . . yes.

I know I shouldn't be concerned. Getting married doesn't necessarily stop you from having adventures. Jacques Cousteau sailed the world with Simone Melchior. Admiral Peary, the first man to reach the North Pole, travelled with his wife Josephine around Greenland. Han Solo had Princess Leia. The Lone Ranger had . . . Tonto.

My concerns about monogamous commitment are nothing compared to my fear about what comes with marriage — for just as a tsunami follows an earthquake there would be children. Those incontinent, demanding, noisy, perpetually overstaying, midget house guests. Quite possibly, only a few short months after getting married, I could be submerged in a sea of nappies, preschool, soccer practice, bagpipe lessons, Wiggles, Teletubbies, Hairy Maclary, and when I finally resurface I will be old, creaky and ready for a blanket on my knee.

I sound out my male friends, nearly all of whom are long travelled down this road. In private they discreetly agree with me that other people's children are often badly raised demon spawn. But, they confide, with only a small application of commonsense parenting skills, I, too, can enjoy a wonderful and richly rewarding parenting experience with well-behaved children like theirs. They nod with pride as Junior upends his pudding bowl onto his head before smugly filling his nappies. After their eyes snap back into focus they equally fervently plea, 'I know! Why don't you have mine for the weekend?'

Or they say 'Kids! Wouldn't give them up for anything . . .' And then more quietly as if reminding themselves, '. . . it's illegal'.

I go to a friend's house. It is only 9am and he is draped, as if deflated, on the sofa, the TV is blaring, the floor is carpeted with neglected playthings while his kids are running around at full speed into walls like wind-up toys.

'Where do they get their energy from?'

His head is lolled back, eyes staring at the ceiling. 'They suck it out of me.'

An additional problem is that I seem to have a strange knack of enraging children, particularly boys of a certain age. It doesn't matter if they are normally model infants, or freshly returned from Sunday school with scrubbed angelic faces and neat clothes. One look at me and they turn into snarling, bum-biting berserkers. I might walk into a room only to find myself seconds later staggering around trying to claw off the one who has straddled my neck, simultaneously gouging my eyes and banging me on the head, while his brother is earnestly laying into my legs with a hockey stick.

'Kevin, please stop winding the kids up,' the parents plead.

Even my cute little four-year-old nephew is not immune.

'Hi Uncle Kev! Can I show you a new trick?'

'Sure.'

'Okay. High five?'

I hold my hand up — he socks me straight in the nuts.

As I topple over to the floor it occurs to me that I really should make the most of the time I have before my life is . . . blessed with offspring. That perhaps in the solitude of the wilderness I will find the wisdom to fully reconcile myself to the domestic bliss of a fruitful union.

The only problem is that this kind of thinking has got me into trouble before.

A few years earlier, after a number of curious episodes including a strange pizza-buying experience, it had become clear to me that I was in fact mortal, and what little life I had left was uncannily predictable. I hadn't known what my future would actually hold, but I had thought there would be more jetpacks in it.

In an attempt to grab control of my life I had quit my job, sold my house, left my previous girlfriend to . . . go and get fat on my mum's couch in Howick at the very Edge of the Known Social Universe. After being inspired by an item on the TV news, I decided to take part in the trans-Atlantic rowing race. This was definitely against the wishes of my new flatmate, who warned that in the unlikely event of me surviving I would be broke, jobless and still living at home with her.

After many, frequently improbable, adventures, I was fortunate to find Jamie Fitzgerald as a last-minute replacement rower, who over the duration of the race had become a good friend. And, of course, I had met the lovely Hot Polish Girl (HPG). I had returned much thinner, less neurotic and much more grateful for everything that wasn't blue, wobbly and wet. (See *The Oarsome Adventures of a Fat Boy Rower*.)

Unfortunately Mum's prediction had been remarkably accurate; I was broke, jobless and still living at home with her.

Then things started to improve. I moved out of Mum's house . . . into a friend's garage. Well it used to be a garage, and while it had been recently renovated, you could still park two cars side by side in my living room/bedroom/kitchen. It was at least closer to the HPG, who has started working in a hospital in Auckland.

Meanwhile, Jamie, after winning a spot on the National Bank's graduate training programme, has recently moved up to Auckland. So I've moved out of the garage and we now have a flat together at the end of a row of two-bedroom units in a leafy street in Remuera.

The flat is a refuge of perpetual maleness. From the Fred Flintstone-sized steaks cooked on the barbecue, to the height of the grass growing around the lawnmower. From the sparse and unmatching borrowed furniture, to the well-used bachelor blender in the kitchen, to the number of surfboards, mountain bikes and other toys in the garage. Other brothers and their beers are welcome. Women bearing agendas and leafy vegetables are treated with suspicion.

After a brief resistance I have succumbed to the inevitable and now have a job back in the corporate world working for a telephone company. What's that? Why am I back working and not say . . . making a documentary about base jumping into active volcanoes to rescue orphans? I'll tell you why — life is not just about having fun. Sometimes you have to apply yourself and work Diligently on your Career. That's why I'm back to the cubicles, fluorescent lights, stationery cupboards and fire drills. That's why I'm back on a slippery slope to despair. Literally. The floor in the chic refurbished warehouse I work in is on a slight lean. Knocked pencils keep rolling until they fall off into the bin. I stick them down with Blu-Tack.

I try to explain to the HPG what I'm working on, why I'm so busy, why it's so important and urgent.

'It's to do with, you know . . . the reaction of anthropomorphological constraints . . . to the conditional barriers to diffusion of . . . intermediate technologies . . . in the future.'

She nods and pats me on the knee.

Jamie is feeling it too. We look at each other in the morning and shake our heads as he puts on his tie and clips his name badge on to his short-sleeved shirt, and heads off to a bank branch in the suburbs.

Standing on the dock in Barbados after rowing across the Atlantic, I had felt like I could do anything. Take on any challenge and win. Face anything except Kryptonite. Life then was nothing but potential and opportunity. Was this job the best thing I could come up with? It didn't seem very wild. Had I let a million sharp cuts of practicality kill my mojo?

On the other hand, I might be expecting too much. When you're building towards your future it's not always going to feel like you're making progress. You're not going to have a crowd cheering at the end of every day. No job is perfect and going to work helps to stop the weekends running together and provides the money to keep HPG and I afloat as we drift down a golden river of picnics, holidays, restaurants and parties.

Only now do I notice that the current has started to quicken and that my canoe·is made of barbed wire. Only now do I hear the roar of the Waterfall of Commitment in the distance. Only now do I see the steely glint of determination in the eye of the helmswoman.

When I arrive home from work one day, Jamie is out on the deck prodding a slab of cow on the barbecue.

'Kev, I'm not sure I'm getting nourishment and spiritual fulfilment from my work.'

'Oh, why's that?'

'I just spent three hours looking for a missing $2 coin.'

'Did you try the vault?'

'That was the problem. There were five thousand of them in there that looked exactly the same.'

'Crikey. Don't worry, mate, the next forty years will just fly by.'

There's a long pause. He starts again. 'You know what? We can't just have one book on the coffee table.'

'What are you thinking?'

'Antarctica. South Pole.'

'Sounds good. Let's go.'

'No, seriously.'

'I am serious. I've always wondered what husky tastes like.'

'Anyway, have a think about it. It might be just what we need.'

So I do.

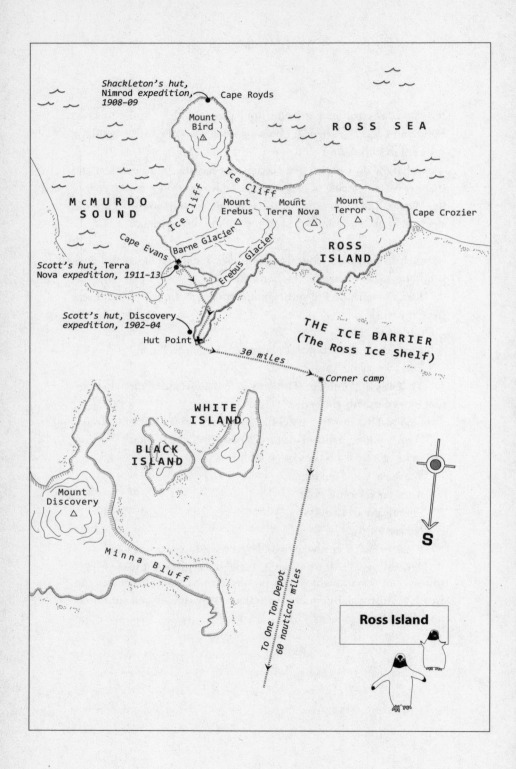

Shackleton's hut, *Nimrod* expedition, 1908–09 — Cape Royds

Mount Bird

ROSS SEA

Ice Cliff

Ice Cliff

McMURDO SOUND

Ice Cliff

Mount Erebus

Mount Terra Nova

Mount Terror

Cape Crozier

Cape Evans

Barne Glacier

Erebus Glacier

ROSS ISLAND

Scott's hut, *Terra Nova* expedition, 1911–13

Scott's hut, *Discovery* expedition, 1902–04 — Hut Point

THE ICE BARRIER (The Ross Ice Shelf)

30 miles

Corner camp

WHITE ISLAND

BLACK ISLAND

Mount Discovery

Minna Bluff

To One Ton Depot 60 nautical miles

S

Ross Island

2. WOODEN BOATS AND IRON MEN, or, 101 WAYS TO DIE IN ANTARCTICA

Men wanted for hazardous journey. Small wages, bitter cold,
long months of complete darkness, constant danger, safe return
doubtful. Honour and recognition in case of success.

— Ad for Shackleton's *Nimrod* Expedition

IMAGINE YOU'RE A JEWEL thief. You have just completed a successful heist. You have split the money, got the girls out of the pool and now need to lay low for a while. Where do you go to hide out? How long will you be able to stay hidden?

Imagine how much harder it would be if you were not your current trim self but have a slight weight problem which makes you twice the size of . . . Australia. But unlike Australia you are ribbed with enormous mountain chains and carry 70 per cent of the world's fresh water on your shoulders in the form of massive ice plateaus several kilometres thick. You're girdled by powerful currents; you change the weather with your vastness and every winter you create voluminous skirts of floating sea ice that double you in size again. Let's just say, it's going to be hard to tippy-toe into Monte Carlo without attracting attention.

It gets worse. For the last thousand years, maps have been available that show where you are. They are mostly just lucky guesses based on sheer speculation, but in some cases spookily given-to-me-by-a-space-alien accurate.

Which brings us to perhaps the most startling fact about the world's most astonishing continent — that it remained undiscovered for so long that the first human footprint was made there scarcely more than a century ago.

With the enormous wealth of the colonies, powerful steam engines and an unshakeable faith in his mission to bring civilisation to savages, Victorian Man could have anything in the world he wanted. What he wanted was wasp-waisted women. Weally.

The expanding middle classes required corsets and corsets required stiffening rods. In those days, the necessary combination of flexibility and firmness required to restrain the bulging bellies of the bourgeoisie could be best achieved with whalebone (more exactly baleen, or whale 'teeth'). Substitutes were being found for whale oil but baleen still fetched good prices.

This was bad news for the whale, who, it has to be said, had not had good news for a while. Certainly not since Norwegian Svend Foyn had invented the exploding harpoon and proceeded to make a fortune blowing up whales — literally. After firing an explosive harpoon into a whale, its carcass was pumped full of air to stop it from sinking. Now, with stocks depleted in the Atlantic and Pacific, Foyn needed to head further south to find some more obliging cetaceans to turn into whale-meat lilos.

So Foyn outfitted a whaleboat, which was sent down to explore the waters around Antarctica in the summer of 1894–95. After shoving through the pack ice into the Ross Sea, they came upon the grim and forbidding cliffs of Cape Adare.

On 24 January 1895 the ship's boat was lowered over the side, and oars were dipped into the inky, freezing waters as it pulled towards the shore. The last great landmass in the world, uniquely untouched, was about to experience its first human boot print. This fact was not lost on any of the boat's occupants, who crouched by the gunnels ready to spring into their place in history.

As soon as the boat reached the shallows there was an unseemly rush over the side and a mad dash for the beach. In their haste, they forgot about the boat boy, who had bravely and quietly got out before all of them to hold the boat steady on the freezing shore break — a sixteen-year-old New Zealander from Nelson, Alex von Tunzelman.

When travelling to America you don't think about scurvy or read up on Christopher Columbus (unless you are planning to fly very cheaply or your flight is going very badly). Of course not — your experience is 500 years and 30,000 feet removed from his.

On the other hand, if you are planning a sledging expedition to the South Pole then your required reading consists of the explorers' accounts written about the handful of expeditions that made up what has become known as the Heroic Age of Antarctic Exploration. Not only did they pioneer the methods and routes, but they set the standards of daring for years to come.

Led by the ruthless and efficient Amundsen, the passionate, scientific Scott, and the swashbuckling Shackleton, they braved the howling gales of the Southern Ocean in small wooden boats and bashed their way through the ice floes to scout out a continent that was *completely* unknown. When Scott found seals with inexplicably large wounds he thought it proof of a southern polar bear, or some other giant snow beastie.

Their reward was pure unadulterated discovery — to see things that no human eye had ever seen before; to be the first to travel in a place so bizarre and novel that they were disappointed if, for example, the trawl net brought up only *few* new species of marine life, and not *lots* of new species.

The price they paid for being trailblazers was suffering and pain, lots and lots of pain. Jamie and I are certain to repeat their mistakes unless we learn as much from their expeditions as we can.

So night after night I open one of their books and find myself milling with the curious crowds on the docks. Each night I read a 'crew wanted' sign and each night I join up only to find myself promptly drowned, splatted, gored, frozen or maddened. I quickly learn that the first survival trick is to be an officer, or at least get yourself a speaking part, because to sign on as just an 'able-bodied seaman' is asking to be flushed off the deck by a large, green wave, cartwheeled into the pitch-black depths of a crevasse, rotted alive by scurvy or starved into a diet of boot and lichen soup.

Unfortunately neither does being an officer always guarantee you immunity from Antarctic hazards. In terms of unhappy endings to be learned from and avoided, arguably none is as excruciating and tragic as the fate of Captain Scott and his colleagues, who died of cold, hunger and dehydration just a few miles from safety.

But that's the end. To understand Scott's tragedy we need to go back to the beginning of the Heroic Age to meet the man who was to set Scott and Amundsen on a collision course. Equal parts dashing hero and dastardly villain, he is the fascinating, enigmatic and contradictory Dr Frederick Cook.

So let's rewind the calendar to the late autumn of 1898 and spin the globe around to the Drake Passage. Here we see a small boat, the *Belgica*, being tossed from side to side as it struggles northwards through the giant southern ocean rollers. A giant wave had swept the deck and dragged a sailor overboard. (Note to self: Use the inside loo in big seas.) A dozen yards behind the boat, his flailing hand manages to connect with the trailing log line, which he now holds in a death-like grasp. Dr Cook is first on the scene and starts pulling him in. Just before the poor man can be reached by outstretched hands, his grip fails and he falls back into immense waves.

The boat is returning from a mission for the Brussels Geographical Society to survey the largely uncharted coast of the Antarctic Peninsula.

The man in charge is the young lieutenant Adrien Victor Joseph, Baron de Gerlache de Gomery, who was apparently fussier about his moustache than the itinerary. For reasons best known to himself, Gerlache did not order the return to South America until strangely late in the Antarctic summer. As they battled north the temperature began to plummet and the sea began congealing into a thick icy porridge, then hard pancakes of ice that groaned as they pushed and squeezed against the side of the boat. Soon the *Belgica* was held fast, locked into the pack ice for the winter.

No expedition had ever wintered below the Antarctic Circle before and they were quite unprepared to be the first, lacking much of the basic equipment and supplies they needed. As the winter progressed, the darkness and cold started to gnaw at the men. When the sun disappeared below the horizon for the duration of winter, the men began to experience a strange and rapid physical and mental deterioration.

Some started to show signs of madness. One announced he was going to walk back to Belgium. Another (worryingly an officer) started to experience heart palpitations and died. Next to die was the much-loved ship's cat. Then the captain couldn't eat and found it difficult to sleep or even breathe. He retreated to his bunk and became certain he would die. With Gerlache also invalided, leadership now rested entirely with Cook.

We become pale, with a kind of greenish hue . . . The night soaks hourly a little more colour from our blood . . . [there is an] air of despondency which has fogged our mental energy.

— Cook

Cook recognised that some of the men were suffering from scurvy. The crew had killed and stored fresh penguin and seal meat before winter, but Gerlache had so despised the taste that he had banned it from the boat. Cook now retrieved the caches, and bullied and persuaded the men to eat the meat. He guessed that somehow the

27

sun, or perhaps heat, was involved in regulating heart rhythms, and had each of the sickest men sit for an hour each day in front of a roaring coal fire. He organised complicated games to distract the men's attention from their grim plight. With unflagging energy and humour, he sustained them through the long dark night and when the first rays of sun returned in spring the men slowly began to improve.

Spring turned to summer, yet the ship remained trapped in ice. When open water appeared some 600 metres away, Cook, once again, took charge, urging the men to cut a channel to it. They worked day and night for a month only to wake one morning to find that the ice had moved and driven the banks of the channel together. All their work had been for nothing. Then two weeks later the crack reopened and they slid through to the open sea and safety.

With the sheer force of his will, extraordinary energy and tenacity, and a little luck, Dr Cook had saved the lives of (*nearly*) all of the men on the *Belgica* and personally nursed many of them back to health. None was more impressed than the young ambitious Norwegian first mate.

This man had learned a lot from Cook about polar survival techniques, how to guard against scurvy, how to wrangle and cajole men through an Antarctic winter (and, more sinisterly, how if you want to keep your authority as a captain don't ever take a doctor on an expedition). He would retain feelings of respect and loyalty towards Cook for the rest of his life. These sentiments would, ten years later, pit him against Scott when they might otherwise have been natural allies.

The first mate was Roald Amundsen.

When the head of the august Royal Geographic Society, the magnificently sideburned Sir Clements Markham, had convened the

International Geographical Conference and implored for an Antarctic expedition, he had of course meant a *British* expedition. It was galling that Johnny Foreigner had ever since been doing all the running around Antarctica, including the recent *Belgica* fiasco.

After all, Captain James Cook had practically mapped the coastline (admittedly without actually seeing it) and then Sir James Ross *had* mapped the coastline, or at least part of it (admittedly without actually landing on it). The British then had moored off it, mapped it, everything but bloody morris-danced on top of it. Antarctica, as everyone knew, was as English as cucumber sandwiches and tea with the vicar!

Time was clearly overdue for a proper British expedition with a serious scientific agenda, and if, in the sober pursuit of geographical elucidation, an Englishman should happen to stand on the South Pole, well then, so be it. Several years of planning finally gained traction when a wealthy industrialist pledged £25,000 towards the expedition.

Markham began making a list of the potential leaders of a new geographic and scientific expedition to the south polar regions. The sixth name on his list was an obscure young torpedo specialist — Robert Falcon Scott.

Scott had worked his way up through the ranks of the navy since joining as a cadet at the tender age of thirteen. Although senior officers described Scott as 'zealous', 'painstaking', 'intelligent' and 'capable', he had to work hard to hide his emotional sensitivity and a quick temper. Throughout his life he struggled for long periods with black moods. While on expeditions he was extraordinarily dynamic and energetic, yet when a fortune-teller came to his house and commented on his 'laziness, untidiness, touchiness and tendency to gloom', his new wife enthusiastically agreed.

For someone in the business of blowing people up, Scott had an aversion to the sight of blood and, perhaps apocryphally, had visited a slaughterhouse to try to cure himself. He particularly hated cruelty to animals. When, during one of his expeditions, he could not bring himself to take his turn at killing huskies, he described his lack of action as 'a moral cowardice of which I am heartily ashamed'.

Yet his strengths far outweighed any weaknesses. Scott's second-in-command for his first expedition described him as 'Athletic, brainy with a keen quick intelligence, great courage and charming manners'. It was a combination of qualities that earned him extraordinary devotion from nearly all his crews. 'I have never known anybody, man or woman, who could be more attractive when he chose,' wrote Apsley Cherry-Garrard, a member of Scott's last expedition.

In June 1900, Scott was appointed commander and leader of the British National Antarctic Expedition, now better known as the *Discovery* Expedition, after the ship that carried them there.

On 21 December 1902 several thousand people lined the docks of Lyttelton Harbour in New Zealand to see off the *Discovery*. New Zealanders had adopted the expedition in the weeks that it had been in the harbour and well-wishers were crowded onto no less than five steamers.

Two weeks after leaving New Zealand, the *Discovery* broke through the pack ice, sailed into the Ross Sea and up to the foot of Great Ice Barrier (now less poetically called the Ross Ice Shelf), the enormous sheet of floating ice, about the size of France, that prevents any further sailing south. They steamed along under frowning cliffs of ice that towered above the masts until they found land and a safe-ish harbour for the winter at Ross Island.

> *The barrier edge . . . looked like a long narrowing black ribbon as it ran with slight windings to the eastern horizon. South of this line . . . a vast plain extended indefinitely, whilst faint shadows on its blue grey surface seemed to indicate some slight inequality in level; further yet to the south the sun faced us, and the plain was lost in the glitter of its reflection.*
>
> — Scott

The main base would be the ship, which they would allow to become iced in, although a hut was assembled on the shore, to provide additional storage and a living room, at a place they called, appropriately, Hut Point.

The days became shorter and shorter, until on 23 April the sun set for four long months. While the blizzards blew day after day, the crew remained snug below deck. When the storms had passed and the moon was up, the men would emerge blinking into an extraordinary, magical scene.

> *The cold white light falls on the colder whiter snow against which the dark rock and intricate outline of the ship stand out in blackest contrast . . . beyond our immediate surroundings is a fairyland. The eye travels on and on over the gleaming plain til it meets the misty white horizon and above and beyond the soft silvery outlines of the mountains. Did one not know them of old it would sometimes be difficult to think them real, so deep a spell of enchantment seems to rest on the scene.*

With spring approaching, Scott did something that hadn't been done by a human being for twenty thousand years — he began to explore the interior of a new continent. His goal was to push as far south as possible.

Scott had originally planned to take only one other man with him — Edward Wilson, the ship's doctor. As well as being an enthusiastic amateur zoologist and artist, Wilson was probably the most popular and well-liked man on the expedition. He in turn suggested taking a third person to increase safety. Scott agreed and they both picked a young, enthusiastic sub-lieutenant, Ernest Shackleton.

Shackleton had been slowly working his way up the ranks of the merchant navy, but not fast enough for his ambitions nor to prove his worth to the object of his affection, Emily Dorman, whom he had been trying to impress for three years. Shackleton's natural preference would have been to join an expedition seeking buried treasure on the

Spanish Main. Those being in short supply when he had heard about the National Antarctic Expedition, he applied immediately.

The southern journey of 1902–03 was a gruesome, horrible ordeal. No amount of kicking and whipping would get the dogs to pull the heavy sled-loads, and for the whole first month they had to shift a half-load 5 miles, drop it off, and then return for the other half. It was risky and heartbreakingly slow, for every mile of progress south they had to travel three.

The UV rays seared their eyeballs, causing agonising pain and temporary blindness. On more than one instance two of the party were temporarily blind and the third only had the use of one eye. Shackleton started to show signs of scurvy, and Scott possibly was as well. They all suffered from hunger; Scott was only spared somewhat by his habit of smoking two pipes a day.

After nearly two months of seeing only featureless ice, they began to make out the peaks of mountains on the western horizon, and veered from their course to raise them higher. This new mountain range appeared to run more or less continuously to the southwest, and so could possibly block the route south.

They were never to find out. By now the dogs were either dead or too weak to pull, and rations were running low. After sixty days of frustrating, painful marching, it was time to turn back. The team had only made it to 82° 11' south. As the skua flies, only around 265 miles from where they started.

On the return trip, Shackleton's health worsened. He was now having violent coughing fits and spitting up blood. Wilson whispered to Scott that he didn't think Shackleton was going to make it. Somehow he did. After three months on the march, they rounded the final cape and saw the *Discovery*. Scott described their arrival:

> *A fairer sight could scarcely meet our snow-tried eyes; and*
> *to mark the especial nature of the occasion a brave display of*
> *bunting floated gently in the breeze, while, as we approached, the*
> *side and the rigging were thronged with our cheering comrades.*

A special dinner was held in their honour but Shackleton did not attend the celebration. 'I turned in at once when I got on board, not being up to the mark . . . It is very nice to be back again; but it was a good time.' Which leads you to wonder what Shackleton would describe as a bad time. A few years later he would be back to find out.

Had you been a penguin sunbathing on the sea ice near Ross Island in the summer of 1908, you would have been surprised to see an open-topped sports car rush past, with a goggled, barrel-chested man at the wheel. Shackleton was back. In style, and at the head of his own expedition.

Since returning from the *Discovery* Expedition, Shackleton had tried to be a journalist, a member of parliament and the secretary to the Royal Scottish Geographic Society, but he had never given up his expedition dreams.

Then his luck started to run. He landed a job as something of a corporate ambassador to the rich industrialist William Beardmore, who was eventually persuaded to put up a highly conditional guarantee for a small loan that Shackleton was able to parlay into real money.

In July 1907, just five months after advancing his plans, Shackleton was off, having purchased an old sealer, the *Nimrod*. After a long voyage, they arrived in New Zealand in mid-December 1907. Antarctic fever gripped the country and fifty thousand New Zealanders travelled over the hills from Christchurch to Lyttelton on New Year's Day 1908 to farewell Shackleton and his men.

For ten straight days, the *Nimrod* was hit by a gale that drove gigantic waves continously over the boat — on one occasion blasting a startled person out of the privy on the stern, on another drowning a dog on its chain. At last the *Nimrod* arrived at Ross Island. A new hut was quickly assembled at Cape Royds, and they settled in for the winter. After the frenetic preparations of the previous months, Shackleton and his men now had time to take stock, consider their position and estimate what their chances were of reaching the Pole.

They were slim to laughable.

Let's start with the good points. No one was going to suffer from scurvy; Shackleton's pantry included Carlsbad plums, eggs, cakes, plum pudding, gingerbread, crystallised fruit, boiled chicken, cans of kidneys, cans of mushrooms and Garibaldi biscuits.

They also had a racy Arrol-Johnston motor car, a present from Beardmore. It had been specially 'polarised' and worked very well provided the ground was flat and there was no snow.

On the negative side, Shackleton's only experience was as the most junior officer on the best attempt so far, and that best attempt had been hopelessly inadequate. The only fact it had proven conclusively was that dogs don't work in the Antarctic. To solve that problem he had brought along . . . ponies.

Yes, Shackleton's Pole party would use Siberian ponies. There was no particular reason for thinking that the ponies were going to be a silver bullet. Pony hooves punch through snow crust much easier than do dogs' paws. Ponies require more food and ponies can't be killed and fed to ponies as a last resort. Ponies also don't like being tossed around on the Southern Ocean. Of the fifteen ponies originally bought, only eight had survived to land in Antarctica and those weren't exactly thriving. Now there were only seven. Make that six. No, five. Wait . . . four.

Then there was the terrain. It was likely that the mountain chain seen on the *Discovery* Expedition would angle around to block the path south. Was Shackleton going to have to be a kind of Antarctic Hannibal, leading his ponies through the alps? Or would there be open water, as he had often predicted?

Then there was the issue with Shackleton himself, who was arguably the most suspect team member. For three weeks in the last expedition, he had been perilously close to death — and a serious liability to his companions. Was it really scurvy that he had suffered from, or some other weakness that would return under strain? Or had it all just been a touch of asthma — as Shackleton now insisted.

The Pole is 859 nautical miles away from Cape Royds. If the team was careful with their food they might be able to spin the trip out for 110 days, which meant they must average 15.6 nautical miles per day. Yet the last time Shackleton had been across this terrain he had covered only 5 miles a day. Furthermore they hadn't had the time to put a depot out on the Barrier to help lighten their initial loads. So as the winter closed in, the expedition had every reason to be pessimistic. But somehow they weren't. 'Shackleton was so enthusiastic and so confident in his own ability that he didn't leave very much for us to think other than success,' an expedition member observed.

On 28 October 1908, Shackleton shut the hut door at Cape Royds and began the march south with his party of three. Every minute was accounted for – there was no margin for error.

Things went wrong immediately. One of the horses went lame and needed to be rested. Another kicked one of the men so badly that you could see the bone in his leg. Another horse bit his way through his tether and ate much of the food on the sleds. So far they hadn't even got past Hut Point.

They rested and restocked. Then on 2 November 1908 they set off again, and climbed onto the Ice Barrier. Slowly, very slowly, they became tiny specks on the vast, white plain.

Since returning from Antarctica, Scott had written a book, become great friends with James Barrie the author of *Peter Pan*, got married to the fiercely strong-willed bohemian sculptor Kathleen Bruce, but most of all he had devoted himself to his career, becoming a battleship commander.

His thoughts kept turning to another Antarctic expedition, but only if it could be done without jeopardising his naval career and his income. As well as providing for his new wife, he was very conscious that since the death of his father (and especially since the death of his brother) he was the sole economic support for his mother and sisters. He had to focus on the practical, on consolidating his financial position and building his future. In other words — he was sticking his pencils down with Blu-Tack.

Then, on 24 March 1909, Scott was walking down a railway platform in London when he saw the four-hundred-point headline of the *Daily Mail* announcing first contact with the *Nimrod* Expedition. Shackleton had come to the end of the Ice Barrier, discovered and climbed an enormous glacier, spent weeks high on the Antarctic Plateau and come within a hundred miles of the Pole before having to turn back.

Scott caught his breath; the prize was still there, waiting to be claimed. Shackleton had not only forged the route but had also shown the method. Bugger a career, there is only so much temptation a man can take. Scott quit his job and started planning for the Pole.

I go to work and get in the lift. The doors open and I walk into the office. Normally by this time on a Monday morning the large open-plan room with its rows of desks is full of people, but today there's just one guy with headphones on browsing the web. I tap him on the shoulder. 'What's going on? Where is everyone?'

He turns around and unhooks an earphone. 'Where have you been?'

'On holiday.'

'Have you spoken to your boss?'

'No.'

He looks left and right. 'Look, I better not say anything. You better hear it from him.'

My mobile rings. It's my boss calling from his car.

'Have you spoken to anyone?' he asks.

'No.'

'Well, sit tight — I'll be there soon.'

And so I find out that our group of more than one hundred staff is to be disbanded and scattered into the rest of the company. My boss is probably going to move on, his boss already has. No one knows exactly what's going to happen, it will all be clear soon. Maybe in a couple of months. Maybe three.

I go back to my desk, and look up at the rows of empty desks and blank monitors filling the floor. All the work I have done over the last year is now meaningless, tipped into a corporate crevasse.

I go for a walk in the park across the street. It's a sunny spring morning; the sky seems very blue and very large. Dogs chasing tennis balls galumph happily through the dewy grass. Kids are laughing and pushing each other as they dawdle to school. A cool southerly breeze blows and the air sparkles with new possibilities.

Scott delayed returning to Antarctica for seven years because he was worried about his financial situation and the impact on his career. I had been concerned about that, too (although now not so much), but mostly because I knew what had happened to Scott.

With his team of Oates, Wilson, Bowers and Evans, Scott arrived at the South Pole on 17 January 1912 to find that Roald Amundsen had beaten them by a month. On the way back, Taff Evans, the largest and strongest, began to weaken and deteriorate. As they came down the Beardmore Glacier he became strangely addled and confused until he finally fell over in his tracks and died.

Next was Oates. He had been suffering from cold injuries to his toes even on the way to the Pole and on the long return trip his condition steadily worsened. As they picked up the depots on the way back there were strange shortages of food and fuel, especially fuel. Winter was arriving and the intense cold made the icy surface cruelly difficult to pull on, but most of all they were slowed by Oates' feet. One morning as a blizzard raged outside, Oates walked out into the whirling white, sacrificing himself so that the others might survive.

Unfortunately it didn't work out that way. Scott, Wilson and Bowers pulled on desperately for the large stockpile of provisions waiting for them at One Ton Depot. Then, just 11 miles out, another blizzard struck. All they could do was lie in their sleeping bags and wait as their meagre supplies of food and fuel expired.

They hoped for a break in the weather, for any chance to make the dash to the depot, but the blizzard was unrelenting. One by one they succumbed to cold, hunger and dehydration.

Scott, alone, in the freezing dark, with the wind roaring outside, finished his journal with these words:

> *Had we lived, I should have had a tale to tell of the hardihood, endurance, and courage of my companions which would have stirred the heart of every Englishman. These rough notes and our dead bodies must tell the tale.*

From the warmth and safety of an armchair, Scott's last words are heart-stirring stuff, but if you think that you might be putting yourself in the same situation then it's another bodily sensation altogether.

Did I have what it takes to haul a heavy sled to the South Pole? It's a question I have been asking myself on and off since seeing Fiennes' lecture all those years ago. Certainly not if it meant going through even half the agony that Scott and his men went through. But surely most of that was due to the fact that those guys didn't have modern techniques and equipment? Nowadays explorers don't suffer like that, do they? I know! Let's see how Fiennes found it.

I pull his book off the shelf and flick through. A paragraph jumps out almost immediately.

*I realised how lucky I had been for fifty years of experiencing
comparatively little pain. Broken bones and teeth, torn-off digits,
frostbite and chronic kidney stones had seemed unpleasant at
the time. But, those nights in Antarctica, I knew real pain for
the first time.*

I give a little cough. Okay. I could do with a second opinion.

'You should talk to Scotty, he's done something like that,' says one
of my surfing buddies about another.

Turns out that Scotty, the shortboarder, is one of the very, very few
people in the world who has completed an unsupported man-haul to
the North Pole. Not the North Magnetic Pole — which you can drive
to — but the actual geographic North Pole, across hundreds of miles
of fragile floating ice, never more than a few metres from the frozen
sea and the drooling snout of a ravenous polar bear.

We meet in a vegetarian café downtown for lunch. Over a bowl of
lentil soup I go through my list of questions. 'So what was the worst
moment?'

'Probably when our sleds broke through the ice and pulled us
under the water.'

'How did you get out of that?'

'Well, luckily I was able to kick off my boots and come to the
surface, and then crawl on my stomach to where the ice was a bit
thicker.'

'Weren't you cold?'

'Fucking freezing.'

'So how did you get warm?'

'Well, first we had to get the sleds. They were bobbing in the
water, but the ice was starting to refreeze again, so we ended up
having to jump in again and pull them out.'

'Did you put the tent up?'

'Fuck off. We just pulled it out of the bag, wedged it behind some
ice blocks and huddled behind it.'

'Did you get the stove going?'

'Fuck off. We just poured the fuel on the ice, lit it and shoved our hands in the flames.'

Okay. I could use a third opinion.

The conversation that kept coming back to me was one I'd had with a guy who had trekked to the South Pole. I had spoken to him even before rowing the Atlantic, and when I had asked him about the cold he had said, matter-of-factly, 'You know it's going to be cold — you take extra mittens.'

This is the key. If we *know* something bad might happen we can avoid it. I had read the adventures of the Heroic Age, I had read Fiennes; we didn't need to repeat their mistakes.

That evening I'm at the flat reporting back to Jamie. 'You know, I think we can do it. You don't have to come back from Antarctica with black stumps.'

'Oh yeah. They only get the stumps when they cut off the frostbite.'

'Ever done any skiing?' I ask.

'Not really.'

'So is that none?'

'Yep.'

'Ever been in snow?'

'Oh yeah. A couple of times. What about you?'

'I worked on a ski field once for a season. Last time I skied, I hit a tree and nearly broke my leg.'

'So it would be fair to say we are a bit undercooked in the expertise department.'

'Sure, but we can learn and if we're good at anything it's pulling heavy things for a long way.'

I slide back in the sofa. The dream again! What would it be like to lean into the harness, to pull my way across half a continent under my own power, to straddle a yawning crevasse with my skis, to breathe in the thin air of the polar plateau? To spend day after day walking towards an open horizon, with every step counting solidly towards a goal? To have life back in sharp focus once more? What would it be like to reach out and *touch* the South Pole?

I could make a pretty good guess. It would be that feeling of reaching the harbour at the end of the trans-Atlantic rowing race. I would be light-headed with elation and relief, and pressurised with pride. I would have a feeling of omnipotence that would last . . . at least until I arrived back at Mum's. To get that feeling again, I had to take on one of my wildest dreams and fight to make it real. Trekking to the South Pole certainly qualifies. In my pantheon of Things That Would Be Really Cool That I Will Never Do, it's right up there with rocking Wembley Arena and landing on Mars, with the advantage that I wouldn't need to leave the atmosphere. I start to feel the nausea that comes with a looming obsession.

But hold on there, Tony Robbins. There's a reason why it's in that box — time and money. If we can't raise the money then I'm going to bankrupt myself back into being Mum's flatmate again, and even if we do get sponsorship then I'm going to spend eighteen months flatlining my career.

Jamie interrupts my thoughts. '. . . and you know it's not always going to be easy to drop everything and do these things . . .'

'What are you saying?'

'You know what I'm saying.'

I thought for a moment. What? NO!

Jamie nods his head.

'It's going to happen one day, and it might be sooner than you think . . .'

Of course, but to another Kevin in a parallel universe.

'. . . then you'll have kids.'

I'm out of the sofa like I just spilled hot coffee in my lap. 'South Pole then — what do you say?'

'Someone has to come and pull you out of the crevasses.'

Scott announced his *Terra Nova* expedition to the South Pole on 13 September 1909. The next day his wife gave birth to their son.

3. THIRD MAN TO THE POLE

YOU THINK THAT SCOTT and Amundsen were a long time ago? Well, what do you say when the third man to travel overland to the South Pole offers you a scone?

'Go on, take one,' says Sir Edmund Hillary. 'You're going to need it.'

We're in Sir Ed's sunny living room, looking out over the rooftops of the northern slopes of Remuera. We are surrounded by mementos and awards, Buddhas, statues, medals and certificates from all around the world.

I haven't seen Sir Ed since finishing the Atlantic row. Although he just now met us at the door with sticks, and seems occasionally hard of hearing, his voice is still strong, and he has the same sharp sense of humour and quick and loud laugh. It isn't difficult to imagine him as a young man directing the unloading of a yak train, or circling the tractors to face an oncoming blizzard.

'So how was *your* trip?' asks Jamie.

At the end of 1956, Sir Edmund Hillary, just three years after summiting Everest, was leaving New Zealand again on another adventure — this time to provide support for the Commonwealth

Trans-Antarctic Expedition, led by the English explorer Vivian 'Bunny' Fuchs. The New Zealand contribution to the expedition was to set up a base camp in the Ross Sea area (Scott Base), winter over and then, using modified Massey Ferguson tractors, lay out depots to within 300 miles of the South Pole. There, the New Zealanders were to wait for Fuchs' party to arrive from the other side.

Although the tractors broke through the snow crust many times or teetered on the edge of terrifying drops, Hillary and his team still managed to arrive at the last depot on schedule.

Hillary then radioed Fuchs to say that he had left the depot to 'prove the route' another 200 miles. And so it was that a week later Hillary found himself just 200 miles from the pole. Through the crackly Morse code transmissions, officials in New Zealand sensed a scandal and told Hillary not to go further. He ignored them.

By this time Hillary's party was committed, only carrying enough fuel to get them to the Pole. He radioed Scott Base to say that he was 'heading hell-bent for the Pole . . . God willing and crevasses permitting'.

On 4 January 1958, forty-six years after Scott, Hillary and his men became just the third team to travel overland to the South Pole.

So now, nearly fifty years later, Jamie and I are in the living room of Sir Ed's house, with maps spread all over the floor and Lady June bringing in the tea and Sir Ed telling the story.

'So the problem we had was that it got so cold that the diesel would freeze in the fuel lines, so then we would have to draw straws, and the person who drew the shortest was given the blowtorch and it was his job to use it to thaw out the fuel lines . . .' He smiles at the look on our faces. '. . . while the rest of us stood well back.'

He leans forward in his chair. 'So what are you thinking of doing?'

Good question.

The problem is that Antarctica is hard to get to. There are cruise ships that visit — but most of them nose around the bays of the Antarctic

Peninsula to look at the waddling penguins and marching seals. But the peninsula is serrated with sharp mountain ranges and no place for a couple of novices to start an expedition to the Pole.

There are one or two cruise ships that get close to the Ross Sea, in the area of Scott and Shackleton's huts, but they only arrive near the end of the summer season. So again, no good for us — unless we want to go 'old school', build a hut and winter over. Which would be a great idea if we didn't mind the near-continuous gales, air-liquefying cold and months of complete darkness huddling in a portacabin listening to the wind peeling off the cladding.

So we have to fly down. Only that isn't easy either, as the signatory nations to the Antarctic Treaty (essentially everyone) aren't allowed to offer anything other than humanitarian assistance to private expeditions. So there is no chance of hitchhiking on one of the several flights that leave from Christchurch to McMurdo Sound every day in summer.

There is, however, a private company, Antarctic Logistics and Expeditions (ALE) who have established a niche supporting teams climbing Mount Vinson, Antarctica's highest mountain, and a small number of expeditions to the Pole each season.

Then once you arrive in Antarctica you have a couple of big choices. The first is where do you start from? The über purists want to start with their boots in the water, or at least on pack ice, a long, expensive plane ride away. Those of a more practical nature start from Patriot Hills base camp, some 24 miles away from the coast. The romantics have established a convention of starting at a place called Hercules Inlet, at 80 degrees south, 80 degrees west, where the land starts to drop under sea level — the beach, as it were.

The second big choice is *how* you travel. Many cups of tea have been spilt by armchair adventurers at institutions like the Royal Geographic Society and The Explorers Club of New York when ranking the worthiness of expeditions in this regard. Essentially, credibility among your peers comes down to how well an expedition is able to uphold the standards of minimalism and self-reliance set by the Heroic Age. So any mechanical assistance is immediately ruled out — with the possible exceptions of pioneering new routes, or moon landings.

The impression you get is if you were to knock on the oak door of the RGS and announce that you had just, solo, unassisted and unresupplied, forged a new route, travelling only at night and in winter, eating only organic pemmican, wearing hand-stitched garments made from the hide of a seal (that has died of natural causes) and navigating by a sextant you've constructed from penguin bones then will you be shown to the armchair next to the fire, brought a brandy snifter, and have an attentive and admiring audience.

If, on the other hand, you had just strolled along a known route with a helicopter dropping off a steak meal and a hot shower every few days, then you can help yourself to a Diet Coke from the vending machine in the staff canteen.

Of all these distinctions there is only one that anyone agrees on — and that is whether or not you were resupplied during your expedition. Which is just as well because being unresupplied means starting off pulling everything that you need, and pulling heavy things is something that we know we can do.

To haul unsupplied to the South Pole from Hercules Inlet would put us in with a pretty exclusive crowd. More than 4000 people have climbed Mount Everest, but only around fifty people have trekked unsupported to the South Pole. But maybe we could do a little more?

Recently, adventurers have started using traction kites to pull sleds. In some respects this is nothing new; Scott and Shackleton used sails on their sleds to help speed them along. Fiennes and Stroud used a modified parachute (until it towed them into a crevasse) and now kites are being used on very long trips. Kites can't help us on the way to the Pole, as we will be dragging into the katabatic winds that howl off the Plateau — but quite possibly could on the way out.

Sir Ed is still waiting for our answer.

'We're going to try to make the first ever unresupplied trek from the coast to the Pole and back. We'll start from Hercules Inlet and then use kites as much as we can to tow us back.'

He raised his eyebrows. 'All of that unsupported? Well, it's good to do something new . . .' He looked dubiously at the map. 'How far is it?'

'Around 2200 kilometres.'

He frowned. 'Are you sure you won't need depots?'

'We'll be laying out the depots we need for the return leg on the way in.'

He nodded.

Sir Ed farewelled us with a strong handshake, a cheery wave and one last bit of advice: 'Watch out for crevasses. We found them all the way to the Pole.'

There were days when a man could happily announce to his wife he was going on an expedition to Antarctica, stuff a jersey into a duffel bag, and then turn and wave from the gate to his spouse on the doorstep. She, with bulging belly and a swarm of young children, would beam back with happiness and pride. And that would be him gone for two or three years or so.

Unfortunately those days were over by Edwardian times. The reaction of Scott's new wife was a pitch-perfect passive-aggressive put-down. Kathleen Scott said, presumably through gritted teeth, 'You shall go to the Pole. Oh dear me, what's the use of having energy and enterprise if a little thing like that can't be done?' You can almost see her boot in his backside as she skittles him out the door, his suitcases following shortly.

As I drive to HPG's house to tell her the exciting news about my plans, I rehearse the conversation in my head. It doesn't matter how I play it — it's going to go well.

HPG will see through this. She will be pleased at the positive approach that I'm taking to put to bed the last of my boyish ways. She will realise straight away that this is just a last hurrah before I settle down to the serious business of matrimonising. In fact, she has probably been expecting it. Secretly hoping for it, even. She will know that my telling her I'm going to Antarctica — well, it's practically a marriage proposal! In fact, am I giving too much away? Am I being too obvious? I don't want to spoil the surprise because if there's one thing I know — girls love surprises.

That didn't go quite as I expected. In fact, there was a bit more silence than was strictly required. Chilly silence.

'Honey, you know how we've been going out for a while,' I had started.

'Yes?'

'And we've been getting on quite well.'

'Yes!'

'Well, I was thinking of trekking to the South Pole.'

'Oh really . . . ? How long will you be away for? Two weeks?'

'More like four months.'

'And what do you know about pulling a sled?'

'Well, not much, but we can learn.'

'I see.' Her forehead knitted into a frown, no doubt concerned about my welfare.

'Honey, it's not that bad. It isn't nearly as dangerous as the Arctic.'

'Oh it's not . . . ?' (Long pause.) 'So where will you be doing your training?'

'The Arctic.'

The look on her face told me this wasn't going well. Pull up! Pull up!

'Actually, it's Jamie's idea.'

4. THE OLD TYRE AND CHAIN

I'M WATCHING TV ON the couch one Sunday night when Jamie returns from a friend's wedding in Hamilton. He had mentioned that his ex-girlfriend Kate was going to be there, so as he drops off his bag in his room I open a couple of beers and settle back to hear what happened. He's not his cheerful self. Instead he seems strangely . . . strange.

He accepts the beer and sits down on the other couch. He takes a breath and speaks to the air a metre in front of him.

'You know, mate. I think Kate's the one.'

'Kate's the one?'

'Yes.'

'You mean . . .' My head spins. 'You don't mean . . . the last one?'

'Yes.'

I look at him closely. His eyes are glazed with emotion. This is clearly a momentous decision for him. Perhaps I should give him some support. 'Are you nuts?'

'Nup.'

'But don't you know what you are giving up?'

'What am I giving up? She's amazing.'

Suddenly the room seems hot and my collar seems very tight, even though I'm wearing a T-shirt. If I had tippy-toed around the edges of the pool of bachelorhood, Jamie had swan dived in from the high board and splashed around doing backstroke and blowing waterspouts. If he's had enough . . . then for some reason that puts a new spin on things.

'I might move down to Wellington after Christmas to be with her.'

'The end of the flat?'

'Yep. Sorry, mate.'

'Bugger. I suppose that means moving back to Mum's.'

'Don't think of it as moving back home. Think of it as moving up to base camp.'

I'm meeting with Jon Ackland from Performance Lab for advice about the expedition. Jon is known as a high-performance coach for athletes, but really he is a chiropractor — he stiffens spines, straightens out heads and works the kinks out of logistics. He had been a big part of our win in the Atlantic race, so I'm back in his office in Birkenhead to get some more high-decibel, double-shot espresso advice.

'You know the drill: TRAIN IN THE SAME GEAR, PULL THE SAME WEIGHT, EAT THE SAME FOOD. When you get down there NOTHING should be a surprise. NOTHING should be new. What's that book that Ranulph Fiennes wrote?'

'*Mind over Matter.*'

'I think I've read it. Is that the one that's basically: "IT'S COLD, IT'S WHITE AND I HATE MIKE STROUD"?'

'That's the one.'

'Isn't there a scene where they have just been dropped off at the start, Fiennes clips onto his sled and complains about how heavy it is? AS IF HE DIDN'T KNOW?'

'I'm sure it was just dramatic licence.'

'I hope so. Why didn't they train themselves into CLYDES-DALES? Your aim is to be so fit that when you hook onto your sleds and start pulling for the first time you shouldn't be moaning, you shouldn't be smiling, YOU SHOULD BE LAUGHING!'

'Yep. Got it.'

'Most people train by pulling tyres, don't they?'

'Yes.'

'Then mostly they get bored and do something else?'

I grin. 'Yep.'

'What are they thinking? If you want to be good at TOWING HEAVY THINGS FOR A LONG WAY, YOU'VE GOT TO TOW HEAVY THINGS FOR A LONG WAY! I can write you a training plan for that, don't worry about it.'

'OK.'

'Now, what do you call those ice features that you have to pull over — the ones people are always grizzling about?'

'Sastrugi.'

'That's right. Sastrugi. You're going to need to recreate those somehow. You should be pulling your tyres up and down the curb and through obstacle courses or something. You need to get used to the frustration.'

'OK.'

He pauses, tapping his fingers on the desk.

'I'm just trying to think. WHERE'S THIS GOING TO GO WRONG? It's going to come down to COLD INJURIES, YOUR GEAR and YOUR FEET.'

'Roger.'

'So where are you going to learn about the cold?'

'We're going to Baffin Island in the Arctic in February to a place called Iqaluit. Then we're going to spend a weekend in a commercial freezer later on to test out our gear. And we're going to spend a week at Mount Cook learning crevasse rescue.'

He nods. 'All right. What about the gear?'

'We're still sorting that out.'

'OK. Don't cut any corners.'

Jon goes back to finishing off the training plan while we talk about foot care. When he's finished, he hands it over to me. 'And Kevin?'

'Yes.'

'IF YOU GET A SINGLE BLISTER DOWN THERE, YOU ARE THE WORLD'S BIGGEST IDIOT.'

We calculate that the sled is going to weigh around 160 kilograms. That sounds like a lot, but it's on snow right? So it should glide. We get some old tyres and chain them up. How many should we use? How does the friction of a fibreglass sled with polyethylene runners on snow compare to a tyre on asphalt? Thinking that it's safer to err on the side of caution, we decide to fill up one tyre with concrete. It's satisfyingly heavy. It takes two of us to get it into the boot of the car. For our first trial drag, we go to the giant car park at the Ellerslie race course, not far from us, where we won't draw so much attention to ourselves.

Jamie gets into the harness and takes a few small steps forward until the ropes tighten. He leans forward, and then leans forward some more. His thigh muscles bulge; he is now in the position of a sprinter coming out of the blocks. Finally the tyres creep forward a few centimetres and stop. With another huge effort, Jamie takes another half step and stops. He looks up at me. 'How far to go?'

We laugh. Then we sob.

'Go on, give us a go.'

So I get into the harness. I lean forward and pull until the thin tapes feel like they are going to cut me in half. Still nothing.

'Get off the back,' I shout over my shoulder. 'Quit messing around.'

Jamie walks around in front of me.

'The bad news, my puny friend, is that it's all you.'

I have to lean so far over that I can almost touch the ground before the tyre even seems likely to move. I take a single shaky step. Training has begun.

The novice surfer, as he takes his board down from the roof rack, looks out at the waves and secretly imagines that today, just for a moment or two, he might look like Kelly Slater. The training cyclist pulls on their shoes, clips into the pedals and for a few seconds feels like Lance Armstrong.

The training sled hauler goes into the garage and hooks onto the tyres, knowing that for the next hour he is going to look like a deranged refugee from a junkyard.

It takes us both a long time to get over the embarrassment of drawing so much attention to ourselves. We initially try just going out at night, or to the reserve at Bastion Point, or the beach, or the race course, but it isn't always practical. It's just plain easier to hook on and pull straight out of the garage into quiet unsuspecting suburbia, chased by four bobbing, weaving lumps of smelly old rubber. They each have a life of their own, wrapping around lamp posts, dropping into drains, gouging up the grass and otherwise scraping noisily and reluctantly along the footpath. Security lights flare, curtains twitch, dogs howl, cars swerve — but after ten minutes you're beyond caring.

I caught up with a friend of mine I hadn't seen for a while who had just come back to Auckland.

'How are you finding it?' I asked.

He makes a face. 'You know the neighbourhood's not what it was. There are some strange people around. I mean there's this nutcase who keeps dragging tyres past our house at night. But anyway, what are you up to?'

We've managed to convince ourselves that the cement-filled tyre is unnecessarily pessimistic, but even with four empty tyres it's hard to get used to going so slowly. After five minutes of hard pulling, Jamie can still get me for a phone call at the house. Going up hills, I put my head down between my poles and jerk my hips forward. Banging away with the sticks like a spastic grasshopper. Sometimes I think things have improved and then I turn around to find that a tyre has become unfettered and is 50 metres back up the road.

Going downhill, depending on the surface, you can either still be pulling or trotting faster and faster with the tyres threatening to lasso your ankles like heavy rubber bolas.

People come up to me — I'm not exactly hard to catch — to ask me what I'm doing. Or they stand at the letterbox while I go past; there's plenty of time to chat.

'Which way are you headed?' one asks.

'The South Pole.'

'In that case, you're heading the wrong way! Hee hee!'

The sight of someone shackled to four tyres often gets a response from occupants of passing cars. But I am still taken by surprise one day when I hear the squeal of tyres and look up to see a car bearing down on me, filled with young guys leaning half out of the windows, pumping the air with their fists like chimpanzees. As they roar by, one of them gently enquires: 'Loser! Where's the rest of your car?'

Jamie comes in from a training session. He staggers through the door of the flat, his mouth ringed with salt. He lunges for the juice in the fridge and empties half of the bottle into his mouth before his chest stops convulsing.

'How was it?' I ask.

'Epic. Legendary.'

'Will the old men sing songs about this day?'

'Verily they will raise their goblets and drink with gusto. Maidens will come a-playing. The fatted calf will be slain.'

'So where did you get to?'

'Bottom of the road and back.'

(In fairness, it's a steep road.)

Jamie pauses for a long time. 'You don't think that this is what marriage is going to feel like, do you?'

Any hopes I had that Jamie's new revelation about Kate might evaporate have been proven wrong. So some weeks later I find myself in Mum's driveway with a Toyota Starlet full of my junk.

Carlos, Mum's Portuguese boarder, is waiting at the bottom of the stairs. 'Eh boy — miss your mamma's cooking? When are you going to come and work in the hotel?'

I go up the stairs and open the door to my room. Chantelle the Evil Cat runs out leaving a trail of white fluff. That's strange. She knows she's not allowed in here.

Carlos is still in my old room, so I'm back in my sister's, who's still overseas. I sigh as I drop my bags on the bed. Nothing has changed. It's all still here. The frilly tassels on the bed, the George Michael poster, the soft toys.

But what's that smell? I look down. Chantelle has regurgitated a large fur ball as a welcome home present for me. I look up to see her little white face peering around the door. If cats had lips there would be no doubt as to the expression on her face.

I sit on the bed. Here I am again. Back at Mum's. The Hotel California of Howick. These last few years my life has seemed to have a nasty habit of repeating itself — like a soap bubble circling the drain hole. If I want to start moving forwards, I need to make a decision, pick a course and hold to it.

Obviously I'm not going to do it soon (and I strongly reserve the right not to do it at all!), but if I were going to do it, what would I do? The room starts to spin and there is a roaring in my ears. I'm just going to sit down for a bit. I'm going to have to do this one step at a time. OK, I need to buy a ring.

Buy a ring? Don't they come in different like . . . types? What kind of ring would she want? Where can I find a jeweller? I don't think I've ever seen one. The way my heart is pounding, I'm going to have to take this very very slowly.

I may not be very smart in the romance department, but one thing I do know is that girls love surprises. Love them. So it's very important that I give away no inkling to HPG of what is (what may be, might be) in store. She will get no suggestion or hints. Any overtures or enquiries from her side must be firmly rebuffed. She has to be put off the scent, as this will only make the proposal (when it comes, *IF* it comes) even more delightful and astonishing.

I find a jeweller's shop in the phone book. I drive to the address.

Yep, there it is. How about that? I must have gone past it a hundred times and never noticed it. I wipe my brow and keep driving. Man, it's hot today.

We need to learn how to fly kites. These aren't the bamboo and newspaper kites we used to make as kids. These are big double-skinned traction kites, scientifically designed to harness their motion through the air to create a very efficient aerofoil. On the ground they look innocent and cheerful, like a brightly coloured duvet just out of the wash. In the sky they hum and howl as dozens of nylon lines, pulled tight as piano strings, slice the air, and scatter onlookers.

The pulling force is exponentially proportional to the kite's flying speed. On calm days you are working the handles continuously in a figure of eight to keep the kite moving to get any power. But in only slightly stronger winds, making the wrong kind of swoop is to risk a ballistic experience similar to Mr Sulu engaging warp drive. The instruction manual is very clear that you must never launch the kite into the area in the sky directly downwind from you — the 'power zone'. If you do, the kite will accelerate into the air right into the most powerful part of its range and deposit you in Oz.

Other than that, it is fun to stand in the grassy fields of Bastion Point, looking over the sparkling waters of the gulf, and have the kite carve graceful arcs in the sky while I imagine smooth white snow hissing underneath my skis as we return from the Pole.

One day I arrive at Bastion Point to find the wind is slightly stronger than I would have liked, definitely too strong for safe kiting. But seeing the trig station, I get a cunning idea. After carefully laying out the kite, I go back to the car to get one of the tie-down straps used to keep stuff on the roof rack. I loop one end around the back of my harness and the other around one of the steel crossbars of the trig. Now firmly secured, I hook the kite on and give the lines a flick. Clever, eh?

The kite comes off the ground unevenly — in three quick bounces it repositions itself directly downwind, pauses for a moment, then rockets into the air. Immediately behind me, the line twangs tight and I'm hoisted off the ground, eyes bulging and legs kicking. I have created a giant slingshot, and I'm the marble.

The kite spins crazily in the sky; the lines stretch, the harness tightens, and there is an ominous groan of steel behind me. With a bang, the tie-down strap snaps and I hurtle forwards as if shot from a circus cannon, before being dragged like a torpedo through the long grass, sieving the paspalum through my gritted teeth, before the kite finally tangles itself to death.

A car has been parked for a strangely long time outside a jeweller's shop. Curious passers-by see a man in intense discussion with the steering wheel.

'Now Kevin, you're here to look at rings. People do it all the time. Looking at rings isn't buying rings, it isn't getting married. It's not like you're going to walk into the shop and walk out with two kids in a pram. Now get out of the car and go in.'

I walk in. With a disquieting thump the door shuts behind me. In the dimly lit room the bright counters eerily light up the faces of the staff, transforming their smiles into leers of the undead.

'Can I help you?' one croaks.

I back out gasping into the street.

Just as Rio de Janeiro has the Corcovado — the giant statue of Christ with his arms outstretched on a hill overlooking the city — Wellington has the Brooklyn wind turbine, an old 225-kilowatt Vestas, swinging its 13-metre arms on a ridgeline 350 metres above the sea.

It is a very respectable climb to run, the views out over the city and harbour are sensational, but it's not the top of the hill. The road keeps winding up further to the white mushroom domes of the Hawkins Hill radar station at some 480 metres. I had done this run only once before, and while I stood there gasping I could see that a dusty mountain-bike track fell away precipitously to the crashing waves of the south coast below. I hadn't been game to try it; I could survive the jog down all right, but then how would I get back up?

Since Jamie had moved to Wellington we hadn't been able to keep good tabs on the other's training. Oh, there had been a lot of crazy talk on the phone about the extraordinary number of tyres that were being dragged and the multitude of Sherpas needed to carry the bottles of oxygen required for the altitude of the peaks climbed and so on. Now I'm down here so we can compare how we are progressing, side by side, on one of Jamie's training routes that he assures me is 'fairly typical'.

From the car park outside the Kelburn Wildlife Sanctuary we grind our way up the hill. Keen to get bragging rights, it soon develops into a race. The trick is to try to get the other person talking, and as they waste their wind you can sneak past them. In this way, we pull up the mountain-bike tracks to the wind turbine and keep going up to the radar station. We suck on our camelbaks and eat chocolate while enjoying the incredible views over the foam-flecked Cook Strait and even to the shadowy peaks of the Seaward Kaikouras at the top of the South Island, more than one hundred kilometres away. The air smells unbelievably fresh. I had read somewhere that when it's been blowing from the south for three days the actual molecules of air that you inhale come direct from Antarctica. Down below us the waves tumble onto the wild beaches.

'Feel like a swim?' says Jamie.

'Serious?'

'Yep.'

'Is this really your normal training?'

'Well, I've done it once.'

'What's it like coming back up the hill?'

He points with his ski pole towards a ridge halfway down the slope. 'You see that little patch of grass?'

'Yeah.'

'That's where I threw up.'

The tyres bob around our ankles as we descend along the switchback bends, down down down to the sea. Halfway. Then we turn around and head back up the hill. With our shoes slipping on the gravelly track and the tyres eager to run back down the hill, we can make only one slippery centimetre at a time. Our legs are burning and sweat is pouring off our noses onto the ground as we lean over to pull. The effort is phenomenal.

'You think this is what the hill from Hercules Inlet is like?' I gasp.

'I hope not.'

It's dark by the time we get back to the wind turbine and wind our way through the trees with our headlamp lights on. Surely nothing in Antarctica can be as bad as that.

I've made it into a jeweller's again.

'Can I help you?'

'Ah no, just looking thanks. Well, what does this one cost?'

'That one? That's on special — $19,995.'

'Oh really?' I squeak. 'How . . . reasonable.'

Now that I have desensitised to the point that I can focus, I buy a diamond from a New York wholesaler via the internet and have it set into a ring. A colourless near-flawless round brilliant solitaire, in a Tiffany-style six-claw setting on a knife-edged platinum band.

It actually looks quite something.

As I hold it in my hand, I imagine for the dozenth time what the expression on HPG's face will be when she sees it for the first time. She will be thrilled and knowing that makes me very happy. There has been a change in me over the last few weeks while I've been putting the ring together — the reality of marriage has come closer. Now it's much easier to imagine myself as a husband and I feel with every smile that HPG gives me, and every time I hold her hand, that I am a very lucky guy.

Until now spending the rest of my life with just one person has always sounded a bit rash. I have always tried to maximise my opportunities. I have been desperately clutching onto my hypothetical future options like a fistful of Lotto tickets in the wind, knowing they are mostly worthless, but unwilling to let go. Unwilling to commit.

Now I can see that this isn't the way to move forwards. I need to commit to someone and take a chance. It's just like deciding to trek to the South Pole. I might fall flat on my face but it might be the best thing I've ever done.

At the end of the day, getting married to HPG won't affect my relationship with Angelina Jolie, and my wonderful real someone is much better than a fantasy nothing.

You know what? I'm going to ask HPG to marry me.

I have the ring. I have made up my mind. There's one last hurdle — asking the father.

HPG's father is a professor of neurophysiology. He teaches at the medical school when he's not finding a cure for Parkinson's. The Professor's fastidious appearance, clipped, accented English, thin moustache and formidable, unsmiling intellect combine to give the impression of a height several feet taller than his actual slight physical stature. Physically, I might get picked for a basketball team before him but psychologically, he slam dunks me. His students regard him with awe. Some say that he exhales argon, others that he composes haikus in Klingon.

He left Poland when the jackbooted heel of General Jaruzelski's martial law descended on the country. Arriving in New Zealand, he had carefully nurtured and guided his daughter through the perils of two and a half decades of the bourgeois Western world. He became anxious when HPG started to date, but was pleased and relieved when she finally brought home a well-educated, charming suitor, who had, it has to be said, clearly excellent physical fitness and was not without some prospects. Unfortunately HPG left him and started dating me.

Since the first time my (well, actually my sister's) Toyota Starlet had farted down their manicured driveway, there seemed to have been a certain coolness in our relationship.

The morning of our first meeting HPG had been of little help.

'So what shall I call your father? Professor? Doctor? Janusz? Sir? Dad?'

She started choking on her cornflakes. 'Definitely not Dad.'

I don't know what he thought his son-in-law would be like but clearly he had at least begun with high standards — which perhaps over the years had been lowered, but I still think he harboured the secret desire that his future son-in-law would at least have a job and not live with his mother. Oddly, our relationship hadn't improved when I moved into the garage.

'I don't think your father likes me. Is there something I could do?'

'Maybe you could get that crack in your windscreen fixed, and replace the wing mirror . . . then become a Catholic, learn Polish and get a PhD.'

At least her father spoke to me. Her mother ignored me so completely I was left doubting my own existence. When I delivered her from the airport, HPG would skip from the car to be warmly embraced and ushered into the house while I was left struggling with the suitcases wondering if I had slipped into interdimensional space.

I had thought things were starting to get better once I got a job, although they took several backward steps when (lulled into complacency by a full stomach after an excellent meal) I pushed back my plate and postulated that (purely statistically speaking) there must have been *some* positive points to living under communism.

It took some time after that before my re-education was complete. Now relations were at last back on a courteous, if formal, footing. Did I really need to ask The Professor for his daughter's hand in marriage? This was a ritual that I would prefer to let slip, except that I knew that HPG would appreciate it and so would he, and so would I were I in his shoes.

By coincidence, Shackleton had also been courting in the months leading up to his first expedition to Antarctica on the *Discovery*. His target, Emily Dorman, was the daughter of a wealthy doctor, whose intelligence and personality had apparently inspired no less than sixteen marriage proposals.

Fearless Shackleton, a man who had sailed in square-riggers

across the seven seas from Shanghai to Sydney, who had boxed his way out of many difficult situations and charmed his way out of the rest — surely he had set an example of tact, grace and fancy footwork that I could follow?

So how did he deal with his prospective father-in-law? He wrote a letter and sent it to him — just *two days* before he sailed to Antarctica. Presumably before the enraged doctor could dispatch the bailiffs onto him.

Does this mean I can send a text message from the departure lounge?

Finally, I couldn't postpone it any longer. My plans were in place to propose to HPG the next weekend. So I call The Professor to arrange an appointment. Surely he knows what is coming; I have never requested an audience before.

Yet he greets me at the door courteously and invites me in. At least he doesn't appear to be armed. But when he goes to the trouble of showing me his roses, we both know that is where he's going to use me as fertiliser. We eventually find ourselves squared off across the dining-room table, separated only by cups of chamomile tea. When the small talk finally runs out there is a long and awkward pause. At last my beating around the bush meets his third language.

'So I would like to make an . . . er . . . long-term commitment to your daughter.'

I wait for his reaction.

It was never going to be 'Well, I'll be blowed! Kev, my boy!', a hearty slap on the back and then off to the billiards room for port and cigars, but I wish he would stop looking at me like he wants to give me a lobotomy with his teaspoon.

'A long-term commitment? What exactly is that? A mortgage?'

Only after three hours of questioning, during which I frantically emphasise my fabulous work for the poor, my loving and adoring devotion to my mother, the unlimited nature of my prospects, the vastness of my land holdings, the exceptional fitness of my genes, the shininess of my new carbon-fibre sled, the completely overstated nature of any risks of trekking in Antarctica and, most of all, the heartfeltedness of my commitment to his daughter, does he put down the teaspoon, and there is a begrudging acceptance.

Oh boy, is HPG going to be surprised!

A few days later on a lovely late summer's evening, I walk HPG along a path that leads up from the beach below. We climb to a point where we can look out at the setting sun brushing the sea, while the Pacific Ocean sobs quietly on the rocks below. I knew it would be perfect. I had scouted the location the week before, to leave nothing to chance.

I start to tell her all the wonderful things about her, and how much she means to me, and how she has changed my life and how I want to be with her forever.

I get down on one knee and produce a little box from my pocket and hold it out to her on my hand. HPG is fluttering her hands at her eyes and blinking back tears. For a moment I pause, feeling a little dizzy. My whole life is pivoting on a point. Everything will always be before or after this moment.

I take a breath. 'Will you marry me?'

The violins soar to a crescendo and pause, doves alight from the heavens and cock their heads, angels peek from behind the painted clouds. We all wait breathless . . . and still we wait.

I see a mixture of emotions cross her face. Surprise, doubt, uncertainty.

Suddenly, I realise what a complete jackass I've been. If it had taken me a year to get my head around marriage, then why should she suddenly be swept off her feet by my offer? Particularly from someone who has been so stonily non-committal for the last few months.

'No.'

That was me that just said 'No'; she had said, 'Let me think about it', before adding hopefully, 'but can I still have a look at the ring?'

After a long talk we walk back to the bach I've rented. HPG is remorseful.

'I've broken it! I've broken it!'

Just before we get back to the house I ask, 'What's your favourite food?'

'Italian, you know that . . . whose car is that in the driveway?'

'That's an Italian chef, who's come to cook our dinner.'

'Oh no, I've broken it!'

I'm just glad that I hadn't booked the helicopter.

Jamie calls me up. 'Mate! How did it go?!'

'Ah. Turns out she's a better judge of character than I thought.'

'Oh . . . bugger.'

There has never been a better time to fly to an Arctic wasteland.

5. THE PLACE WHERE EVERYONE IS BEAUTIFUL

If you are ugly, in Iqaluit you are beautiful. If everywhere else you have no friends, in Iqaluit you are popular.

— A woman living in Iqaluit

THE FIRST AIR INFLIGHT magazine has a map which makes it all clear — the world is top-heavy. At a latitude of 47 degrees south there is nothing but ocean between the bottom of New Zealand and Antarctica. Yet in the northern hemisphere, 47 degrees north is still well short of the border between the United States and Canada. So Canada then is much further north than New Zealand is south, which helps explain why Ottawa gets up to 4 metres of snowfall a year. Yet Ottawa is in the very south of Canada; it's on the Canadian Riviera. If you ask Canadians for a place where *they* think it's cold they point to Iqaluit as a good place to start.

Lying two thousand kilometres due north of Ottawa, Iqaluit, on the bottom of Baffin Island, is right in the middle of Canada's far north, where on a map the land gets distorted into a bizarre, fractured archipelago afro. It is only just below the Arctic Circle and for eight months of the year you can ice-skate on your swimming pool. You'll need a torch, though — in winter it's dark for as many as twenty hours a day.

Iqaluit is a seaside town — but not very often because for most of the year the sea is frozen solid. Sometime around the start of July the ice melts enough to let a few boats into the shallow harbour; by the beginning of October it begins to freeze up again.

I'm here to learn how to handle the cold from renowned polar guide Matty McNair. For the past twenty-five years she has been cutting trails through snow, pitching tents in blizzards, cracking whips over dog teams and kicking polar bear arse.

She has been to the South Pole three times and the North Pole twice, and has even travelled around Baffin Island in winter by dog team. Just a year earlier she had, with her two teenaged children, trekked unsupported to the South Pole, where they picked up their snow kites and skis, and kited back to Hercules Inlet. There is, by all reckoning, not much Matty doesn't know about travelling on snow or ice by dog, ski or kite. Once or twice a year she offers polar training from her base in Iqaluit. I was very much hoping that she would chew tobacco and wear spurs.

Unfortunately I'm not with Jamie, who has had to stay behind because of commitments in New Zealand. But he has promised to listen attentively to everything I tell him when I get back. We'll return later in the year for kite training, but by then it will be warmer. One of us, at least, has to find out what this cold stuff is they keep complaining about in books. This is why I'm here in February, in the very middle of winter.

After picking up my bags I go outside to a line of taxis. A driver sees me coming and helps me get my bag into the boot. It's not all *that* cold, but we leave the talking until we're both back inside.

'Where are you off to?'

'Apex, what will that cost?'

'Five bucks.'

'What about the supermarket?'

'Five bucks.'

'What about across the street?'

'Five bucks.'

Unfortunately for him I upset the average and ask him to take me to the other side of town, over the hill, five minutes, 5 kilometres and five bucks away.

Iqaluit is the sort of town that only needs four-digit phone numbers. You feel like you could say 'Take me to Jo's' and the taxi driver would know where Jo lived. But my driver is new, too, having only arrived that winter, and is still coming to terms with the place.

'Any bars in town?' I ask.

'You could go to the Frobisher Inn or The Legion. I haven't been there but I've heard it can get crazy. You know there was a wire-mesh screen between the Inuit and European sides of the bar until a few years ago. This your first time in Iqaluit?'

'Yes.'

'Everyone in Iqaluit is very friendly. Until you ask them what they did before they came here.'

I can't resist.

'What did you do?'

'I owned an ice-cream truck.'

In the long silence that follows, I look out the window at what will be my new home for the next three weeks.

Town is only a few streets, some commercial buildings, a couple of hotels, a supermarket and two ice-skating rinks. There is something of a utilitarian Eastern Bloc atmosphere, particularly about the government buildings. Most are cubic, grey and a little short of windows.

Yet it's not the differences that are striking; it's how much the town looks normal. Those cars parked outside the fast-food place could be anywhere until you look closer and see that they are all plugged in to keep the engines warm.

The driver drops me off outside the B&B with some advice. 'There's some bad weather coming. It's going to be really cold tomorrow.'

'How cold?'

'Well, you might want to put on long pants.'

The B&B's living-room window has an arresting view out over the bay. On the shore you can see the warehouse that was the Hudson Bay Trading Company's outpost. Here started the process whereby exquisitely evolved and adapted animals, eking out a precarious existence in the brutally hostile Arctic wilds, were knocked on the head and turned into charming hats in return for pots and old blankets.

In front of the warehouse lies the vast expanse of white flatness that is the frozen ocean. I had never seen frozen ocean before. It looks white . . . and flat. It runs for miles and miles until it reaches some low sinuous hills in the far distance on the other side of the bay. There is a strange absence of sharp peaks. They must have got a good scrubbing during the last Ice Age.

I'm used to wilderness being tightly defined — places that have been set aside with boundaries drawn around them, with rules and park rangers. I'm used to The Great Outdoors being a place you visit. Here it's the other way round. Here the wilderness completely dominates. It doesn't have to be mollycoddled and patted on the head — it's big enough and bad enough to take care of itself. We humans are the ones who need to be protected. There are no roads into or out of Iqaluit. The town is in the middle of nowhere — a single full-stop of semi-civilisation on an otherwise white A3 page. Everything here is either flown in, or shipped in during the brief time the harbour is wet. There is something of the Berlin Airlift in the sight of another plane dropping out of the leaden sky.

I think I might show the locals some Kiwi heartiness and walk back into town. So I put on my warmest pants and jacket, and stride outside, shutting the front door behind me. Oh it's not that cold! It's just bracing. I did my paper round in worse weather than this and in bare feet. Now I have my new boots, which give me a manly week-in-the-saddle swagger. I take my swagger for a few more steps, enjoying how the invigorating cold enlivens the senses — like a slap in the face with a piece of wet lettuce.

Two breaths later, I feel a prickling sensation as the hairs in my nostrils freeze into spikes, and my face and lips turn into stiff rubber. Now my head is aching and my ears are solid. I bring my hands up to them. While my attention is distracted my feet fall off. My clothes have turned into paper. I turn around and shuffle on frozen stumps the few metres back to the house, pawing at the front door until I fall inside. When I can say consonants again I order a taxi into town.

I ask the driver to take me to the supermarket so I can get out of the cold. I'm not the only one who has thought of this; there's a welcome party of tipsily courteous Inuit by the sliding doors, their faces flushed, with more or less toothless smiles. They are carefully positioned to get some warmth from the air leaving the sliding doors, yet just out of range of the glaring store security.

I walk around the shelves; at first glance it looks like a supermarket anywhere. But this isn't anywhere; it's the wild frontier. This brightly coloured abundance seems jarringly out of place against the scarcity of pretty much anything outside. Most items on the shelves I could find in a supermarket in Howick — except for the snowmobile gauntlets and snow chains. Except that the packaged meat comes with the warning label 'not to be eaten raw' (which puzzles me for a bit). And prices that would stagger a moose. At the pharmacy counter, bottles of mouthwash are on the same shelf as the prescription medicines.

'Why is the Listerine back there?' I ask.

The clerk looks at the town's newest greenhorn.

'Because it's got booze in it.'

'Oh.'

The next morning I'm sitting around the dining-room table at Matty's house, not far from the supermarket. It's warm and snug, and smells of baking cookies. There's local art on the walls and a profusion of pot plants on every flat surface.

Matty doesn't wear spurs. She's in her late forties, small, quite petite even, with a high, almost girlish voice and a mass of frizzy grey hair. After a hard morning out on the high tundra lassoing reindeer, she likes to come home and sew up a pair of oven gloves and do a little embroidery.

The other people doing the course are a Swiss businessman, who has already bagged several of the world's highest peaks, and his delicate, fashionable wife; an Israeli adventurer; a World Bank executive; and a Canadian woman from Montreal, who works at the local tourist office.

Matty starts with the house rules. Services are expensive. Showers need to be short, and if it's yellow let it mellow, if it's brown, flush it down. This raises an interesting point — how do they stop poo freezing in the pipes? Do they flush with hot water?

Over the morning we start to grasp the intricacies of polar equipment. We learn about the different deniers of tent nylon and the pros and cons of SNS versus Baffin boot bindings. We look at burn rates of stove fuel and different polar-fleece grades and the need for layering. We discuss the controversy about Gore-Tex in the cold (stops the wind but may not breathe); and the need for and uses of vapour barrier liners (stops your boots from getting iced up); about why you don't walk in your down jacket (you get too hot), and why it should be stored outside (too much moisture in the tent).

The most important item in your clothing arsenal is the polar-fleece neck warmer, which is truly the Swiss Army knife of clothing. Used in accordance with the manufacturer's instructions, it can keep your neck warm, but pulled up a little further it creates a barrier to help pre-warm your breath. Up a little further and it stops your nose from getting frostbite. Further still, and it's an eyeshade to allow you to sleep in the constant daylight of a polar summer.

We learn the tricks of the trail, such as using chapstick for stove maintenance (lubricating the pump shaft); how to prevent condensation on electronic equipment when taking it into a tent (let it warm up inside a bag); why and how to shorten the skins on your cross-country skis; and some techniques to help keep your goggles fog-free.

'By the time your body sends you a warning signal it will be too late,' says Matty. 'You have to manage yourself consciously. You need to eat before you get hungry, drink before you get thirsty, take off your jacket before you start sweating, stop before you get too tired to make camp.'

This sounds very important but I'm still jet lagged and struggling to pay attention as one of the four hours of winter sunshine now hits the window, refracting through the sparkling crystal dreamcatcher. A big snowdrift is pressed a metre high against the glass of the ranch slider, showing a cross-section of the snows of the winter.

Matty's house is right next to the 'beach', and not far away there is a loose line of small boats of various sizes on trailers or frames, or just pulled up on the snow, frozen into crazy angles. Every flat surface, from the handrails around the deck to the boats' cabin tops has a delicately poised plump mound of snow on it.

Behind the boats, the first hundred metres of sea ice has been crumpled by the tide, and beyond that is the flat smoothness of the bay, with grey humps marking some islands. The black dots in the middle distance are Matty's sled dogs, chained just far enough apart so they can't bite chunks out of each other. The wind is blowing little eddies of snow. There are black clouds on the horizon. Looks like some bad weather is coming. A rhyme runs through my drowsy brain, 'She sews snow shoes by the sea shore . . .'

'Got that? OK, everyone. Dress up, we're going cross-country skiing.'

You don't walk out of Matty's living room into the street. You walk into a changing area, similar to an airlock, where you suit up for the vacuum of the Outer Arctic. There is plenty of time as you tug on your boots to look at the few centimetres of ice that coat the *inside* of the actual front door before you go outside where it's really cold.

The 15 or so metres to the minivan is done at a jog. The engine of the van has been running for the last ten minutes to warm it up. Still, it's so cold that as you slide across the seat your pants stick to it.

Would you *please* shut that door?

A few minutes later the van rolls to a stop at an abandoned air strip at the edge of town. It could be anywhere as squalls of snow whip past on all sides hiding any landmarks.

By the time Matty has finished handing out skies and poles, I'm already freezing.

'Right, take off your down jackets.'

'Is this really a good idea?' I chirp in an unfamiliar soprano.

'You want to wait for spring? Let's go.'

Faster than you could skin a beaver, Matty has clicked into her ski bindings and shuffled off, head down, into the flurries.

Cross-country skis are like downhill skis, except much skinnier and floppier. The bindings clip in by the toe, while the heels are left free to help you fall over. Which is very easy to do: if you cross the tips you can be striding along one second and a crumpled heap the next.

By the time I've picked myself up off the snow, the little group has long since moved off. I should have paid more attention. Everything is wrong. My goggles fog up almost immediately leaving me flailing about blindly. The wind whistles through my hood which won't stay up. The ski poles suck the heat from my hands and my sleeves don't overlap the top of my gloves, leaving my wrists to freeze into bands of ice. Worst of all it's claustrophobically, panic-inducingly cold. I thought you were supposed to warm up?

After half an hour, Matty raises her ski poles in a cross above her head to indicate a break. She produces a thermos and pours hot chocolate into a ring of trembling plastic mugs. The base of the cup is hot but the hesitantly rising steam turns to ice by the time it's reached the rim. The nuts and raisins in my snack bag taste like a mouthful of gravel.

Matty squints at me. 'Hey big guy, your nose is going white. Quick, press your hand on it like this.'

'Wha?!' I say, frozen raisins exploding out of my mouth.

If she's nervous about my nose, I'm nervous about my nose.

Back at the house, I'm now a model pupil. I have a needle in my hand, stitching a fur liner on the hood of my ski jacket, and pushing my way to the front of the queue for the patterns for the wristlets.

The next day Matty announces, 'Tonight you are going to be sleeping outside.'

Cool. I haven't slept out on a lawn since I was seven. So that afternoon we set up the tents on the snow in the space between the house and the boats, and later that evening, after one last hot chocolate in Matty's living room, we make a dash for our accommodation.

I'm wearing most of my warmest clothes, inside not one but two thick sleeping bags, which are on top of a foam mat on top of a Therm-a-Rest. But I'm still shivering like buggery and I don't know which way the delicate heat balance is going to go. By the time I realise I'm not heating up, will I be too cold to do anything about it?

When I turn off my feeble LED torch it's somehow colder. I try to poke the bag away from me because wherever it touches, it stabs like ice. The air is so cold that just drawing it into my lungs shocks me awake. I turn the torch back on to see my breath falling as tiny particles of snow. I try to take a photo of it but my camera battery has frozen. OK, so this is the type of cold that stops chemical reactions.

While I wait to find out if I'm going to warm up, I gingerly open Scott's journal from the *Discovery* Expedition. It seems that even with the boy racers on their snowmobiles howling past outside I'm in the Ritz compared to the conditions Scott had to endure, with three men sharing a reindeer-hide sleeping bag.

It doesn't do to dive straight in, for we may land in the centre of someone else's anatomy, so we shout, 'All right for coming in?' There is a scuffling, then 'Right, oh!' and we dive with a blind lurch towards our own corner . . . The first half hour is spent in constant shifting and turning as each inmate of the bag tries to make the best of his hard mattress or to draw the equally hard covering closer about him. There is a desultory muffled conversation broken by the chattering of teeth. Suddenly the

bag begins to vibrate, and we know that someone has got the
shivers. It is very contagious, this shivering, and paroxysm after
paroxysm passes through the whole party . . . Presently we hear
our neighbour ask him if his feet are cold; he explains their exact
state in the most forcible language at his command.

By now the LED light has nearly expired in the cold, so I put the book
away and turn it off. The night is quiet, the snowmobiles must have
all found their slippery corners and lamp poles. I shape the sleeping-
bag liner around my face so that it creates a little chamber where the
outgoing air warms the incoming air. I've managed to shove away all
offending places where the sleeping bag is placing a freezing hand.
I'm not warm exactly but, if I stay very still, I think I will make it.

Damn. I really need to pee.

Now that we are veterans of sub-Arctic suburban camping, Matty
has decided that we can go on a little mini-expedition out to the bay.
The weather forecast isn't promising, though; blizzard conditions are
coming.

'Perfect,' says Matty.

That afternoon we pick our way through the rubble of the shore ice
to get to the smooth ice of the bay. We've weighed our sleds down
with large sacks of dry dog food. I've made mine up to 160 kilograms,
which forms quite a cargo. The fibreglass sled is buckling a little bit,
but it does slide over the exposed ice. It's harder to get going than
the tyres, but a lot easier to maintain momentum. The problem is
when the sled hits a little lip of ice, it takes a huge effort to get the
load moving again. So I'm last getting out to the campsite next to
Monument Island and have to put up my tent in the twilight.

Matty has a circular tent large enough for everyone to cook in,
and with all the stoves going it gets quite warm inside. I go outside to
cool down in the still but freezing air. I look up to see the stars and
instead see a magical sight, a shimmering banner of green light. It is

as if a giant translucent glow-in-the-dark shower curtain is hanging in the sky. It seems to be static, then, between blinks, changes into a new shape. It is completely entrancing, but the cold is intense and soon drives me into the safety of my sleeping bag.

The next day we are pulling sleds over a rutted ice plain. With so much emptiness, the islands form a kind of visual oasis as we trudge for miles in the thickening gloom to the next camping spot. You don't want to give too much thought to the fact that you are walking over the sea. I wonder how thick the ice is.

At the island, to get out of the threatening weather, we pull up into a little cove. It's very sheltered but as a result the snow is soft and absurdly deep. Each step punches a hole through the snow up to my thighs. For the last few metres, it's easier to crawl like a dog.

I see that the trick is to watch what Matty does. While the rest of us flop about sucking on our hot chocolate, she is constantly in action. Washing, cleaning, fixing and stowing. No time is wasted.

One minute it's sunny and still — even hot — and we are standing around the sleds laughing at some joke, while Eric, Matty's son, changes his top into something less warm. I have the zips of my fleece undone and am thinking of changing myself — I'm always too hot or too cold. Then a gust of wind almost takes the jacket out of Eric's hands, the temperature drops and we aren't laughing any more. The air becomes thick with fine rushing particles.

Hoods come up, goggles go on, our world becomes a muffled tunnel. People are moving off, I don't know why or where, but moving seems like a good idea. The cold is already taking the function out of my fingers. The person in front of me is a grey outline in the flying snow, and it's all I can do to keep them in sight. I hope they can see the person in front of them, otherwise I'm just following them into the gloom, and with no tent or stove in my sled, how will I survive? Could I crawl under the sled cover? Can you eat dog food?

What about the person behind me? Where are they? I turn around to see a figure struggling over the rough ground. Then they slip over and slowly start the process of untangling themselves and getting on their feet. I shout for the person in front to stop but the wind whips away my voice. Now what do I do?

I wait until the person behind has got up, then dash forward. As soon as I see a shadow in front of me, I stop and wait for the person following to appear out of the murk. This is going very badly. It's starting to read like an accident report.

Matty seems to be leading us around the island. I don't know how she knows where to go — the cliffs of the island have completely disappeared. Then a grey lump resolves into a group of people stopped at a spot that's a little out of the wind. We slowly erect what tents we can in a tiny area of flat ground and cram in. We lie top and tail in our sleeping bags, looking up at the tent poles bending in the wind.

The Israeli guy tells us about an expedition he was on that crossed the Greenland ice cap. They were caught in a storm, got their tent up but it was ripped apart by the wind, so they had to dig a snow trench and barely survived the night. A Swedish expedition close by wasn't so lucky.

'This is nothing,' he says, curling his lip. He pulls down his hood and goes to sleep.

Nothing? Then I would hate to see what a bad blizzard is like. While we wait in the tents for the weather to clear outside, I find myself thinking of the last days of Scott.

I don't know when I first learned about Captain Scott and his tragic death, probably at primary school. For a while, every child of the Commonwealth was taught it over Marmite and Bovril. The book written about the expedition, *The Worst Journey in the World*, by one of its youngest members, Apsley Cherry-Garrard, has been in almost continuous print since it was written in 1922. In the Second World War it was even recommended to soldiers as an example of British pluck.

Unfortunately stories about stiff white authority figures dying nobly for King and Country didn't sit well with the revisionist 1970s and Scott fell out of fashion, replaced in popularity by tales of the apparently less aloof, more egalitarian and charismatic Shackleton. Out with Cliff Richard — in with Keith Richards.

Now I'm older, the potted version of Scott's obituary wasn't quite so tidy. I mean, what was the rest of the expedition doing? Why, when they were barely a week away from the coast, did no one come out to help pull them in? Why did he die so close to One Ton Depot? Why did Evans die so much earlier than the others? Why on Earth were they found with thirty-five pounds of 'geological samples' — i.e. rocks — in their sled. What kind of madness was that? Why didn't they jettison everything? Perhaps Jamie and I would find the answers in Antarctica.

The next day there is a break in the weather and a few days later I'm back in Ottawa, calling Jamie to begin the process of transferring my new polar expertise.

'It's really cold, eh.'

'So jandals are out then?'

'Well, you might have to bring your wool jandals.'

HPG has been rotated to a hospital down in Wellington for the next few months. She picks me up from the airport and we drive back to her flat in Mount Victoria. We have hardly seen each other in the month since I proposed. She isn't saying very much, and we sit rather awkwardly.

As I go to the sofa I see a piece of paper cut out from a magazine on the cushion, on which was originally the word 'eyes', but the 'e' has been cut off.

'Honey, why is there a . . .' I pause to process why a 'yes' might be stuck on the bottom of my coffee mug. I look over and see 'yesses' of various types going all the way up the stairs.

I look over at HPG who blinks twice, smiling sweetly. 'But honey,' I ask, 'what's the question?'

Her lips purse and her eyes flare. I remain resolute.
'You'll just have to wait until I ask you again.'

6. NO BUSINESS LIKE SNOW BUSINESS

YOU KNOW THE HARDEST part of going to Antarctica will be raising the money. So you give that the highest priority and start the gruesome business of making phone calls and knocking on doors of potential sponsors. In the meantime you have to assume that the expedition is going to happen, so you start paying for bits of equipment and training and travel that can't be delayed. These costs continue to mount, so to avoid bankrupting yourself, you set a firm deadline to get commitment from sponsors or it's all over. You will pull the plug and give up on the idea. No point throwing good money after bad.

Then that deadline passes and you give yourself another one.

In this way, Jamie and I had solemnly agreed to abandon our plans if we hadn't raised the money we needed by December — now it's the start of May. Soon we will have to pay the deposit to ALE for our flights to Antarctica and that is an eye-wateringly large stack of cash. This causes the type of anxiety that has you staring at the ceiling at 4am. Particularly now that Jamie has left his job with the bank and is working full-time on expedition preparations.

Getting money for polar expeditions has never been easy. The original British Antarctic Expedition took eight years to get off the ground. Often the money doesn't come until very late — Shackleton was left with only five months to get his boat ready for the two-year *Nimrod* Expedition. Most often it doesn't come at all. For his North-West Passage expedition, Amundsen slipped his moorings and snuck out of the harbour in the middle of the night to avoid his creditors. You haven't heard of the feats of the Belgian Antarctic Expedition of 1907, led by Henryk Arctowski, even though it was announced at the very same function where Shackleton declared his *Nimrod* Expedition, because they never managed to get the money together.

Beggars can't be fussy. Admiral Peary, to help fund his expeditions to the North Pole, gladly accepted money from Morris Ketchum Jesup, one of the founders of the YMCA and a staunch supporter of the New York Society for the Suppression of Vice. Jesup presumably didn't know that Peary was fathering Inuit children out of wedlock.

All the successful leaders were very creative when it came to money-making ideas. Shackleton charged the public for the thrill of viewing expedition equipment before it was loaded onto the boat. For the *Terra Nova* Expedition, Scott accepted two men — Apsley Cherry-Garrard and Titus Oates — who, while not exactly paying passengers, had their applications reviewed favourably after they coincidentally made sizeable personal contributions of around £75,000 in today's money.

Shackleton did take a paying passenger. As the *Nimrod* was setting off from Lyttelton, a sheep farmer called George Buckley asked on a whim if he could travel down with the ship to the ice. Since he had just donated £500, Shackleton readily agreed.

Certainly none were better at hustling than Shackleton. His employer at the time of planning the *Nimrod* Expedition, the very wealthy Scottish businessman William Beardmore, had been charmed by Shackleton . . . but not very much. To get the expedition rolling,

Beardmore begrudgingly offered him, not cash, or even a conditional pledge, but only a guarantee on a loan for £7000. A fraction of what was required.

From this gossamer thread, Shackleton built a tissue of promises, IOUs, deferred payments, guarantees on the condition of other guarantees, book rights, speaking rights, film rights, forward sales, exclusive news rights, gifts, sales of postage stamps and otherwise leveraged just enough money to get a barely suitable boat on the water to New Zealand.

On the journey out Shackleton developed the alarming habit — at least in the eyes of a crew expecting wages — of charging for public lectures (4000 attended his speech in Melbourne) but then donating the entire proceeds to local charities.

Despite these foibles Shackleton was still better at financial engineering than nautical engineering. It had become clear on the voyage out that it wasn't possible to carry enough coal on the *Nimrod* to get her to the Antarctic and back. Lesser men would have quietly returned to port and expired from embarrassment — not Shackleton.

When he arrived in New Zealand he graciously accepted the £1000 offered by the government and brazenly requested the services of a ship that could tow the *Nimrod* down to the Antarctic Circle. In return, Shackleton assured them that the *Nimrod* would assist in carrying out magnetic and oceanographic surveys (which were never done).

The one thing that all the early expeditions had in common was support from newspapers. The first group to winter over on the Antarctic mainland — the *Southern Cross* Expedition — was supported by George Newnes of the *Westminster Gazette*. The *Nimrod* had a deal with the *Daily Mail*, and Peary and Cook by fierce rivals the *New York Times* and the *New York Herald*. The *Terra Nova* had an exclusive contract with the Central News Agency, a rival to Reuters. Great lengths were taken to ensure that the sponsor's paper got the scoop. Shackleton waited off the coast of Stewart Island for a special Morse code operator to arrive at the town of Oban to send the news of the expedition in secret code.

In a similar way, we are working with a modern-day 'newspaper' — the Xtra internet portal — and waiting for those negotiations to crystallise into cash. In the meantime we have to continue as if the expedition is going to happen, and as the spring has sprung in the northern hemisphere, it's time to fly back to Iqaluit — this time with Jamie.

We're going to learn snow-kiting from Matty's son Eric. At twenty-two he is a downy-cheeked veteran of crossing the Greenland ice cap with snow kites, and trekking to the South Pole, using kites on the return. He's also perpetually cheerful and enthusiastic in a way that's inexplicable from someone who spends a large chunk of the year mostly in darkness.

Eric's there to meet us at the airport. As we walk to the car, a light sprinkling of snow falls.

'Hey, it's snowing!' says Jamie of the Arctic.

Eric looks at him sideways. 'You haven't seen snow before?'

'Ah well, you know, I've been in snow, sure — but I've never seen it snowing!'

'Mmm-kay.'

With the arrival of spring there is a softness to the air. The icicles on Matty's roof are dripping, the sea ice at the harbour front is breaking up, and we have to ski out through slushy rubble. Away from shore, the spring snows have covered up the hard ice of February, coating the harbour in a pristine white duvet — a million hectares of perfectly smooth kiting rapture.

We set up camp out next to Monument Island, just outside the arms of the harbour but still sheltered from the prevailing wind. Only there isn't any. We are baked by sun, and the snow is melting so fast that we have to reset the tent pegs every day. Jamie sits in a deckchair putting on sunscreen.

'Kev mate, just quietly, were you maybe talking up a bit how cold it gets here?'

While we wait for the wind to blow, Eric starts instructing us on the theory. The first lesson of snow-kiting in Antarctica is to never launch your kite without being connected to the sled. He tells us that there was a Polish explorer, Marek Kamiński, who was doing a solo-kiting expedition a few years ago and set up his kite in a strong wind, nearly a blizzard, thinking he would launch first and then hook onto his sled. He never got the chance. The last thing he remembered was flying through the air. He regained consciousness to find that he was being dragged along by his kite, his head being used as a battering ram against the sastrugi. When he finally managed to disconnect himself, he had no idea where he was or which way his sled was. Then he noticed blood dripping from a gash in his head, leaving a pink stain on the snow. So he walked upwind, guided by the trail of blood, for nearly 2 kilometres until he somehow managed to find his way back to his sled.

The wind starts to blow and it's time for us to watch and learn. Eric can sniff the breeze, toss the kite into the air, where it snaps into perfect shape, and then, before you can say 'Bastard!', he's going 30 kilometres an hour, raked over with one hand trailing along the ground.

On the other hand, mortals, like us, have to be very very careful about the launch. First, the kite has to be taken out of its bag and laid out flat on the ground, then a carefully assessed amount of snow is put on top — enough to keep it in place, but not so much that it can't be pulled loose when you're ready to go. Then you need to back away slowly, carefully unwinding the kite strings as if laying out the detonation wires to a bomb. Once you get to the handles, you walk back to double-check the strings, cursing if you find a knot. As you painfully pick at it with freezing fingers, you are always careful not to inadvertently tug on the kite to release it from where it's flapping menacingly under its pile of snow.

By now you have trudged back and forth from the kite to your skis several times in the soft snow, and it is a relief to finally click into your bindings. You pick up the kite handles and prepare to launch.

First you back up about half a metre to tension the lines and give them a flick. One edge of the kite stubbornly won't lift, so you side-step awkwardly in your skis, arms above your head trying to tug the kite from a slightly different angle, not aware that the line between you and the sled is slack. So when the kite leaps into the sky (at the wrong angle and far quicker than you had expected), you are shot forward, at least until the line to the sled goes tight. Now you are yanked to an abrupt halt and it is the sled's turn to surge forward; this yo-yoing continues while the kite explores every corner of the sky with the frantic logic of a released balloon. After a few lively seconds of this impromptu line dance, you are yanked over on your side.

Your cursing abruptly stops when you remember that your 100-kilogram sled is coming at you from behind with the deadly accuracy of a fibreglass cruise missile. You roll to one side just before it slides past. But while you were briefly distracted, the kite has regathered itself and you are yanked miraculously upright, but now in the confusing situation of chasing after your own sled, which then comes to a stop broadside across your path. In a moment of madness you try to jump it, only to have both skis hit the side. Thankfully the bindings give way before your knee ligaments do, and after a brief flight you land, arms out, face down on the snow. Then the sled arrives and gently rolls over your leg.

Eric glides past. 'Try bending your knees,' he suggests.

You raise your snow-covered face to see him tack, via a deft aerial pirouette, and accelerate into the distance.

I'm sitting on the snow untangling my lines for the umpteenth time when I see two snowmobiles buzz away from the town and make their way around the point. One of them peels off and heads towards me. It's a young Inuit guy with a rifle over his shoulder. He pulls up alongside and sits there smiling.

'Hi,' I say.

He smiles and nods.

'Where are you off to?'

'Hunting!'

'Is that your dad? Where is he going?'

'Hunting!'

'Hey, isn't this a school day?'

He nods.

'Why aren't you in school?'

'Hunting!'

We laugh, then he revs his engine and takes off after the receding dot in the distance. Maybe he'll be back later and we can talk about snow.

For the next two weeks, if there is wind, we're out sliding and lurching, steadily building our skills, and soon the times between getting alarmingly airborne become fewer and fewer. Although if the breeze is strong, there's never an opportunity to get complacent; I look over to see Jamie making good use of his helmet as he is lifted and dashed back into the ground.

Hour after hour in the lengthy twilight evenings, we practise doing long, long downwind runs, with the sleds bumping behind, while the kite does giant figures of eight in the sky. I'm thinking that if Antarctica will be like this then things won't be so bad.

We want to test out the latest version of our equipment and routines, so we plan an expedition of a few days down the coast.

'Oh, you are definitely going to have to look out for polar bears,' warns Eric.

As a child I used to have a large polar bear soft toy, which may have left me with the wrong instinct — if a polar bear came up, it would probably be a bad idea to try to give him a cuddle, unzip his tummy and get out my jammies . . . because in reality that's what it wants to do to me. Polar bears are basically sharks with fur and, although they aren't very cheerful at any time of year, they are particularly bad-tempered in spring.

Female bears make a den, typically in a snowdrift on a hillside where they don't eat or drink (or, ahem, poo) for several months. In the darkest days of winter they give birth to a pair of cubs. So come springtime, Mrs Polar Bear emerges from the snow cave a little worse for wear and as mentally stable as you would be after spending the winter, mostly in darkness, cooped up in a small room with the kids. Not only that, she's eye-crossingly constipated, thirsty and, most of all, ravenous.

Polar bears are extraordinarily stealthy hunters. More than one expedition to the North Pole has gone to sleep after telling themselves they were only imagining that they were being followed — only to wake up with a paw coming through the tent.

'You'll need to take one of these,' says Eric, handing me an aerosol tin, about the size of a large can of fly spray.

'What is it?'

'Bear repellent.'

'Do we spray it on ourselves?'

'No, you spray it at the bear.'

'Does it work?'

'It will for me,' says Jamie. 'While you're messing about with the bear deodorant, I'll be running for help.'

Over a few days we pull our pulks down the coast, testing our gear and bedding-down routines. We try to get our heads around the long days on the trail, the deceptions of snowy landscapes, particularly the way an apparently close feature takes hours to reach, and the feelings of being quite alone (hopefully) in an immense wilderness.

As we trudge past spurs of land, we sometimes look up to see the silhouettes of inukshuk, simple human figures made of blocks of stone that stand like symbolic scarecrows to guard places of interest to the local Inuit or to warn of dangers. Hmmm, does the one we are passing now look like a man being attacked by a polar bear?

On our last night heading south we decide to stay in a little hut for a treat. When we eventually find it, perched on a peninsula, it doesn't look that sturdy. In fact, it looks like the second of the Three Little Pigs' houses, except the bullet casings on the floor, complete with what looks like wolf prints outside, create more of an impression of the Three Little Pigs' Last Stand.

We scramble up to the top of the ridge next to the hut. Thirty kilometres away, across the frozen white bay, 600-metre-high hills rise up. To the south, though, the hills peter away as the arms of the bay open out onto the Labrador Sea.

Long before he became known for being the first man to the South Pole, Roald Amundsen came this way when he began a journey over the top of the world on the start of an expedition that would make him famous.

In 1903, Amundsen sailed in the *Gjøa* out of Oslo Harbour in search of the North-West Passage — the legendary shortcut across the top of North America that had been luring, bewildering, and frequently killing, adventurers for four centuries. The difference was that this time, two and a half years later, Amundsen walked into the telegraph office of Eagle, Alaska, to announce to an astonished world that he had found it, mapped it and sailed through it.

Amundsen's fame had been achieved; he was now a household name and would never have to buy another glass of aquavit in a bar in Norway again. Of course it wasn't enough. In 1909, Amundsen began to turn his considerable energy and expertise towards putting together an expedition to claim the Pole. The *North* Pole. Who should upset these plans? His good friend, the heroic Dr Cook.

When we last left Cook, he had just escaped death on the gruesome *Belgica* voyage. In the intervening years, Cook had also continued a life of adventure. He had become the first to summit Mount McKinley, North America's highest mountain, and more recently he had disappeared, rumoured to be exploring in the Arctic.

We now catch up with him in the summer of 1909, emaciated and long-haired, stumbling into the whaling station of Upernavik in northern Greenland. He bangs on the door of the house of the Danish governor, who, after checking if Cook is free of vermin, invites him in. Cook announces that he has been travelling with two Inuit companions for many months. Nearly dying several times, they somehow managed to survive a winter in an underground den north of Baffin Island, at one point becoming so hungry that Cook had not only eaten his boots but his laces as well. However, his most sensational claim is that during his meanderings he had succeeded where 600 expeditioners had failed and had become the first man to reach the North Pole.

The governor put Cook on the next boat out, which just happened to be going to Copenhagen. When Cook arrived in the Danish capital he was met with gushing adulation. He had audiences with Danish royalty, ambassadors, ministers and mayors. The night of his arrival, while thousands lined the streets hoping for a glimpse of this hero, a banquet for 400 people, 'many of them ladies' it was coyly noted, was put on in his honour. A toast to 'our noble guest' was followed by no less than nine hurrahs.

Then, two days later, while the Danish capital was still cheering, the telegraph machine clattered out another message:

'Stars and stripes nailed to the Pole — Peary.'

Commander Robert Peary was an American naval officer, who had given up twenty-three years of his life and eight of his toes on various attempts to get to the North Pole. On 6 September 1909 he telegraphed indignantly from Indian Harbour, in northern Canada, that *he* had just returned from reaching the Pole and what's more, 'Cook's story shouldn't be taken too seriously. Two Eskimos who accompanied him say that he went no distance north and not out of sight of land.'

Cook was asked to produce his journals and log books. He said that he would be delighted to — except that he had left them in Greenland somewhere. Meanwhile, Peary's own claim required believing some heroic mileages, which were doubtful enough to contribute to a lively and prolonged debate on whether either man had made it to the North Pole.

The *New York Herald* went into bat for Cook, while the *New York Times* sided with Peary. For months, they slugged it out in a series of partisan articles and fiery editorials. As the *Wall Street Journal* put it: 'The question used to be what lies about the North Pole, now it is, who lies about it?'

Back in Norway, Amundsen considered his options. He could continue going to the North Pole, in which case, depending on how things were resolved, he would either be the first, the second or the third person to get there — but more likely no one would ever know. Moreover, if he continued with his current North Pole plans he could be potentially offending his friend Cook, as it would imply that Cook hadn't made it.

Brooding through the long winter nights, Amundsen finally came up with a bold solution — he would keep his ambition to be first to the Pole, but swap *north* for *south*. It was a daring plan, and to maximise his chances of polar priority he decided to keep this reversal secret from everyone, including his patron, the government, his sponsors and even his crew. Everyone except his brother and the captain of his new boat the *Fram*. For the long months leading up to the departure of the expedition, he scrupulously maintained the façade. No one must know, least of all Scott.

But then — who was that knocking on the door of Amundsen's house in Bundefjord. It couldn't be! Yes it was: Captain Scott.

In March 1910, Scott visited Norway to observe trials of the motorised sledges that he was planning to take to Antarctica. After finding out that Amundsen lived nearby, he decided to pay a visit. It was public knowledge that the great Amundsen was planning an expedition to the North Pole and Scott wished to coordinate measurements of the magnetic fields between the two teams. Before travelling to Norway, Scott had tried to call several times but, unfortunately, Mr Amundsen was never at home, at least not to Mr Scott.

Scott arrived at Amundsen's house and waited downstairs.

Amundsen's embarrassed brother said that he had passed on the message that Scott was coming and that Amundsen must have stepped out for a minute. After waiting an hour, Scott finally left. Seven months later, when Scott stopped off in Melbourne en route to Antarctica, he was handed an enigmatic nine-word telegram:

'Beg leave to inform you. Fram proceeding Antarctic Amundsen.' Scott knew exactly what it meant. The race was on.

When we arrive back in Iqaluit from our mini-expedition there is an email waiting for us. The deal with Xtra has turned into money. We can start breathing again. The fundraising is by no means over, but now at least we know we are on our way.

While cash was still proving elusive we had been having more luck with our scavenger hunt for clothing and equipment. The New Zealand distributors of international brands had been exceptionally generous. After my first Iqaluit experience, I was worried about our clothing and had started looking for alternatives. Our comfort had taken a huge step up when we switched to using The North Face as our main clothing supplier. Our down jackets were now particularly impressive — fat as a whale, light as a bee and orange like a traffic cone. The MSR distributor provided three of their highly compact and reliable stoves (not so different in principle to Scott's), as well as a tent, specially modified with large flaps around the groundsheet so that we could anchor it down in the Antarctic winds. We had also received a half dozen one-litre Nalgene bottles, made from a super-tough plastic that doesn't mind being frozen or boiled which made them perfect for holding everything from fuel to pee.

We had made small modifications to some of our other gear. We had the sled canvas fitted with more pockets to save time at the break trying to find and retrieve things from the main compartment. We had special sleeping-bag liners made with a breath chamber to warm the incoming air, making it easier to sleep when it gets exceptionally cold. We had put little transparent windows in the sleeves of our North Face jackets so that we can more easily see our watches. Jamie came up with the idea of sewing possum fur into the crotch of our trousers for a little added thermal protection.

'We should make sure the possum's dead first,' he suggests.

The general kindness and hospitality of New Zealanders are well known to every stranger who has visited the country, but in our case there was added a keen and intelligent interest in all that concerned the expedition, and a whole hearted desire to further its aims.

— Scott

One of the main problems we will face is getting video back from Antarctica to keep our website and TV commitments. There are no communication satellites over the South Pole, at least not ones that civilians can use, which means relying on the slightly erratic (only gone bankrupt once) Iridium system. You can send video data through it, but it's so slow it's practically semaphore. Then we figure out that mobile phones are very good at taking video clips and compressing them into relatively small packages. The quality is only barely good enough to use on TV, and a short clip would still take half an hour to send, but now it is possible to do something that to the best of my knowledge has never been done before — send video back from a tent in the middle of Antarctica.

The people at Vidcom have done a sensational job of integrating the communication system, and building a rugged battery box that, as well as holding the main charging battery, will also house all of our charging components for our electronic equipment, which now includes a video camera, a digital still camera, two iPAQs, two iPods and two satellite phones.

Perhaps the coolest of all our new toys is an audible navigation system. Worried about how difficult it will be to navigate to our caches while kiting, Gary Nicholson, a very talented and obliging programmer, has developed a hands-free navigation system that sits on our GPS-enabled iPAQs, and will provide audio instructions through the headphones built into our kiting helmets.

But still no cash.

Then we discover that a quietly successful and innovative Hamilton-based company called Architectural Profiles Ltd (APL) is about to launch a new type of highly insulating window joinery called Thermal Heart™. It's a very cunning product. Aluminium is a sensational conductor of heat, so even if you have double-glazing, the joinery surrounding the panes of glass is still bleeding warmth away and thus undermining the whole point. Thermal Heart solves this by incorporating a strip of toughened nylon into the frame to physically separate the warm inside from the cold outside. We arrange a meeting.

When Rob Hamill and I were knocking on doors trying to get sponsorship for the trans-Atlantic race we occasionally, mostly through bad luck and misunderstandings (asking for coffee at a tea company, that sort of thing), failed to make a good initial impression with potential sponsors; it was a mistake I was keen not to make again.

Fortunately, when we meet APL's CEO Craig Vincent and head of marketing Shane Walden, I am immediately taken aback at their devastating sartorial elegance as well as their shrewd and insightful business thinking, a combination that would have been intimidating had it not been for their easy charm and near supernatural good looks. (Did I forget to mention their exceptional intelligence, work for charities and kindness to animals?)

We soon find common ground. They are looking to promote a product called Thermal Heart that is about staying warm in the cold. Our product is trekking to the heart of the coldest place on Earth while trying to stay warm.

The only way it could have been a more fortuitous and agreeable match is if the APL marketing department had been trying to figure out how to sell a new window frame called 'Kevin and Jamie go to Antarctica' and we had been planning to tow a double-glazed glasshouse to the Pole. Even the Thermal Heart logo, which shows the profile of the joinery, looks remarkably like a cross-section of Antarctica.

So, just two months after arriving back in New Zealand, we are again trudging through mist in our ski gear. Then the dry ice clears and the crowd claps as we walk into APL's regional conference. We are very proudly launched as the Thermal Heart Antarctic Expedition.

Immediately, preparations pick up pace as the expedition grows by a few hundred enthusiastic supporters and some very capable and willing hands. Their marketing department swings into action to start promoting the trek. I'm startled one day to see a large delivery truck go past, bearing a photo of Jamie and me. While Xtra will run the expedition website, APL marketeers will be the daily conduit for the content coming from us in Antarctica.

Our tame inventor, Shamus Fairhall, who had helped so much in preparing for the Atlantic race, has, with his typical flair and cunning, designed away our heavy kite ski boots and replaced them with a kind of aluminium exo-skeleton. These will wrap around our soft cross-country ski boots to provide ankle support, yet still fit into the bindings of our kite skis. At least they do on the computer screen; to make them we need four lumps of high-quality aluminium, cut and ground within micro-millimetre tolerances by a five-axis CNC mill. Where are we going to find one of those? APL again. When the freshly milled footplates arrive from APL's Hamilton factory, Shamus assembles the rest of the skeleton and soon I'm stomping around his workshop, astonished at how light they are. They are going to save several kilos a *boot*, as well as making us look like RoboCop. How good is that?

The Don's new Jaguar scatters stones as it sweeps into the car park of Snow Planet, an indoor ski slope just north of Auckland. He steps out wearing a dark suit and a white silk shirt and puts on his sun-glasses.

The Don is a successful but enigmatic businessman who I had met in preparing for the Atlantic race. Since then we have kept in sporadic contact.

We go to the canteen where we can look out through the giant windows over the slope where I have just finished testing some changes that have been made to the ski-boot shells. The Don realises that he is about to put the sleeve of his Armani into some tomato sauce. He takes out a handkerchief and wipes it away. They don't do table service, but for the Don they make an exception. Soon we are waiting for his third choice of bottled water brand to appear.

In the corner below us, Jamie is doing a photoshoot for the University of Waikato, one of our sponsors. He's wearing all his expedition gear, while some assistants hold up the lighting reflectors and others with shovels take turns throwing snow at Jamie, who is trying to look grimly resolute. The Don gives a rare smile as a lump of snow hits Jamie in the face.

He asks about my family. I ask him about his recent holiday in the Caribbean. He shrugs and raises a heavily ringed finger and leans forward.

'I wanted to talk to you before you go. You don't seem as confident as last time. What's going on?'

This catches me off guard.

'Well, I'm not sure . . . was I that confident before the Atlantic? Things are going fine. We've just come back from doing the last train-ing at Mount Cook. Learning crevasse rescue and trying out our final gear setup. It was . . . fine.'

'But?'

'There is a lot of risk in this one. Antarctica isn't like the Atlantic. There are a lot of things that could go wrong.'

'Like?'

'The cold, and crevasses. What if one of us falls down and the other can't get him out? Then there's the weight — very few people have tried to pull this much weight across Antarctica. It could all go bad very quickly and we could disappoint a lot of people.'

'This is what challenge feels like. This is what you signed up for. Whatever the outcome of this, at least you two are putting yourselves on the line.'

'What do you mean?'

'By the time you get to a certain age, it is easy to become very good at fooling yourself about where your life is at, which is just as well as otherwise you would self-destruct with loathing. Look at people as they get older — they get fat, they get lazy, they expect life to get easy. But life isn't easy, it has never been easy, and it's not going to get easier. At least you're not giving in to that. At least you're pushing yourselves.'

'We might be pushing ourselves into a crevasse.'

'You might be. Or maybe you'll make it. At least you'll find out.'

Just like marching armies, the key to every successful expedition is logistics — the boring business of making sure that you get not most things but *everything* you need (including the 00-size square-head multi-tool adapter that undoes the tiny screws holding the ski skins on) to the start. APL has again helped us out by giving us the keys to the storeroom in their Auckland office. Within a few days you have to be careful how you open the door against the piles of brightly coloured and freshly embroidered Ozone kites from England, sleds from Holland, packets of delicious freeze-dri meals from Backcountry Foods, food of many kinds from Victoria Park New World, precious camera equipment from Regency Duty Free and electronics from Dick Smith.

There's a quote from Peter Blake that goes something like, 'I don't care if you've checked it, check it again.' Now that I've left my job (just before another restructure), I keep hearing these words as Jamie and I spend many hours organising, checking, rechecking and stowing our gear.

A year and a half of training and testing, fundraising, shopping, researching and inventing, publicising and packing is over. We're nearly ready to go. Just one more thing to do.

One evening HPG and I are sitting in her favourite Italian restaurant. There's a live opera singer to provide entertainment between courses. After the mains I go to the bathroom and when I come back HPG has a coy look on her face.

'Honey, why did I just get a text saying "Congratulations?"' She shows me the screen of her mobile phone. 'Do you have a little surprise for me?'

Wak! I told her friends not to call until after nine! What can I say to put her off?

'No baby, you're not going to hear a proposal from these lips tonight.' She seems a little miffed by this and turns darkly toward the dessert menu. Soon she brightens. 'Oh look, they have "Pannacotta Polska". How funny! Oh and look, "Amore Eterno — guaranteed to give you a lifetime of happiness" . . .' Her voice trails off and she looks at me strangely. I make a face of perfect innocence. By the time she gets to 'Muchos Bambinos — lots of little bundles of joy made with love' — she is blowing her nose into the napkin.

'Shall we have the tiramisu?' I suggest. 'It's only 50 cents.'

A few moments later the tiramisu comes out. The icing on the top spells out 'Will you marry me?'

She laughs and hugs me, sobbing.

'Umm. Why aren't you saying anything?' I whisper nervously.

'Check your phone.'

I pull it out of my pocket. I've received a text message.

One word.

'Yes.'

And the night explodes into a thousand shiny pieces.

7. ADAM'S FINGERTIP

HPG AND I DECIDE that she shouldn't be at the airport on the day I leave. I know it's going to be madness with so many people around and things going on that I won't be able to do her justice. So she is up a week earlier to say goodbye.

After the weekend we're at the airport departure gate, with her about to get on the plane to fly back to Wellington. The awkward silences are getting longer. There's a chance, however small, that I won't make it back, and she will have to live with that fear every day until I return.

I try to change the conversation to a happier subject. 'So when shall we send out the wedding invites?'

She looks at me with a face of stone. 'When you come back with all your bits.'

Finally, departure day is here and we're at the airport checking in to a LAN Chile flight with the eighteen North Face duffel bags, each weighed to be within 3 grams of the maximum allowed. The guy at the X-ray unit almost spits out his coffee when the battery-charging box goes through the machine. It turns out, as he later explains with some relief, that it has a very unfortunate X-ray image.

Friends laugh and wish us well. We take photos, shake hands and kiss cheeks. Kate tries to smile. My mum is trying to be brave. She wishes me good luck and tells me to come back safe, then gives me a brief, awkward hug and rubs my arm. Last of all is Jamie's mum. She is too beside herself to talk, just shakes her head and presses 'fragile' stickers onto our chests as we go through to customs.

At last we're on the plane; my head hits the back of the headrest and I let out a long silent whistle.

'Do you think it's going to be cold in Chile?' asks Jamie.

'I don't know . . . are people starving in Hungary?'

'Good point . . . are they busy in Russia?'

It's twelve hours of flying (including two hours of punning) from Auckland to Chile and none of them south. It's not until we reach Santiago, where we donate several hundred dollars' worth of pecans to the Chilean Customs Christmas Fund, that we turn right and start heading towards Punta Arenas and Antarctica. I look out the window at the snow-topped Andes passing beneath us in the moonlight. My attitude is sinking with the latitude.

An eyeball appears between the seats in front of us.

'You wouldn't be a couple of Kiwis, are ya? Are you the Thermal Heart crew?' says a guy with a thick Australian accent. A burly, energetic middle-aged man pops his head up and introduces himself as Peter McDowell, one of the owners of ALE.

'You must have seen a few expeditions go wrong down there,' says Jamie.

'Crikey, I'd say so,' he snorts. 'Just last year we had the guy who got out of the plane then hooked on his sled and twisted his back in the first two minutes . . . reckon he might have made it if his mates hadn't sent him packing. Or the guy who put a knife through his hand while slicing cheese . . . that must have smarted a bit. Or the two blokes who thought the other was holding onto the tent, and they both let go . . . bloody miracle they didn't freeze to death before help got to them. Or those ladies who only lasted a couple of days . . . got a bit cold for them. Or those Koreans . . . the one I saw at the end was going to need a skin graft. Fair dinkum. Or the . . .'

'I've heard it can get pretty windy in Punta Arenas,' I interrupt desperately.

'Windy? Struth. Blow a dog off a chain. When it's really bad, they put a rope along the streets so people don't get bowled over. Oh no, you boys are going to have a great time — more fun than a barrel of possums. You'll see.'

So where exactly is Punta Arenas? Try bringing to mind an image of Michelangelo's painting *The Creation of Adam*, the one where God and Adam languidly reach out to touch fingers. Now, with the help of a good swig of your Pisco Sour, if you can think of God's arm as the Antarctic Peninsula and the gap between their hands as the Drake Passage, then Punta Arenas is at Adam's fingertip, very nearly at the end of South America. Although for a small, battered town at the very 'bottom' of the world, quite a different and unbiblical anatomical comparison is also possible — and much more frequently made. So far it doesn't look promising. But no town should be judged on the drive in from the airport, particularly at 3am after seventeen hours of flying.

We're staying at the Hotel Condor del Plata, the last warm bed of choice for Antarctic expeditioners for the past ten years. After breakfast, I'm in the lobby waiting for Jamie to come downstairs, chatting with Nicholas, the portly, well-dressed proprietor of the hotel, and killing time by looking at the photos of expedition teams on the walls. There are many framed shots of small cheerful groups, their faces beaming with hope and excitement, with messages of gratitude to the hotel and Nicholas scrawled across them.

There's also an old photo of the original *Condor del Plata*, a wood and canvas biplane that was used to explore Patagonia in the 1930s. Two nattily dressed guys wearing leather hats and flying goggles stand with arms draped over a wing. Now that's the way to see a country, soaring over the scenery, carefree as a bird and home in time for tea.

'What happened to the plane?' I ask Nicholas.

'Eet crashed somewhere. They drown-ded.'

When Jamie comes down, we go outside. It only takes a few steps before we realise that although it's sunny, it's also windy and very cold.

Jamie sniffs the air. 'Crikey, I think I can smell Antarctica.'

'Only five degrees today apparently. By the way, why are you wearing shorts?'

'I'm psyching out the locals.'

'Good thinking.'

It turns out that the centre of Punta Arenas is full of scruffy two- and three-storey stone buildings all painted in the same shade of peeling. They are mostly obscured by a complicated cat's cradle of electricity and phone lines, as if everyone in the town had laid out their own private line to everyone else's house. Each pole is like a giant topiary, moaning quietly in the wind. Gangs of semi-feral dogs lope along the roads. They have baggy skin and an awkward gait, almost as if they are people wearing dog suits. They are chased by plastic bags flicked by the constant wind.

Nicholas had assured us (with a look of aghast horror and wounded civic pride) that Punta is perfectly safe. If so, it might have something to do with the fact that nearly every house has 3-metre-high security walls topped with broken glass, and angry dogs that bash themselves at the wire gates as you walk past. We watch as three security guards get out of a heavily armoured van. Two set up a perimeter, each with a jumpy hand on their gun holster, while the third puts cash into a money machine.

As if to complete the wild frontier-town feel, one of the town squares has large speakers playing crackly mariachi music. Any moment, Butch and Sundance are going to come busting out of a bank, guns blazing.

We're the first team to arrive for this season of Antarctic travel and for the next few days we have the hotel to ourselves. Our one remaining job is bagging all our food into convenient calorie-correct portions.

So we turn our hotel room into a production line, weighing and combining muesli and milk powder and butter, cheese, chocolates, salami and freeze-dried food into two-day and four-day portions all neatly heat-sealed. We have five million kilojoules of food. It's going to take days.

The fifty-third bag of white milk powder looks very much like the fifty-second, so we start watching the local Chilean music-video channel. It seems permanently stuck in the '80s. I watch, delighted, as they play videos I haven't seen in years — Duran Duran, Terence Trent D'Arby, Milli Vanilli (they'll be back), Cyndi Lauper and The Weather Girls.

Other times we turn to the movie channel. We watch Russell Crowe in a fight scene in *Master and Commander*.

'You know,' says Jamie, 'he's pretty good with a sword.'

'Not too many captains have had experience as a gladiator.'

'That's the thing, he's been doing this for 2000 years.'

Nicholas is excited. "annah has arrived today. You should say 'ello to 'er, she ees veery nice.'

Hannah, it turns out, is a young, tall Englishwoman with long blonde hair who is almost continually smiling or laughing. She's as bubbly as champagne opened on a plane. With her rosy cheeks and creamy complexion, she looks like she should be a schoolteacher on the prairies or a nanny in an Edwardian children's story, rather than someone whose life is more or less a non-stop adventure. Among other things she has already raced ocean yachts around the world, walked to the South Pole on a resupplied expedition and spent a couple of seasons hunting for fossils in the Sahara. Most recently, though, she has been based in Tasmania, preparing a yacht for sailing trips down to the Antarctic coast. The work on the yacht meant that she hadn't been able to do as much of the training as she would have liked. However, what she lacked in physical activity, she made up for in the quality and quantity of her carbo-loading.

As she follows Jamie and me up to our room to get something, she squeals with laughter. 'You lads can't go to the Pole yet — your bums aren't big enough! Ha ha!'

By that measure Hannah is well ready. The bed creaks alarmingly as she flops onto it. She lays the back of her hand dramatically to her forehead. 'Please say that you get puffed walking up those stairs too? Ha ha!'

Hannah is going to make an attempt on the fastest solo, unresupplied trek to the Pole. Despite appearances she's not all muffins and Mary Poppins. She had learned a lot from her previous polar trip and there's something in the way that she considers advice and then does her own thing (often with a resourceful and clever twist) that reveals flashes of steely determination. She also has the huge advantage of being a woman. The record of forty-two days that she's hoping to beat is held by a woman, Fiona Thornewill, who herself had taken the record from another woman.

As the resident polar veteran, we grill her with questions. Hannah is very reassuring.

'Oh bless! It's easy-peasy. You walk for a bit and then at the end of the day you have lots of lovely hot chocolate. It's great fun. You'll be fine. Ha!'

Nearly a week after arriving, we are still packing food when a slight, silver-headed man puts his head around the door to our room and asks in a soft American accent, 'Hey, are you the guys who rowed the Atlantic? How are you? It's great to meet you! I'm Ray Jardine and this is Jenny, my wife.'

A younger woman with short grey hair and a smiling face comes in and we shake hands.

'We rowed it, too. Not as fast as you guys. When did we row, Jenny? It wasn't last year . . . it was . . . a few years ago . . .'

'It was 2002, Ray.'

'Was it? Oh, I forget.'

It turns out that he has good reason to misplace a little thing like rowing the Atlantic. He and Jenny have been doing an adventure more or less every year for the past thirty years. In his humble, good-natured, slightly forgetful way, we hear about his life.

He and Jenny have, at various times, spent three years sailing around the world, cycled across America more than once, walked the 3500-kilometre Appalachian trail, and the even longer Pacific Crest Trail (three times). He has done more than 2500 sky dives, flown hang gliders for hundreds of hours, as well as gone on long sea-kayaking trips through Alaska and north Canada. Along the way, Ray developed his own philosophy about hiking. He has written some books about it and is now considered the father of lightweight backpacking.

The more I ask, the more extraordinary the story becomes. 'So what did you do before that?'

'Oh, I invented some rock-climbing equipment.'

'And what were you doing before that?'

'I was a rocket scientist.'

'A real one?'

'Yep. I worked on orbital mechanics for the Apollo missions.'

'So what do you think of those people who say the moon landing was faked?' asks Jamie.

'You can't say that!' I hiss.

'Oh no,' says Ray, 'I'm one of them. When they took us to see the lunar excursion module, I thought there was no way that thing was going anywhere.'

Ray and Jenny are planning to trek to the Pole from Hercules Inlet, get resupplied and then kite back. They aren't even going to fly to Hercules Inlet — they are going to walk or kite down from Patriot Hills. This means that they are actually planning to go further than all of us. Respect!

So now there is a happy chatty group of us that heads across the road each night to the dark recesses of our local bar, Santinos, for a Pisco Sour. One night the conversation moves on to the shortcomings of the local laundry.

'Yeah, I'm not sure my jeans came back very clean,' I complain.

Jamie nods, 'Yeah, my socks were still pretty stinky.'

Peter McDowell rolls his eyes. 'The problem with these guys is that they think they are going to get a date halfway to the Pole.'

I find myself talking to Mike Sharp, the dapper boss of ALE, about the flight in the Soviet Ilyushin plane that's going to fly us down to the ice. I'm interested in the views we might get. 'Are there any windows on the plane?'

He frowns as he thinks. 'About five. The pilots use most of them though.'

I know Mike and Peter are experts at figuring out who is going to make it to the Pole. I have heard that they even take informal bets.

'So what do you think our chances are?'

He looks at me, with just enough of a pause to indicate that the bidding isn't entirely one-sided, then says, 'Oh, you'll be fine.' He ends the conversation with a sip of his Pisco Sour.

'How are the Twin Otters doing?' Ray asks.

'Still snowed in,' says Peter.

'What's this about Twin Otters?' I whisper to Hannah, and she explains.

It all comes down to skis. Antarctica, as you know, is covered in snow, which means planes need skis to land. But only the American military has the technical know-how to use skis on big cargo planes and they aren't telling. So that means that the rest of us are left landing a wheeled plane on ice. Except there aren't many places on this side of Antarctica where you can do this. You need to have a hill of the right height that's at right angles to the prevailing wind. This creates turbulence on the downwind side which scours away the snow, revealing the hard blue ice underneath — hence the importance of the hills at Patriot Hills. Even though you now have a runway your problems aren't over. As it is in the lee of the hills, you risk trying to land with a crosswind and wildly fluctuating downdraughts. To avoid this you need to wait until you have perfectly calm weather conditions, which means having someone on the ground to put a finger in the air and make the call. So how does that person get there? They fly on a small sturdy twin-engine plane called a Twin Otter.

Over the last few days a pair of Twin Otters, based in the far north of Canada, had flown nearly halfway around the world to the tip of South America. From there they had flown over the foaming Drake Passage and down the Antarctic Peninsula to Patriot Hills.

The pilots had tried to land but due to bad weather had been forced to circle back out to Hercules Inlet, where they had become separated. They had both managed to land and anchor down the planes in fifty-knot winds. One of them had narrowly missed a crevasse. The other had had his tent rip apart, and was now hunkering down in the plane waiting for the weather to improve.

When the pilots finally get to Patriot Hills, they have to dig out a large snow blower stored in an underground cave, start it up and clean the remnants of snow off the ice runway. Only then can they start watching the weather and make the call to send the Ilyushin down.

The team that is going to make up this season's Patriot Hills base-camp staff are starting to arrive from all around the world. Adam, the bushy bearded and softly spoken Radio Guy from New Jersey; John the quick-witted and phlegmatic doctor from the UK; the cook, and snow-kiting legend, Ronny from Norway; and others.

The patient Nicholas is putting up with sleds being tested up and down his stairs; kite lines being laid out and measured in the hallways; solar panels hung up in the windows; skis being waxed in his kitchen; and loud debates about preferred routes and the location of crevasse regions being hammered out in the dining room.

Hannah is trying to find a fur ruff for her jacket. This isn't going to be easy — ours were bought from an Inuit hunter in Iqaluit. In the meantime, she has set up her tent in the kitchen and is inviting everyone to go in and sign the roof.

One night in Santinos we meet the other two expeditions who will be on the first flight with us. There are two teams from the UK forces: one from the RAF and the other from the Royal Marines. The RAF and Marines are both hauling unresupplied to the Pole; the RAF are going to start from Hercules Inlet and the Marines from Patriot Hills. After getting resupplied at the Pole, the Marines are planning to kite back.

The Marines had recently been stationed in Iraq and listening to them talk about fighting street by street through Basra, you understand why they think walking to the South Pole might be a nice break. These genuinely pleasant, interested and very interesting guys kick down doors and dodge bullets for a living. They seem so normal, except perhaps their eyes flick around the room scanning faces a little more than strictly required.

Both teams are reeling from the hospitality of their Chilean hosts and have already seen a lot of ice — bobbing in their gin and tonics. They're very much looking forward to reaching Antarctica, if only to dry out.

Today, ALE came to weigh our sleds and take them to the airport. Our sleds will be bang on 160 kilograms once the fuel cans are added at Patriot Hills. I step on the scales myself and see that my carboloading has topped out at a waifish 110 kilograms. Hannah pushes me away and steps up. I get a glimpse of '105' on the screen before she jumps off laughing.

Now with the food bagged and sleds packed and taken away, there is little left for us to do. We go out to dinner with the Jardines and Hannah to celebrate.

'Any luck finding a ruff?' I ask Hannah.

'Oh yes, I got one. I found a Buddhist who likes to go hunting. Ha ha!'

'Any news of the Twin Otters?' asks Ray.

'Apparently they can see a little patch of blue. They are going to call in tonight to say if they have got into Patriot.'

My fork stops halfway to my mouth.

'What's up?' says Jamie.

'I've just had a thought. If the weather is good enough for the Otters to arrive, it might be good enough for them to call in the Ilyushin and then good enough for one of the Otters to take us out to the coast.'

So that means in just a few hours we could be pulling towards the Pole. Wine glasses are put down and stay untouched.

After stopovers in Cape Town and Melbourne, Scott's ship the *Terra Nova* arrived in Lyttelton on 29 October 1910. As it was nearing departure for Antarctica, the Bishop of Christchurch came on board to bless the ship. One of the crew, Taff Evans, somehow managed to fall off the boat, probably assisted by a skinful of booze. It was not the first time he had disgraced himself drinking. The night they had left Cardiff, he had become so drunk that it had taken six men to carry him onto the boat. So Scott dismissed him and sent him home.

Yet a few days later when the *Terra Nova* arrived in Port Chalmers to top up with coal, a remorseful Taff Evans was waiting for them. He had travelled down by train and now begged to be reinstated. Scott relented — Evans was extremely valuable. As one of the most experienced sledders, he was very likely to be part of the final push to the Pole.

Just two days south of Dunedin, the *Terra Nova* struck a tremendous gale in the Southern Ocean, and wave after enormous green wave crashed over her. So much water was washing over the deck that one of the dogs was swept away — then flung back on board by the next wave. Somehow they survived.

After a slow journey through the pack ice, the ship finally broke through and steamed down to Ross Island, this time to Cape Evans. Another hut was quickly assembled, and Scott, making use of as much of the summer as possible, went off to lay out a supply depot on the Barrier at 80 degrees south.

Meanwhile the *Terra Nova* was sent along the Barrier to look for a place to drop off a geological survey team. It sailed into an inlet in the ice front known as the Bay of Whales. There, to the captain's surprise, he found a ship. It was the Norwegians.

Amundsen and the *Fram* had arrived in Antarctica just a few days after Scott and had headed straight for the Bay of Whales, where they set up camp a few miles back from the ice edge.

While Scott was planning to lay siege to the Pole with a combination of man-hauling, motorised sleds, two small dog teams and ponies, Amundsen was doubling down on dogs only. He had put together a crack team of dog handlers, and a happy yelping scrum of more than one hundred of the best Greenland huskies. Amundsen was not only already on the Ice Barrier, and 60 miles closer to the Pole than Scott, but by the time he had settled in for the winter he had managed to lay out depots all the way to 82 degrees south.

The Norwegian had only a couple of things to worry about. Well, three actually. The first was that large chunks of the front of the Ice Barrier were known to break away periodically. In fact, when Shackleton had passed by in the *Nimrod* he had also considered making camp in the Bay of Whales, except he was spooked by the fact that there was much less ice there compared to just a few years earlier. Amundsen believed he knew better, and was willing to gamble that the ice was shelved up on some shallow land and more or less permanently fixed.

The second problem was that Amundsen had no idea what was waiting for them as they pushed inland. There might be mountains — there probably were. He *could* simply angle over to the Beardmore and retrace the route of Shackleton, but he had no intention of doing so. He wanted to take the fastest, most direct route possible to the Pole, and hoped that if there were mountains he could find a way through that was smooth enough for the dogs.

The third problem was perhaps the most serious and the most maddening (even more annoying than his having forgotten to bring any snow shovels). In a colossal blunder, Amundsen had forgotten to bring the 1912 Nautical Almanac. Without the tables it contained, he couldn't determine their latitude from a sun sight after 31 December 1911. They had to be at the Pole on or before that date, otherwise no one would believe that they'd got there.

Throughout the dark winter, as the blizzards howled outside, Amundsen and Scott looked out through the rattling windows of their huts, across miles of dark and frozen snow, to their competition, and wondered when the other would try to start out for the Pole.

Tuesday, 7 November. Today is our theoretical departure day. We aren't going to be flying; the weather at Patriot Hills isn't good enough. Yet the countdown clock has already started ticking. We have calculated it will take us fifty days to get to the Pole, and twenty-one to get back with our kites, plus three days to return from Hercules Inlet to base camp. Patriot Hills closes down on 27 January. We have to be back at Patriot Hills by then or else the Twin Otter will have to pick us up at a cost of some thousands of dollars an hour. At the moment we have 81 days to do a 74-day trip, so we still have some slack. If we don't fly for another week or two — well, eventually there will come a point when some tough decisions will need to be made.

Now we get phone updates every six hours. If the weather clears then we have half an hour to get ready and meet downstairs for the minibus. So we sit in our room, nine-tenths packed, watching the music channel (if I hear Rick Astley another bloody time I'm going to give *him* up) and waiting for the phone call. Every time it rings and we are told to 'sit tight', the bolt through my neck gets another quarter turn.

I come out of the shower.

'That was a long shower,' says Jamie.

'It was my last shower for this year.'

'You said that yesterday.'

'It was true then too.'

Jamie's come back from town with movies to put on the iPods.

'What did you get?'

'Touching the Void.'

'Isn't that about one bloke dropping his mate into a crevasse?'

'Yeah, I thought it might be hard case to watch on the ice.'

Hannah is spending her time baking and making sock puppets. She brings us fudge and little bags of pork crackling, 100% fat, salty and delicious. The Jardines give us two small slim Christmas presents and we promise not to open them until the day.

On 8 September 1911, just two weeks after the sun had reappeared, Amundsen could stand the tension no longer. With seven men and all his best dogs. he set off for the Pole.

His second-in-command, Hjalmar Johansen, had been opposed to starting so early, arguing that the temperatures were still too cold. He was right. A week later they were back at base. Five of the dogs had frozen to death and two of the men had serious frost damage to their feet in temperatures that had dropped down to ‾56° Celsius. One of the men would have died in a blizzard had it not been for a heroic rescue by Johansen.

Johansen quarrelled with his leader over his actions, which he believed had unnecessarily endangered the life of the men. Amundsen, who insisted on absolute loyalty, was furious. Johansen was pulled from the Pole team.

I'm babysitting, watching TV while two young boys are asleep. At least I think they are. I hear screaming and come round the corner to see one of them using my cell phone as a hammer on his brother's head. It's ringing in his hand.

'Kev, Kev.'

I open my eyes; Jamie is holding the phone.

'Wake up. Get ready. We have to walk to the South Pole.'

Oh, thank goodness.

Off to one side, away from the airport's main terminal, squats a strangely bulbous and menacing high-wing plane. It looks a lot like an over-inflated Hercules. This is the Ilyushin.

The Ukrainian crew are milling around having their last smoke. They are normally in the Middle East somewhere, waiting to be hired to help fly bags of milk powder into refugee camps in Botswana, or ping-pong balls from Moldova to Libya.

I look at it dubiously. I've never travelled in anything built in Tashkent, Uzbekistan by the sullen workers of the Fatherland. How much care and attention do you get for two roubles and a roll of one-ply toilet paper every other month? The Soviet empire has given us such technical marvels as the Skoda and the Trabant — if these are anything to go by we'll be lucky if the door handles don't fall off.

We make our way across the tarmac and walk up the fold-out stairs into the hold. Inside it's enormous; it's twice the height of a person and as long as a cricket pitch. You could park a double-decker bus inside if it wasn't already so cram-pack filled with supplies. We pick our way around the piles of cargo, including an entire prefabricated radio hut strapped down with rope netting.

The decor is from the Utilitarian School of Design. There is no attempt to conceal the lines of piping and wiring that snake up the walls. There is only a single row of bench seats running down each side. Decadent and corrupting niceties like cushions or soundproofing are in limited supply. I expect I'll see pack ice when the toilet flushes.

We take our places and belt in. After a long take-off roll and a reluctant howl, the plane crawls into the air. Once we've finished climbing we're free to stand up and, to the extent there's room, walk around. Earplugs are handed out and we stuff them in as the crew grin at our delicateness.

I go to try to find a view. Up the front, the navigation cockpit droops underneath the fuselage like a glass jowl. It's almost entirely windows. It would have stunning vistas but unfortunately all that can be seen is a layer of flat white clouds. I'm fascinated by the navigator's control panel. It looks like the result of asking an engineer in the 1930s what they thought the 1990s would look like.

It's hard to make conversation. It's too noisy to do anything other than shout and everyone seems very thoughtful, staring into space or scribbling in diaries. Even Hannah seems pensive. Ray stands with his knees bent forward a little, giving him a schoolboy look; yet he will become one of the oldest men to have walked to the Pole. The RAF guys are wearing strange fishnet shirts. Apparently they're the latest thing in thermal protection but instead make them look like they are ready for a sweaty night in an edgy German disco.

Jamie shouts in my ear, 'Did you know that the RAF have now decided to start from Patriot Hills?'

'Really?'

'Yep. One less team to beat.'

'Not that it's a race.'

'Oh no.'

For the first couple of hours we all feel an added tension. If the weather worsens at Patriot Hills we can still be sent back to Punta Arenas. But the engine drones steadily on as the wild Southern Ocean passes beneath us.

Then Peter McDowell shouts out, 'Take your seats everyone — we're about to land!'

8. BAPTISM BY FROST

*Glittering white, shining blue, raven black, in the light of the sun
the land looks like a fairy tale. Pinnacle after pinnacle, peak after
peak — crevassed, wild as any land on our globe, it lies, unseen,
untrodden.*

— Roald Amundsen

THERE IS A MAD flapping of down jackets, then we sit back in our seats,
uncomfortably large and warm like overstuffed day-glo penguins.

The plane starts making a series of steeply banking turns. There's
a flash of crisp, jagged peaks in the window above me. Antarctica!
The circling continues as the pilot checks the runway — such as it
is. No landing lights, no air traffic control, no ILS, no radar, no fire
crews, no painted white lines. Only a few forty-four-gallon drums
set out by the advance party to assist one hundred and fifty tons of
aircraft land in a crosswind, on a few hundred metres of shiny blue
ice. The type of ice they warn you about in traffic reports. The type of
ice that if it appeared on the runway of any airport in any other part
of the world would shut it down.

I decide to be only as worried as the people who know about these things. I look at the RAF guys — they seem to be checking the location of the emergency exits. Even the Ukrainians have lost their swagger; one of them is putting on his seatbelt.

I turn to Peter who is sitting next to me. 'So how many times have they done this?'

His lips move but I can't quite make out his reply.

'Sorry, did you say "forever"?'

'No, I said "never". First time, new crew.'

We descend once again, and glimpses of white cliffs fill the window. Lower, lower, then we feel the thump and rumble as the wheels hit the ice. Everyone breaks into smiles. The big jet taxis to a halt and the engines are cut.

Wow. Antarctica!

The door opens, letting in a blast of cold air and bright sunshine, and the steps are unfolded down. A figure climbs up the stairs, and pulls back their hood. It is a woman, her eyes wide open. 'Well, helloo guys! How was that?' she says in a cheerful Scottish accent. 'Did you enjoy the slide? You were a bit sideways there!'

Soon it is our turn to back awkwardly down the stairs, stepping onto thick hard slippery ice. Now this is the way to arrive in a country! No miles of grey, stained carpet, no stale air-conditioning, no surly customs officials, no passports. Just throw open the door and walk out into the sunshine.

I take in a lungful of air, shockingly cold and startlingly fresh. This is pure oxygen! Every pristine and pure molecule has been forged on silver anvils by magic elves, then polished by a million years of sunshine. I look over at Jamie. He's playing air guitar.

My toes feel alive, the back of my little fingers feel alive, my nose . . . I can't feel it any more. It's like I have lowered my face into a bowl of freezing water; I pull up my fleece neck-warmer and look around.

I've travelled to Antarctica hundreds of times in my head, imagining the landscape. Turns out I got it completely wrong. It's bigger, much bigger. In my head the snow only goes to the horizon; here it goes on to infinity.

I spin around trying to orient myself. Well, there is no mistaking Patriot Hills, a steeply sloping range just beside the runway. On the other side of the plane, several hundred metres away, is a radio antenna and a single small prefabricated hut. A short distance from the hut are the two Twin Otters, tied down. There is nothing but a large mountain range that stretches off into the distance. Our massive plane now seems as fragile and spidery as the Apollo lunar lander. We haven't flown to another continent; we have landed on another planet. Soon we're going to have to leave these people and head into the wilderness. This seems very reckless. I have the standing-on-top-of-a-bungee-tower feeling.

The crew aren't wasting time. They are unloading the aircraft as fast as possible so they can get back in the air before the weather changes. The ramp at the back of the aircraft has been lowered and all the cargo, including the pallets with the sleds, is being pulled out.

Our sleds are easy to tell from the others. The bright-yellow covers are sausage-skin tight and stand up to mid-thigh. Compared to ours, the other sleds look like they are missing something — like all their food. The Marines turn towards us, but their expressions are lost behind their face hardware. The rest shake their heads and look away.

I grab the harness of one of the sleds with my hand and pull it clear. On the hard ice the sled glides easily. The weight is not too bad at all. We follow the others to a previously unnoticed small low hump a few hundred metres away. As I get closer, I see it is a wooden bunker, mostly covered in snow. Steps have been cut down to get to the door, which is almost under the surface. Peter McDowell is there passing out tins of fuel.

'Have a look inside,' says Peter.

I walk down the steps into a surprisingly large space. There, dangling from the ceiling, is the fuselage of a small single-engine plane, the wings hanging alongside. It is just the sort of highly improbable plane in a hangar that characters in books come across when the authors have written themselves into a corner.

'It's even been to the Pole once,' Peter explains, 'but it's getting pretty old now. We're taking it out at the end of this season.'

(Author's note: But in the meantime I'm going to leave it here in case I need it later!)

I can hear the high-pitched whine of the jet engines starting up. We come outside to see the Ilyushin taxiing along the runway. There is a yawning roar as it lumbers into the air, banks and is gone. The air feels a little colder.

We pull our sleds up to the single small portacabin near the radio tower. The camp manager needs to talk to each team to confirm logistic details before we go, but there is only room in the portacabin for a couple of people at a time. The Jardines go first, while the Marines and ourselves try to keep out of the wind that is now blowing strongly from the mountains.

As bundled up as everyone is it is difficult to work out who is who, but that looks like the RAF putting up their tents, and that over there is probably Hannah. She is going to spend a few days acclimatising and testing equipment before heading off. Man, it's *cold*.

The Jardines finally emerge ready to go. Ray gets out his GPS and after a few moments studying the screen confidently points to a spot on the horizon where Hercules Inlet should be. It doesn't seem right. I double-check with my own GPS. After a few moments the score is Instinct 0: Modern Navigational Aids 1. My heart rate goes up another five beats. We give the Jardines a hug and wish them well. Without any more ceremony they start skiing off. We watch them for a while as they get smaller and smaller. It seems very brave.

Now it's our turn in the portacabin. I'm much happier than I would like to admit to be out of the freezing wind. There's nothing much to discuss, just confirm that we will text in our position, the time we'll make the satellite phone call if texting doesn't work, what equipment we need to be resupplied with (none), what we need dropped off at the Pole (also none), and where our equipment and food that we will need at the end of the expedition is to be kept. Then we're on our way with a warm 'Good luck'.

Jamie and I grab a sled each and start to pull them towards the plane. The surface here is no longer ice but sugary snow, and our loads seem to be sliding a lot less effortlessly. I bet it's mostly because I'm just pulling it with my hand. And I'm not in the harness. And I'm at an awkward angle. Yeah, yeah, that must be it.

We get the sleds over to the rear door of the Twin Otter. I hear a bang and the plane shakes. Another bang. I look underneath and see a man swinging something like a very large sledgehammer onto one of the plane's skis.

When he sees me, he comes around to my side and pulls his neck warmer away from his mouth. 'It's to break off the ice. You ready to go?'

'Yep.'

'I'm Stefan by the way,' he says, putting out his hand.

He jumps into the rear of the plane. The floor of the cabin is at shoulder height, and so he crouches down, slaps his hands together and holds them out to me.

'OK, pass it up.'

We were told by the maker of our sleds to avoid scratches on the runners at all costs because they enormously increase friction.

'Are you sure? They're pretty heavy.'

'Come on,' he says, clapping his hands again. 'I'm no pansy.' So Jamie and I pick up a sled and lift it as much as we can. We can't quite make the height of the door. With a nasty scrape along the runners, the sled gouges its way on board.

Now Stefan wants to know where we want to be dropped off. I get out the map and show him the spot at Hercules Inlet — the famous 80 degrees south, 80 degrees west.

'Eighty degrees 1 minute will be bad because then we'll have to come back. Seventy-nine degrees 59 minutes will be bad because then we'll have to waste time walking away,' I explain.

'Yeah yeah, I got it. Hey, you've got plenty of space back here, I'm going to see if Peter wants to come along for the ride.'

With Peter and us strapped into the back, the plane takes off into the wind, which means directly towards Patriot Hills, before steeply banking around and flying the other way towards the coast. Without the cold pinching my brain, I can pull off my hood, take off my goggles and, with the bright sun and the view coming in through all the windows, get some perspective.

On the left-hand side of the plane, the mountain peaks march out more or less infinitely until they are lost in the dazzle of the sun glare. The view out the front and to the right reveals a vast, vast, white, snowy plain, occasionally punctured by the top of a mountain peak. This isn't a map my fingers can walk over. This is a gigantic continent and the scale is inhuman. I feel like I'm being diluted into homeopathic insignificance by the immensity. We are so pathetically inconsequentially small. We are microscopic bedbugs about to take on a white super-king duvet. This is fricking nuts.

'How does it feel?' Jamie shouts.

Like I'm about to go over Niagara Falls in a barrel.

'Ahh . . . according to plan.'

Oh yes, I had been planning to wet my pants about now.

Then far beneath us I see two tiny dots. Two figures shuffling mechanically across the snow.

'Look, the Jardines!'

They are minute compared to the ocean of white around them, as small as the fly specks on the window. So small that Jamie and Peter can't sight them before they are lost once again. Still, we fly on, and every minute in the air is at least another hour we will be hauling back.

On the left of the plane, the low sun reveals the textures of the land. Occasionally, large patches flash and glisten, declaring that they are mostly ice. Nice smooth slippery ice. But as it pours like clear blue toffee around rock ramparts, we can see enormous crevasses. Hey, they don't look fenced off! Someone could hurt themselves down there.

Now, without any fanfare, a billion tons of ice and snow start pouring over an enormous escarpment. It's a colossal frozen cascade, a thousand white and frozen Victoria Falls. This must be Hercules Inlet. I try to film but the video camera isn't working. I plug in the external battery pack. Also nothing. The cold has got to them already.

Now we are in the inlet with mountain ranges on two sides. On the map, we had carefully picked out two peaks, or 'nunataks', poking through the snow as marking the gateway to the best route up the hill onto the plain before Patriot Hills. But from the air there are now dozens of peaks, any two of which could be our nunataks. Nothing looks like I expected.

There is a whine as the flaps come out, the engines throttle back and we start to glide down.

'It was somewhere around here that the Otters had to land and wait out the bad weather,' shouts Peter. Hang on. Didn't they find crevasses around where they landed?

We fly low and slow over the snow with the pilot checking the conditions. Now that seems a very good idea; I don't want to sink up to the windows in soft snow or be flipped upside down by rough sastrugi. Then just as the skis touch the snow, the power comes on again, and we lift off and start to loop around. We line up again. Lower, lower until this time the skids skim the snow for a few seconds. Just when I think the engines are about to cut, they get louder and the plane shakes clear and lifts away. What? Was he about to run over a penguin?

'He's grooving a runway,' shouts Peter.
We circle around and begin another approach. We've landed. No we haven't; the power comes on and we rumble back into the air. Jamie and I look at each other. More circling and now we come in again, this time at a different spot. Then again. This is starting to get on my nerves. Just open the fricking door, will you, and I'll jump out.

The next time the power eases slightly after the initial thump, and the plane decelerates abruptly. Before it stops the tail swings around in a sharp turn, and we taxi back down to the landing point. The engines are revved again and the plane veers around until it is finally pointing back down the twin tracks. The engines are still on and pulling hard as if Stefan's set for a quick getaway. Why is he flying this plane like he's stolen it? Why the rush? I was hoping maybe we could have a cup of tea and discuss things.

Stefan takes off his headphones, jumps out and comes around to open our door. He shouts over the engines, 'We're at 79 degrees 51 minutes south — is that OK?'

Well, is it OK? Will you get out of the plane?

After Scott had the hut assembled at Cape Evans, he had one last important task to complete before battening down the hatches for the winter — establishing a depot out as far he could on the Barrier to provide a resupply base for the following year. His goal was to get to 80 degrees south.

Over the next three weeks, five horses, two dog teams and six men struggled south. It was difficult travelling, with the ponies sinking up to their bellies whenever they came onto soft snow, which was often. The only horse that was not affected was wearing special horse snow-shoes. Titus Oates, who was responsible for the ponies, had only brought one set of the shoes — the others were sitting back at Cape Evans — much to Scott's frustration and annoyance.

Then a blizzard struck and they were held up for three days. Although the men tried to build shielding snow walls, the ponies, without their seasonal winter coats, suffered badly from the cold.

Finally, one of the ponies fell over with exhaustion and was set upon by one of the expedition's dog teams that happened to be passing. The dogs savaged it badly until they were whipped off. Although the pony survived, Scott, who hated to see animals suffer, had decided that they had gone far enough.

So they built an unmissable six-foot-high cairn, and stockpiled some 2000 pounds of fuel, food and equipment; hence it became known as One Ton Depot. It was 31 miles short of 80 degrees south.

Oates had argued to press on and make the distance, killing the ponies if necessary and caching the meat. Scott refused; the ponies were needed for the polar trip the following summer and what difference could 31 miles make? It was two days' march, three at the most.

It was to be the difference between life and death.

So the plane has finally stopped, the engines are roaring, my stomach is flipping. It's showtime. Stefan is shouting something I can't really understand.

'We're at 79 degrees 51 south, is that OK?'

Hang on, that's not 80 degrees.

'It's not great — we don't want to waste time pulling north to get to 80 degrees.'

'No. No. This *is* further north.'

Shit, he's right. We aren't closer than we want to be — we are further away. Nine nautical miles. Well, that's not too bad, it may take us the rest of the afternoon.

'What do you reckon, Jamie? Good enough?'

'Yeah yeah.'

'Cool. Let's get going.'

With two more sickening scrapes the sleds are ejected and thump onto the snow. The blast from the propellers is crazy cold. We loop the traces over an arm and pull the sleds off to one side as fast as possible. We briefly shake hands with Peter, who looks very happy to be getting back on the plane. Before I can even get the camera out, the plane has taken off.

The only other living things within a million hectares are speeding away from us at 160 miles an hour. In seconds, the plane is just a dot against the background of the mountains, the engine quieter than a mosquito's buzz. Now quieter than the sound of the blood pounding through my freezing ears.

9. 'SHOULDN'T WE BE LAUGHING NOW?'

Superhuman effort isn't worth a damn unless it achieves results.

— Ernest Shackleton

WE ARE UTTERLY AND completely alone. Two tiny bags of kilojoules in a place that wants us cold and dead. We're not supposed to be here. We're not equipped. We should have thick fur and 10 centimetres of blubber all over (and not just on our backsides). All we have is a few handfuls of goose fluff, a dead possum strapped to our groins and sleds filled with hydrocarbons.

'Let's see where we are on the map,' says Jamie.

I take a look.

'We aren't on the map.'

'Well then, which way are the nunataks?'

I look around at all the peaks, nothing stands out. Everything that isn't flat looks like a nunatak.

'I don't know.'

I get out the GPS.

'I think maybe that way.'

The terrain gradually shelves up to our left and behind it there seems to be a small peak that's more or less the way we want to go. There are supposed to be two of them, but from this angle they would be almost in line and so I'll take what I can get.

Jamie takes the GPS and confirms it.

'Better get going then,' says Jamie. 'Five hours?'

'Five hours.'

'OK. Let's try to make it to 80 degrees, or maybe even to the nunataks today. Do you want to take the first shift?'

'OK.'

'iPods on?'

'Yep.'

I snap the carabiner onto the traces of the sled, step into the ski bindings and shuffle forward to tension up the lines. Twenty-four hundred kilometres to make, 3000 metres to climb. Here we go. I bang my poles firmly into the snow and lean forward.

Nothing. My sled must be behind a little lip or something. I jerk my waist again and again with increasingly violent thrusts. The runners break the crust and the sled moves a few centimetres. I shuffle forward a little to take out the slack and jerk again. Only a few more centimetres. That's strange — I must be in a soft bit of snow. By flaring my skis out like a duck and pushing on the poles, I can just get the sled to move a few more centimetres. Are we on a hill or something?

'Hey Kev!' I hear Jamie shout.

I turn around to see Jamie, framed by the sheer mountains behind him. He has pushed up his face mask to speak, dismay is clear on his face. 'Shouldn't we be laughing now?'

Shit. He's right. We're supposed to be so strong and the ground so hard that we should be galloping along. Instead it's just like the day I pulled six tyres through the sand at Eastern Beach for the sick fun of it. That's what it is! This thick snow is as gritty and dense as sand. Behind me the sled has carved deep tracks.

As it grates across the snow, the sled is making a loud rasping and growling sound. It has the drag coefficient of an apartment block, complete with satellite dishes and clotheslines. It feels like I am pulling a bathtub, the old-fashioned claw-footed kind. With a walrus in it.

The heel of the advanced foot is never planted beyond the toe of the other, and of this small gain with each pace, two or three inches are lost by back slipping as the weight is brought forward. When we come to any particularly soft patch we do little more than mark time.

— Scott

This is just settling in, right? It's going to get better isn't it? What about all that nice slippery ice we saw on the flight down?

In the meantime it's just a bitter struggle. There's not even the comfort of repetition; every step is planned and conscious. Take a step. Heave. Take another step. Heave.

There is one good thing, though — there is no wind at all. It's sunny, in a kind of late afternoon sort of way, and perfectly still. Menacingly still, like the wind-up before the punch.

When I stop for the break, Jamie is behind some way. He comes up puffing.

'I'm going to lose the skis, eh? I'm slipping too much.'

'Good idea.'

After a piece of chocolate, some nuts and a little water plated with thin ice, we start off again. Now it's Jamie's turn to lead, I can keep to his tracks, and maybe it will be easier.

It isn't. I turn up the Kylie Minogue coming through my headphones until she drowns out the gasping and grunting coming from my mask.

Very slowly it is becoming clear that we are moving . . . very slowly. As I rise to the top of what seems to be higher ground, I stop and look over my shoulder. Our trail undulates up and down, back to an area of disturbed snow. Surely just over there is not where we started from? There is no way that at this rate we are going to make the nunatak, or whatever it is we're heading towards.

We keep going for another three hours. Time doesn't seem to pass because the sun doesn't get any lower. My watch, though, says it's now late at night Punta Arenas time, and my legs are trembling from all the effort.

We are pulling through rough snow when, just as we come up to the end of the shift, a perfect little tent-sized patch of smooth snow appears ahead. As soon as Jamie reaches it, the wind switches on and starts to blow.

There is a twitching in my left calf and suddenly the muscle spasms and clenches tight. I stop and try to stretch it out. Then the calf muscle on the other side cramps. Now the big muscles of my left quad all squeeze together excruciatingly. I'm standing bolt upright in surprise as if called to attention, as Antarctica takes control of my body from the ground up.

'Come on!' Jamie shouts. I can't move. I'm stuck in place like a scarecrow. One and a half legs, from calf to thigh, have locked up in a painful contraction. I wobble forward on my useable leg and manage to break the cramp before it completely sets in. My muscles are left jumpy and trembling, ready to grip at the least provocation.

By the time I've made it to the campsite, Jamie has unhitched the tent from the sled and pulled off the outer bag. The tent flaps on the ground, unrecognisably distorted. I've never seen it look so tangled or so fragile. How bad would it be if we couldn't get it up? Watch it! You're standing on that corner!

My heart rate finally drops to a canter when the tent pops into its familiar dome. Jamie goes inside to start the cooking and I stay out to secure the guy lines. I use all the skis and tent poles. It doesn't seem enough, so I haul a sled around to each side of the tent and anchor more guy lines around them. Now let's see you try to blow us away, Antarctica you frosty bitch.

Without the warmth from hauling the sled, I'm starting to feel the fierce, intense cold. At the tent flap, about to go in, I take a last look around. We are in a vast, vast white desert ringed by forlorn mountain peaks, all but drowned in the creeping, smothering ice.

There is nobody. There never *has* been anybody. The loneliest spot that I've been in is jostling madness compared with this. The landscape is completely and utterly indifferent. We are as insignificant and ephemeral as any two of the billion flecks of snow that are rushing past us on their way to oblivion. I bet when the first two people land on Mars they will feel the same thing I'm feeling now — *we've got no place being here.*

The floor of the tent is completely covered with hastily chucked gear: sleeping bags, cameras and clothes, battery box and kitchen box. At least it's a familiar and human-sized mess. Now that we're out of the wind and with the stove going, it's warm enough so that it doesn't seem completely suicidal changing out of my trail clothes.

I undo my sleeping roll, and sit on top, staring at the stove. Jamie pours water into a mug to make a hot chocolate and hands it to me. I stare unblinking at the rising steam, haunted by the last five hours of effort. I keep opening my mouth then closing it again as I realise that what I'm going to say is always a variation of 'You've got to be kidding me'.

So instead I say conversationally, and only slightly hysterically, 'Shall I see how far we went?'

'Go on.'

I turn on the GPS.

'3.3 nautical miles.'

Jamie coughs. 'What's that? About 7 ks?'

'More like 6.'

We haven't made it to the 80-degree line. We aren't even close to the nunataks. We aren't even on the frigging map. Six kilometres in five hours. That's just over 1 kilometre an hour. That's as fast as a sloth. That's a slow sloth. That's a sloth on the way to school. Worst of all is how far behind we are from where we were supposed to be.

There are two ways to gauge how we are doing. One is the Average and the other is the Schedule. The Average crudely tells us how far we need to go each day. We were supposed to be trekking 600 miles in fifty days, or 12 miles a day. Now we are 606 miles away with forty-nine days to go. That makes 12.4 miles a day. That innocent-sounding 0.4 looks like a rounding error, but at our current speed works out to be around forty-five minutes of hard pulling. You could say that so far all of our efforts have *added* forty-five minutes of hard work onto *every* remaining day of our trip.

The Schedule is the Average with a human face. The Schedule tweaks the Average to allow for the fact that we won't be starting out with full days of six shifts while we play ourselves in. The Schedule even includes a day in the tent in case we are caught by a blizzard. The Schedule assumes that we will get faster as our sleds get lighter. So the Schedule starts off easier but finishes harder than the initial Average. Due to our unusual starting point, we are now about 10 miles behind the Schedule. Great.

Jamie hands out the freeze-dri and we eat in a stunned silence.

At this rate we're not going to be able to get *to* the Pole, let alone get back. Have we made a colossal blunder? Was our whole plan really only relying on brute strength? We have to go faster — dramatically faster. But how? It's not like our sleds are going to sprout wings. It's not like we can start laying out caches early because we aren't even coming back here! How can this be anything other than hopeless?

I want to talk, but Camp Rule Number One is that you don't say anything that will bring the vibe of the team down. No moaning, no complaining, no exceptions. So I chew and try to swallow down a strangely tight throat.

What would Scott do? Write beautiful, poignant prose in his diary, halve the rations, double the efforts? Tally ho and sally forth? Actually he would relay. He would have both of us pull one sled for a mile and then come back and get the other. So it means hauling 3 miles to make 1 mile forward. Would we really go three times faster if two of us were pulling one sled? No, we wouldn't. It's not a solution.

'We're fucked, aren't we?' Whoops, it just slipped out.

'Yep. That was utter shit.' Jamie chews his Thai chicken curry thoughtfully.

'I tell you what — it was never going to be easy. No one has ever tried pulling 160 kilograms out of Hercules Inlet.'

'What about Fiennes and Stroud?'

'They started from Berkner Island.'

'Oh yeah! I think part of the problem is that we haven't been doing a lot of exercise lately. I think our muscles have got city lazy.'

'Yeah. They'll soon harden up, and at some point we've got to get to the icy stuff we saw from the plane.'

'True! And our sleds will be lighter tomorrow, from eating dinner and breakfast and burning the fuel.'

'Yep.'

Soon we've convinced ourselves that as tough as the day has been, tomorrow, we will be skipping through fields of daisies, or at least have it a little easier.

Jamie gets out the satellite phone to leave the voice message that will appear on our website in the morning.

```
November 12. 79 degrees 54 minutes south. Hello,
it's Jamie here. We have travelled for five
hours after being dropped off by the plane and
have covered a disappointing 3.3 nautical miles
because of the soft snow we have encountered
here on the coast, but we are excited for the
potential progress to be made from now on in.
Temperature is minus 15 degrees Celsius with light
winds . . . all in all a sunny happy day. Bye.
```

I look at him.

Right:
Enjoying my last days of being
warm and well fed in Punta Arenas
with fellow adventurers Jenny and
Ray Jardine and Hannah (right).

Below:
Jamie (right) testing MSR stoves
with AMPRO's Matt Meehan.

Above:
Blizzard on demand:
Jamie doing a
photo shoot at Snow
Planet for Waikato
University.

Above:
I knew I shouldn't have pulled
my Mercedes through the rough
part of town . . .

Below:
Training in Iqaluit — surely
Antarctica won't be as bad
as this?

Above:
The harbour at Iqaluit:
Monument Island, the frozen
ocean and home of the world's
toughest boaties.

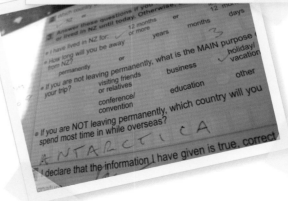

Above:
Jamie nears the top of the
Tasman Glacier.

Above right:
Woof! Towing 160 kilograms
of dog food all day in
Iqaluit began to affect me
strangely.

Right:
My New Zealand departure
card: not sure if it was a
holiday, but it certainly
wasn't 'visiting friends'.

Left:
The view from the Twin Otter on the
way to Hercules Inlet.

Below:
About to hook on to our sleds — our
last smiles for three weeks.

Above left:
Day 5, last shift: hauling
into the midnight sun.

Above right:
Camp 3.

Left:
Day 7. Climbing Foxy Pass
and looking back over the
first week of sledging.

Above right:
Count the fingers to
find the degree we've
just made!

Right:
Jamie under the sock
and mitten drying line.

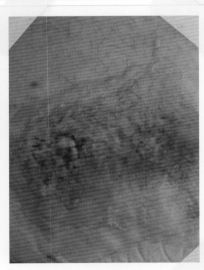

Above:
That bruise at the top of my leg . . .

Right:
. . . isn't a bruise.

Left:
Kevin of Antarctica.

Below:
Downed up during a
break.

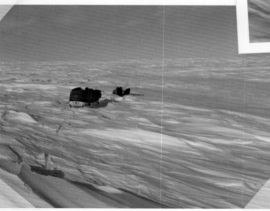

Above:
Hmmm, there's no snow
under that snow . . .

Left:
Can you spot the crevasse
in this photo?

Right:
A typical day in the sastrugi.

Below:
No one had the heart to tell Kevin his snow pony had melted.

Right:
Whiteout — inside the ping-pong ball, waiting for the white ninjas to attack.

Left:
The Antarctic Plateau at 88 degrees 30' South — sledging nirvana. If only it was all like this . . .

Left:
Approaching the Pole.

Below:
At the South Pole after
52 days — we've made it.

The first Kiwis to
walk unsupported to the
South Pole.

Left:
Jamie before: full-cream version.

Below:
Jamie after: low-fat, freeze-dried, shrink-wrapped and 23 kilograms lighter.

Above:
Jamie and Kate wedded.

Right:
Kevin and HPG hitched.

'Did you just say a "sunny happy day"?'

He looks back impassively. 'It's sunny, isn't it?'

'Yes it is.'

Jamie fills our Nalgene bottles with hot water and turns off the stove. Then we zip off the vestibule and retreat into the sleeping area to slither into our sleeping bags. With the stove off, the temperature starts to drop quickly.

I should write in my journal but the pen is a telegraph pole, my arms are bags of wet cement and my head is filled with static — when it's not tuned into the Disaster Channel. Nor do I want to do anything to upset my fragile truce with our situation.

> . . . *the exceptional exercise gives bad attacks of cramp.*
>
> — Scott

It's hard to block out the light. I pull my neck warmer over my eyes but there is always a little needle of white coming in from somewhere, pricking my brain into consciousness. So I lie on my inch-thick Therm-a-Rest, on top of the half-inch-thick RidgeRest, on top of 1 millimetre of groundsheet, on top of 4 kilometres of ice. With each squirm, Antarctica injects a finger of freezing air deep into my bag. As it strokes down my leg, every muscle spasms tightly. My leg shoots out and I groan and bang and massage it, trying to shake the cramp free while not letting more cold air in. Finally I realise that a hot Nalgene bottle pushed against the muscle helps it to relax, and I lie back breathing shallowly and twitching a little. I stare up at the latitude lines that Jamie has drawn on the inside of the tent. We aren't even on the tent map.

Don't think about progress for the first week was Eric's advice. It seems like a good idea, so I lie not asleep frantically not thinking about the progress we're not making. Meanwhile, through the earplugs, I can hear the muffled rumble of the tent shivering and shaking in the wind. There's also a rhythmic hissing sound, as if shovelfuls of sand are being heaped on us. That's *exactly* what it is. Just like the silvery excrescence that an oyster grows over the irritating speck inside it, Antarctica is gently trying to bury us.

DAY 2. THE DAY THAT WE FORGOT

I HAVE BEEN STARING at the roof for some time, listening to the crack and flap of the tent before Jamie starts to stir. The wind has definitely got stronger.

It hadn't been much of a night. With the sun never having set, it hadn't been anything of a night. It's still up, grinning like a deranged clown: 'Still he-re!' I never appreciated how much the night is a big black reset button. It gets dark. You go to sleep. You wake up again and everything is rebooted. Imagined fears have vanished, problems have been untangled, and you have new energy to attack the day. Not here. It's still the same day and we still have the same problems.

The rising and setting of the sun is the most basic and primeval of rhythms; when it doesn't happen it's profoundly disturbing. What other rules don't apply? Are things going to start falling up?

Despite this, I do feel marginally better. The sleeping bags have worked. We haven't been buried alive. The tent hasn't split. We have survived one night, we can survive more. By 4.30am, it's time to get up.

I split the muesli into our bowls, Jamie puts in the water and then garnishes with a glug of grapeseed oil. I can get the greasy goo in while it's still warm but by the time I'm halfway through, it's cold and as appealing as a block of lard.

'I could finish that for you, if you wanted?' offers Jamie.

'Sure.'

Once the stove is off, it quickly gets too cold to stay still. So it's boots on and time to go. I make a dash to get the down jackets from the sleds. Outside it's sunny but the wind is blowing hard. It is also shockingly cold. Over the next two hours we slowly pack the tent away and onto the sleds. Everything has to be placed just so, nothing can be left unheld for a moment or the wind will whip it away.

When everything but the tent is stowed, we stumble back inside to regain some composure. I zip shut the flap behind us, pull off my goggles and sit breathing hard, shaking my head free of snow.

'How hard do you think that wind's blowing — twenty knots?'

'It's gotta be thirty.'

Man. This is really tough.

'Hey, when Bruce Banner gets angry who does he turn into?'

'The Hulk.'

'And when The Hulk gets angry who does he turn into?' says Jamie.

'Chuck Norris.'

'Exactly. Are you ready?'

'Right behind you.'

'OK, here we go. On three. One, two, three.'

I yank the zip up and step out.

DAY 3. BACK TO THE START

WE'RE EATING BREAKFAST WHEN Jamie asks, 'Can you remember what happened yesterday?'

I think for a moment. 'Actually, not very well, no.'

'Me neither. That's weird.'

'What does it say in your journal?'

He looks it up.

'*3.6 miles. Slow. Painful. Four tyres with concrete. I broke the towing rope.*'

An image flashes into my head: Jamie's face emerging from the snow. Now I remember.

I had turned around and seen Jamie pulling low down, like he was in the front row of a rugby scrum, or a sled dog. He was jerking forward to try to get the sled to move over a little lip. There was a bang, and then he had hurtled ahead, landing face down in the snow. His harness line had given away. He had lifted his head up and bellowed, 'That fricking Stefan!'

'Have we had any new texts?'

'Yeah, here's one from Kate. She's saying that the RAF and Marines are complaining about the snow conditions around Patriot Hills.'

'Anything from Adam the Radio Guy?'

'No.'

Because we were working to a different schedule from the other teams, we had arranged with Adam to text in the information he needed to track us each day. He would respond with a confirmation text. If we didn't get one from him we had to assume that he wasn't getting ours, which was bad, because if he didn't hear from us for forty-eight hours, they would send a plane to look for us.

The back-up plan is to call him at the time he is getting the Sched calls from the other expeditions, which is at the end of their day but in the middle of ours.

'We're going to have to call him this afternoon.'

It's another bright, sunny and viciously cold and windy day.

We are trudging alongside a big escarpment, like a long four-storey-high sand dune. It leads right up to the nunatak we have been plodding towards for two days. Slowly, during the morning, the nunatak resolves into two peaks separated by a slope leading out of sight. The start of the legendary hill out of Hercules Inlet.

I'm leading when I feel a yank on the sled. Jamie has grabbed it, and is pointing at the top with his ski pole.

'What?' I shout.

He lifts up his mask.

'Where's the ski?'

One of the kite skis is missing from the top of the sled. Shit.

I look behind the sled. There is just a million hectares of whiteness. The blowing snow creates a ground drift that obscures everything below knee height.

'Wait here!' I start to run back down our increasingly faint tracks. Unshackled, my limbs swing so very easily, weightlessly. I could run

132

all the way to the Pole. There's no sign of the ski. We can't lose a kite ski — we don't have any spares! How can this get worse? *By you getting lost.* I start looking over my shoulder to make sure I don't lose sight of Jamie.

Two hundred metres away, there it is in the snow. I pick it up and jog slowly back.

At the break after the third shift, I check the GPS while I wait for Jamie to catch up.

Hey, we've made 80 degrees! After a two-and-a-half-day diversion we've finally crossed the start line. I'm not happy, but I'm positively Jim Carrey compared to Jamie, who is still going slowly, occasionally slipping over. He pulls the sled alongside, puts on his down jacket and sits with a dejected thump on the back.

I try to cheer him up by showing him the GPS.

'Look. We've started, and we did over a mile in that last shift.'

Two kilometres in one hour and twenty minutes of trudging. That's 1.5 kilometres an hour. That's the length of a cricket pitch a minute. I think there is a species of bamboo that grows that fast. Nevertheless, it's something to celebrate.

'Supersonic,' he says dryly. 'That fricking Stefan.'

I could swear that we are almost at the base of one of the nunataks, yet it's not until just before the end of the next shift that the terrain noticeably starts to rise. It's time to call Adam. We pull the sleds together and I unzip the bivvy bag from its pouch at the back of one of the sleds.

The bivvy bag is a temporary shelter that is stitched into the sled cover on one side and on the other side can be anchored under the bum of a person. We can pull the very fine nylon material all the way over us and tuck it under our boots, creating an instant shell against the wind. After a few frantic seconds we're inside, blinking in the green, filtered light, pleasantly out of the biting wind.

The noise of the wind hammering the thin nylon is so loud that I have to yell down the phone. I shout out our position, and then close my eyes and hold my gloved hand over my ear to hear Adam's tiny voice. When I open my eyes again the air is thick with a fine powdery snow that has somehow found its way in. We are sitting in a mini-blizzard, like a shaken Christmas paperweight.

Then a big gust shreds the bag around us and I'm scampering to get my hood up and the satellite phone under cover.

'What did he say?' shouts Jamie, stuffing the remnants of cloth back into the pouch.

'He said the Jardines never made it down here. They turned back on the first day, they're going to restart from Patriot Hills. Everyone else is going slow and complaining about the snow.'

At last we are at the base of the dreaded hill out of Hercules Inlet, the one that we had been scaring ourselves with when training for all those months. It is, in fact, a gentle slope. If you were in a car you might not even change gear. But it is definitely up. Even imperceptible grades have slowed us and this is definitely perceptible.

We start to climb straight up, but we are slipping, even wearing our boots, so we begin to tack back and forth. At the end of my shift, I'm happy to swap over with Jamie and look forward to having an easier time hanging out in his tracks. Jamie charges, with a rhythmic clockwork pace, and for the first time I'm working hard to keep up. He must be feeling better. Damn.

By the time the shift ends, even Jamie is starting to flag, and I'm exhausted. In the tent, I manage to get off one boot and am tugging on the other when I give up and fall back onto the Therm-a-Rest.

Jamie hands me a drink and I'm halfway through it before I find my voice.

'So, that could have been worse.'

'Oh yeah. I was holding back today.'

Jamie is lying back on his sleeping bag with his mug on his stomach. He talks to the ceiling. 'In fact, I was thinking I might go for a run to burn off some energy.' He drapes an arm over his face.

'You know,' I say, 'I keep thinking of that scene from *Rocky IV*.'

'When he fights that Russian guy?'

'Yeah. He goes out into the wilderness to train, and he's running through the snow up to his knees with a big, like, railway sleeper across his shoulders.'

'Just a railway sleeper? I'd kill for a railway sleeper.'

I'm getting changed when I notice I have left a pair of socks that I need for tomorrow in the sled. Bum. The sled, though, is right outside the door. I could almost, but not quite, unzip the flap and reach out and get them. Almost, but not quite. Instead, I'll have to go outside, and I've already taken off my outside armour. I'm only wearing long thermal undies, a polar-fleece top and down booties.

Do I really need to put all that stuff back on? The sled is just there. All I need to do is unzip the flap, step outside, unzip the sled cover and grab the clothes bag. I'll be back in the tent before I've had a chance to get cold. It'll be a bracing and invigorating little dash.

'I'm just going out to get some clothes,' I say to Jamie.

'Don't you want to put on your jacket?'

'Nah, it's going to be bracing and invigorating.'

A few seconds later I am standing next to the sled, fiddling with the zip on the cover with my bare hands. It's amazing how fast the wind cleaves away any warmth. I reach in and yank out my clothes bag. It's upside down and the drawstring isn't tight. Clothes spray in an arc into the wind.

Shit.

> *We were flying over the ice as fast as we could after our lost garments. The incidence would have been extremely funny had it not involved the possibility of such serious consequences.*
>
> — Scott

The heavy clothes don't fall far but the smalls start tumbling down the slope immediately, with the glove liners leading the way like a mad party of dancing crabs. I start running after them, picking up the big items first, creating a bundle tight against my stomach. Soon there are only a couple of pieces left but as I pick them up, others start falling out.

Then there is only one glove liner happily scampering down the slope and for a second I think maybe I should leave it. No! Bugger Antarctica. I'm going to get it. So I keep running, even when one of my down booties starts to flap off, and I'm very close to sprinting only in my socks before I stop to sort it out. I run on and get close enough to try a one-handed dive. Missed! I get up and chase again; this time I finish the dive with a faceful of snow but the glove liner in my hand. Ha!

My feeling of satisfaction lasts until I turn around to face the savagely cold wind and see the tent silhouetted against the sun, maybe three hundred metres up the slope. As I walk I drop my head down and try to hide my face and hands in the bundle of clothes to protect them. What a stupid thing to do! I'm very cold before I get close enough to the tent to start shouting, 'Door! Door!' The zip comes down, and I tumble in without stopping.

'Was that bracing and invigorating?' Jamie asks half an hour later when I've finally stopped shivering and have got back out of my sleeping bag.

I don't seem to have any injuries — with the exception of a single large blister on my right middle finger. The first sign of frostbite. I pop it, suck out the fluid and wrap it up as well as I can. The books say that if it were to get cold again while it was still healing . . . well, my repertoire of offensive hand gestures might be seriously affected. Antarctica is trying to kill me. Correction: I'm trying to kill me — Antarctica is happy to help.

'So how far did we go?' I ask.

Jamie gets out the GPS. 'In six and a half hours we did . . .' the numbers blink up, '. . . 4.3 miles.'

'At least we're on the map. Eighty degrees 2.4 minutes south. We've started.'

'That fricking Stefan.'

So now we know how much time we've lost. Three days. We have to get to the Pole in 47 days, not 50. The Average is up to 12.7 miles. The Schedule says that we should be passing Patriot Hills, instead we are just leaving Hercules Inlet.

Hercules Inlet! We are paying a huge price to start from down here rather than Patriot Hills. It's a distinction that matters to us but does anyone else care? Are we losing sight of the big picture? Are we being too stubborn?

Look at the Jardines. They wanted to start from Hercules Inlet, but they turned around. They wouldn't have done that if they hadn't done the maths and figured out that it was the smartest thing for them to do. And they don't come tougher or more trail savvy than them. I turn to Jamie.

'You know, just an idea, I'm definitely not suggesting we do it but just so we've talked about everything and looked at all options. We could ask to get picked up and start from Patriot Hills. Maybe they could send down a snowmobile. We might be able to save three days. Get back on schedule at least.'

Jamie is quiet for a long time while he pulls off his cross-country boots and puts on his down booties. When he's finished, he looks at me. 'You know what? I would rather fail trying to do something big than succeed at doing something small.'

I sigh. 'Yeah. I agree.'

Actually, getting a tow probably wouldn't make much difference. Unless our rate of advance improved, we would still be going far too slowly just in a different place, and grinding to a halt in some other white featureless spot well short of the Pole.

I should like to keep the track to the end.

— Scott

So that's how it's going to be then. We're going to haul until we're nearly out of food, then turn around and kite back. We've just bought ourselves seven weeks of pointless, gruesome, bone-bending slog. This is going to be a long lousy summer, unless we fall into a crevasse — then it will be a short lousy one.

Jamie is scribbling earnestly in his journal.

```
During the day I hit the wall. The third shift I
wondered if I was the right man for this challenge.
I questioned myself many times if I wanted the
glory but couldn't hack the pain it required.

In the last two shifts I tried eating more
butter and it worked wonders. Felt strong
going uphill. I was pleased my legs were
starting to show Kev something (finally).
```

I still can't bring myself to write in mine. There is nothing to look forward to. Just the slow disintegration of all of our hopes. We are the punk contender in a mismatched heavyweight fight, who hears the bell and steps out of his corner straight into a knockout uppercut. Now our unconscious body is beginning its slow-motion descent to the head-smacking, mouthguard-spilling collision with the mat.

The wind, if anything, is increasing. I push back the neck warmer to see the tent fabric drum-tight. The seams are exposed and the stitches working hard. Please let them hold. I'm trusting my faith in some person I've never met, some procurer of thread who's never been to Antarctica, to whom breaking strength is just a number, and ripstop just a concept.

It now sounds like the outside of the tent is being sandblasted. The Jardines told us about being nearly buried in snow while training in Greenland and the number of times Ray had to get out in the middle of the night to dig their tent free.

Don't think about the straining fabric. Don't think about the lack of progress. Don't think about the unavoidable failure. Don't think about the pain that you are going to have to go through tomorrow. Don't think about the people you're going to disappoint. Don't think about the snow piling up outside. Don't think.

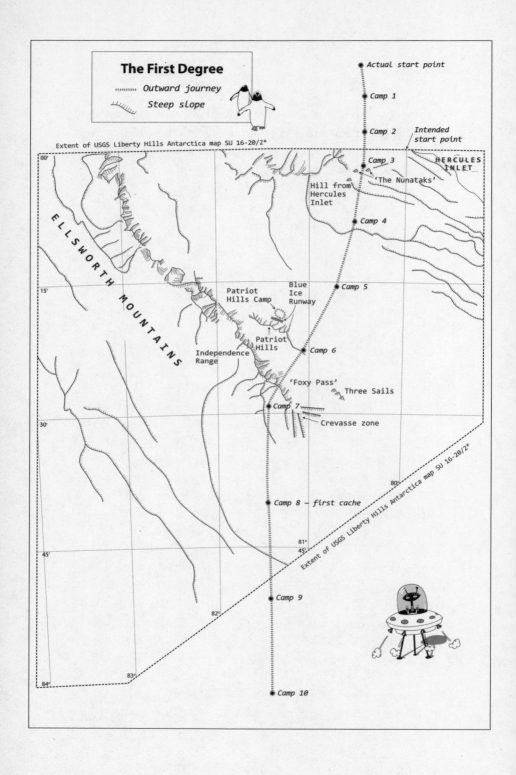

The First Degree

········· Outward journey

‿‿‿ Steep slope

Extent of USGS Liberty Hills Antarctica map SU 16-20/2*

Actual start point

Camp 1

Camp 2

Intended start point

Camp 3

'The Nunataks'

HERCULES INLET

Hill from Hercules Inlet

Camp 4

00'

ELLSWORTH MOUNTAINS

Blue Ice Runway

Patriot Hills Camp

Camp 5

15'

Patriot Hills

Independence Range

Camp 6

'Foxy Pass'

Three Sails

Camp 7

Crevasse zone

30'

80°

Extent of USGS Liberty Hills Antarctica map SU 16-20/2*

Camp 8 – first cache

81°
45'

45'

Camp 9

82°

84°

83°

Camp 10

10. MURDER IN THE FIRST DEGREE

DAY 4. THE HILL FROM HERCULES INLET

MY EYES OPEN. SOMETHING is missing. It's quiet. I take out my earplugs. It's still quiet. The tent isn't flapping. I unzip the fly and peek out. The sky is clear and sunny. Not a speck of snow stirs. The great bowl has been charmed into supernatural stillness.

I don't fool that easy. This is the inhale before the sneeze. I bet the Mother of All Blizzards is grinding its teeth just behind the ranges, waiting to smash us as soon as we let our guard down. The straps are going to be pulled an extra few centimetres tighter today.

It's only 4am but Jamie can't sleep either and soon the stove is going and we're having breakfast. I'm aching with hunger, cradling my bowl of muesli and rocking back and forth like Gollum with his Precious.

Jamie looks at my last few golden oily spoonfuls. 'I could help you with that if you wanted?'

'Fuck off.'

The early start means there is time for first aid. We decide that the deep fissures that have started to appear in the tips of Jamie's fingers

141

and my frost blister probably warrant a call to Dr John at base camp.

He sounds uncharacteristically anxious. 'You've taken the fluid out? OK, then wrap it up. Whatever you do, and I mean WHATEVER you do, don't let it get cold again. It's very serious. Do you understand?'

And as for Jamie. 'Did you get that superglue I told you about?'

'Yes.'

'Well then you can just glue the cracks back together.'

'Are you serious?'

'Yes, it works very well.'

So Jamie gets out the tube and gingerly starts sticking himself back together.

'Be careful what you touch! Actually, I think there is something in your nose.'

'Oh ha.'

> *On long cold journeys one's fingers were liable to split and crack about the nails, and this was both painful and troublesome.*
>
> — Scott

Later, as we are getting ready to leave the tent, Jamie puts on one of his boots and holds the other one upside down next to mine.

'I thought so! Check this out.'

'What?'

'Look at the tread!'

The swirls and ridges on the soles of his brand of boot are much lower.

'I see what you mean.'

'That's why I'm bloody falling over all the time!'

'Yeah, maybe we should try wearing the crampons.'

'On the snow?'

'I think it's worth a try.'

We get out the crampons — the skeleton of hardened alloy jaws that strap onto our boots and bite into the ice. The metal teeth are crazy, angry sharp. They have shredded the layers and layers of foam that they've been wrapped in. It's as if they don't actually have to touch anything to cut it; if they are just close to a sock or a glove then a hole suddenly appears. We walk around the outside of the tent very carefully as we collapse it and put it away.

They do feel like they're gripping more. So with more hope we hook onto the sleds and lean forward.

On 1 November 1911, on a bright, clear spring morning, Scott's main party left Hut Point and set out for the Pole. For the next six weeks the ponies did most of the pulling as they trudged towards the base of the Beardmore Glacier. There, the men were organised into three four-man teams, with each team pulling a single sled weighing around 360 kilograms. They headed for the glacier's lower reaches.

As soon as they started to climb, they found soft, deep snow. Even Bowers, who was the Energizer Bunny of the expedition, was appalled by the effort required:

> We stuck ten yards from the camp, and nine hours later found
> us little more than half a mile on. I have never seen a sledge
> sink so. I have never pulled so hard, or so nearly crushed my
> inside into my backbone by the everlasting jerking with all my
> strength on the canvas band around my unfortunate tummy.

I'm thinking of Bowers as I jerk with my waist to get the sled started.

I'm going to have abs like a samba dancer by the time this is over. It's like the sled runners are Velcro hooks and I'm pulling over something fluffy. At least now our boots aren't slipping and I can take a line as direct up the hill as my screaming Achilles will permit.

The hill is one of those evil, perfect parabolas, so that from any point the crest only seems to be a few hundred metres away. Yet a few hundred metres later we are still looking at a crisp, horizontal line a few hundred metres away. For the first time, we have no landmark to pull towards. I try to use the sun and the rock outcrops on either side to keep a straight course.

Now Jamie takes the lead, and again sets a furious pace. In my Gore-Tex shell, I start to warm up and I have to unzip my jacket and even pull off the hood to try to bleed off some heat. My holiday is over. Jamie has found his form.

At the next break, by the time I arrive, he already has his snack bag out, with one leg resting rakishly on his knee, nibbling on a block of butter.

'So what are you listening to?' I ask.

'The Rocky theme.'

'Anything else?'

'No. Just Rocky.'

On the trail nothing happens quickly; over the next hours the horizon line develops a tiny bump, which turns into a single peak. Then another, and slowly our plodding is rewarded by raising the tops of the Independence Range, some 19 miles away.

According to the map, we are now trudging over a vast plain. In reality, the terrain very gently rolls and folds, although the contrast is so low it is hard to tell exactly what is happening or going to happen. We only know that the mountains in front are slowly getting larger.

We're doing a fifth shift today. As a special treat we even start off wearing our down jackets for a few minutes until we warm up. But by the time we stop and shuffle back to the sled, take off the jacket and stuff it into the sled then we're cold, and it almost hasn't been worthwhile.

Soon after we start, mean little shreds of clouds start to slide in from the horizon, coalescing until we're creeping into a near featureless grey, our view of the mountains almost obliterated. It's very late local time, nearly midnight, so we're heading into the sun when it is at its lowest point in the sky, due south. In the glancing light, icy patches shine in the gloom like bright pools. I try to join the dots to give our sleds the chance to run slightly more sweetly.

By the time the shift ends, I'm dizzy, light-headed and exhausted. I stumble round the camp, tripping over the guy lines as I set up the tent.

Inside, the GPS reports only 6.3 disappointing miles. We're now 19 miles behind the Schedule. The texts from home tell us that the Marines are walking very slowly, that the RAF have had some things go wrong with them, although what exactly isn't clear.

Jamie writes in his diary.

```
Felt strong all day. Kev led well in the second
shift, so I worked him to the ground in the third.
My legs were pistons for most of the day (get
your hand off it, Darryl). I realised you only
have to feel a little stronger than the other
person for the world to look rosy. I can't wait
to talk to Kate tonight, thinking of her a lot.
```

DAY 5. THE WHOLE NINE HOURS
NO WIND AGAIN. ALLAHU Akbar. No horizon to the south either. It just isn't there. It's not exactly mist or fog. Grey snow blends to grey cloud blends to grey sky nearly seamlessly. Only the vaguest hint of a single mountain peak hanging in the sky helps to straighten our meandering furrow.

Today we've scheduled for the first time to do a full day of six shifts. At least nine hours on the trail if we're snappy with our breaks, nine and a half if we're not. It's going to be a long day.

On the Atlantic the best way of passing the time was to talk with each other, listening to or telling some outrageous story. No chance of that here as we're skiing in single file and the wind snatches away anything but shouts. So that leaves the iPod.

While rowing it was also very helpful to listen to non-fiction audio books about people in worse situations than ourselves, like *Into Thin Air* or *Black Hawk Down*. There was nothing like gasping for breath in Everest's Death Zone, or having RPGs rain down as you fight your way out of Mogadishu to put a little sunny paddle into perspective. This time, instead of choosing ever more gruesome books, I have decided to go for some light distraction like David Beckham's biography *My Side*.

At the start of the second shift, after we take off our down jackets, I shuffle back to position, hook onto the sled, pull out my iPod and push the play button with the same sense of relief as Han Solo engaging warp drive to escape from the Imperial forces. Nothing. The screen is blank. Frozen into a lifeless lump. I clamp my teeth together in irritation. This is doubly annoying because we had been warned that it might happen, so we had internal pockets stitched in to our thermal tops. The battery is so close to my skin that it couldn't be any warmer if I swallowed it. We had no trouble with our iPods in Iqaluit or in the freezer, but here the cold seems to have some extra venom to it. I glumly set off. I'm sure the iPod will start working again when it thaws out in the tent, and maybe I can find a warmer spot for it, but in the meantime I'll have to face the rest of the day without any mental anaesthesia and the miles will be extracted from me every single bone-jarring moment at a time.

I have a theory that over our lives we hear so many songs so many times that thousands of verses slowly descend until they become part of the ooze that sloshes around in the basement of the brain. The Subconscious swims around in this like a creature from the depths. Having no words of its own, when it wants to communicate a thought or feeling, it ties a balloon onto a relevant lyric and sends it floating back to the surface. So sometimes when a song drifts into your head, you might find if you play along that you come to a couple of words or a line that perfectly sum up how you are feeling.

Now, with no other distraction, my brain is like a crazed radio station burping out bits of different tunes. I can understand why I'm getting 'She's So Cold' by the Rolling Stones, but why 'It's Raining Men' by The Weather Girls?

As disturbing as this is, at least it's not action songs. I despise action songs. Or worse yet, that song that is so sticky and catchy that I dare not think its name. The song from the Disneyland ride. The one about it being a tiny planet — that's about as close as I'm prepared to go. Then the shift ends and all is forgotten as I have to face a far more serious problem.

The very first thing I do at the start of each break is to pull out my down jacket from the back of the sled, and push my gloved hands into the sleeves and out through the snug elasticised bands around the wrists. This is very satisfactory.

The problem comes ten minutes later when I try to reverse the procedure. Now, like a lobster caught in a trap, it is impossible to withdraw my hands unless I take off at least one outer glove. In the few seconds that my slightly moist, thin glove inner is exposed to the cold, it chills my hand so much that I spend the next half hour trying to bring life and feeling back to it. This has happened so many times that I'm determined to remove the jacket without taking off my gloves.

What starts out as gently and ineffectually plucking at my sleeve, quickly escalates into snarling vicious fury as I try different, increasingly violent techniques to no avail. Jamie looks on bemused as I jump around and beat the jacket on the ground with both arms still locked in. I'm hopping about on one foot, trying to use my boot to push the jacket off my wrists. Then I flail at the ground like a rock guitar player trying to destroy his instrument.

Jamie has finished his snacks, reconnected to his sled and is looking at me curiously. Finally I manage to compose myself, stuff the jacket into the sled and hook on, wild-eyed and breathing heavily.

Just you wait until we get into the tent, Mr Smarty Pants Jacket.

The way I understand it, your body is a furnace and to keep itself going it has stores of glucose, glycogen and fat — which have the relative potency of gasoline, coal and damp cardboard respectively. You only have a litre of gasoline, a few bags of coal, but a warehouse full of the cardboard. (As a last resort your body can also consume the protein in your muscles — the equivalent of throwing the furniture on the fire.)

The body burns anything but the brain only accepts gasoline. The body does have a process for making gasoline from the cardboard, which it will do in a pinch, but it isn't very efficient. Road cyclists, for some reason, are particularly prone to using up all their glycogen and glucose. Then they stop and fall over.

I'm thinking about this as I look into my snack pouch during the last break. We have stretched out our four-day snack bag to five days. I haven't been able to ration very well. When I look inside there is almost nothing edible, just a few greasy smears and some nut fragments pushed into the corners. I nibble at them while the hunger takes great bites out of me.

It's midnight local time, the clouds are obscuring the sky. We can barely make out the terrain and the cold is sucking our sleds to the sandy snow as we trudge towards a dull, cold neon ball. A very fuzzy neon ball, as my goggles are fogging up badly. I push them up to look at my watch. The screen is blank — the cold must have got to it.

There is nothing to distract my brain, which in desperation starts counting steps. No! I refuse. I'm not counting steps. I'm not counting steps again, I'm not counting steps for the third time. Think of something else. My subconscious disc jockey gladly obliges with the first verse of 'YMCA'.

No, please no. Not action songs. But my energy-drained brain is powerless to resist. There isn't any strength in my legs either. They dangle limply from my waist. I'm moving by lifting up my hips and letting my leg swing underneath. I would give anything to stop and just wobble for a bit. I'm burning wet cardboard. My perception of time passing has slowed so much it's like I've entered another plane of consciousness. As I stomp my ski pole into the ground the snow arcs up gracefully like those super-slow-motion clips of a drop of water hitting a puddle and making a little crown.

But even infinity has an end. We stop in a grey patch in the grey murk. I'm confused. I look at things and barely recognise them. I grab things and take them places. I pick things up and put them down. It all seems very complicated. What was I doing? That's right, shovelling snow on the flaps.

It takes the sugary fingers of my second hot chocolate to coax my consciousness out of the back of my limbic system, and for my thought processes to return to normal. Now the GPS has had time to unthaw I take it out. In nine hours we did only 7.46 miles.

I look at the dregs of my hot chocolate.

'You finding this hard going?' I ask.

'Yep.'

'How hard?'

'This is hard like trying to rub your stomach and pat your head at the same time.'

'I know what you mean. This is like when you're playing Scrabble and you're trying to get a word out and you haven't got any vowels.'

'It isn't that hard. Now you're talking it up.'

Antarctica is beating us, and it's time to strike back. I'm going to start with that jacket. Desperate times call for desperate emergency gusset making. I unfold the scissor attachment from the Gerber multi-tool and, with a leer of satisfaction, make a 15-centimetre slash down through the right wrist of my down jacket. Then I just need to sew up each side of the cut, to create a gusset-dart thingy. Down is starting to billow out, so I pinch the edges closed while I poke through our little repair kit for the needle with another finger.

That's funny. It's got to be around somewhere. I rummage

increasingly frantically while down continues to escape. There is everything *but* the needle. It must have dropped out in Punta. Bugger! There are some safety pins, though, and I use all of them to carefully fasten the edges together. I hold it up in front of me when I'm done.

'How about that, eh! Punks to the Pole!' I turn to see Jamie's reaction.

The tent looks like a goose exploded. Jamie shakes his head as he blows a piece of fluff off his nose.

DAY 6. PASSING PATRIOT HILLS

HANNAH IS IN THE radio hut with Adam when we call in the next morning. She has been spending the last few days doing a shakedown trip around Patriot Hills. I point out that there is only a very passing similarity between the breezy walk with lashings of hot chocolate that she had described and this grim muscle-snapping, ligament-tearing reality.

'Oh bless! If I told you what it was really like you would never have gone. Ha ha!'

The wind is back. Snakes of blown snow dart and curl around our boots. With them comes devastating, probing cold. There is an urgency around the breaks that makes them deeply unsatisfying. It's just unhook, pee, jacket on, chew, gulp, take off jacket (yes *much* easier, thank you), shiver, hook on and trudge off, thinking, Was that what I just spent the last hour and a half looking forward to?

I'm worried about my nose. Though protected by my neoprene face mask, it still constantly feels cold. I would hate to get frostbite and lose my nose. I would look very odd at the wedding. I'm even more worried about my hands. They are often painfully cold, particularly after breaks even if I keep my outer gloves on. It's a vicious cycle; the colder the fingers the less blood the body pumps to them. The hurting is less scary than the numbness. Once they go numb then you don't know what havoc the cold is playing.

I keep working them, trying to make fists then relax, until finally there is some creeping warmth — just in time for the next break.

Today is the closest that we get to the Patriot Hills base. On our right-hand side, hidden a few kilometres away in a fold in the landscape, are snug tents, cheerful sympathetic companions and hot food. In just a few hours we could be there, sitting in a warm tent with warm hands, and eating hot food, and drinking beer . . . and dead of shame.

Jamie is leading this shift, so all I need to do is keep my head down, stay in his tracks and focus on keeping up with the North Face sticker at the back of his sled. Leading is quite a responsibility. You're both helming the ship and running the boiler room. The thing that you must never do when you are leading is to stop. Only with progress towards the goal do we get the slow drip of satisfaction that sustains our hope. Stopping means upsetting the rhythm of the person behind you and whacking them with the if-we-keep-going-like-this-we-will-never-get-there stick. It means interrupting their daydreams and bringing them back to the horror of the present. It also means tipping the delicate energy balance back towards cold, and forcing them to spend the next ten minutes going unnaturally fast, puffing hard, burning excess energy to warm up. Just as you wouldn't loudly break wind in polite company in the normal world, you wouldn't stop while you're leading the team in Antarctica.

Ten minutes into the shift, Jamie looks over his shoulder and then stops. Oh come on! I've only just warmed up. He motions for me to come up alongside. This had better be fricking good. He pulls down his neck warmer.

'Your fly's undone.'

'Oh is it? Ta.'

Ice keeps forming inside my goggles. I try to rub it off but most of it is in between the inner and outer lens. For a few moments I get some tiny patch of vision, then after a couple of exhaled breaths it's like looking at the world through wax. I weave and bob my head like a boxer trying to find a clear spot, until I give up. What is there to see anyway? The snow is flat, it's not like I'm going to hit a lamp post or a bus stop. The sun is bright enough so that I can navigate just by keeping its orange glow in the middle of my goggles. But it is very unnerving.

Trying to learn from yesterday, I have saved two precious squares of chocolate for the last break, to help get through this shift. It's making a difference; I can't exactly do a Sudoku in my head but at least I'm still mostly coherent when the shift finally ends.

We set up the tent in a river of flowing snow. Lines of sinewy white smoke race by at calf height. I angle the sleds in front of the tent in an attempt to divert the stream around either side. Before I go in, I take a quick look around.

We are surrounded by a magical white billowing carpet. To the right of the tent I can look down the valley between the Patriot Hills and the much larger Independence Range. The lonely sentinels of the Three Sails rear up five miles away on our left. If you were watching from inside a heated glass dome with a mug of hot chocolate, it would really be quite something.

We only did 6.65 miles today. This is only a little more than half of what the Schedule requires. We're still falling more and more behind, ploughing on to a glorious defeat. We're still firmly on track to be an extremely obscure Antarctic Trivial Pursuit question. Perhaps we won't even make it to halfway.

In the meantime my fingers feel strange. I prod the tips of them with a safety pin. Up to about halfway to the first knuckle there's no sensation. The skin is pink and looks normal, but apparently the nerves have retreated to warmer climes. Do nerves grow back? Or will I never need to use oven gloves again? Jamie is watching.

'Yeah, mine aren't great either. Makes you wonder how the old fella is coping, eh?'

That's right! Hopefully the possum fur is working. A quick examination confirms that there's no need for the safety-pin test. There is a large blue bruise on the top of my left leg, though. It must be from the waist strap of the harness.

DAY 7. FOXY PASS

FOR 300 KILOMETRES, THE Ellsworth Mountain group marches alongside the Ronne Ice Shelf. Then, at a spot right in front of us, its last extension, the Independence Range, finally plunges down under Antarctica's snowy mantle. The great ice sheet pouring down from the Pole has to flow around this point, and as it does it fractures into enormous crevasses. To avoid these potential death traps we must either detour in a wide arc to the east or go over a sneaky little saddle at the end of the mountains. Hannah referred to it as Foxy Pass and for lack of a better reason, so do we.

A pass conjures up llamas and prayer flags. This isn't that sort of pass, it's just a moderate-sized gentle hill. A green run on a ski field, framed by two small picturesque rocky outcrops. Steeper than the hill from Hercules Inlet, but also much shorter. It looks a few hundred metres long, so it is probably only four or five times that.

Last night I thought that we had camped at the bottom of the pass, but today it takes two shifts to get there. The iPods didn't take any charge last night, so it's a helpful distraction having the impending pass to add drama. Did I just say that? Just a week ago entertainment was rugby test matches, a new Bond film and flaming tequila shots — now I'm happy with several hours of a small hill coming closer.

Jamie stops at the bottom and looks up as I pull alongside. During the last few days we have detoured to avoid anything higher than a freckle and now here we are about to climb up this monster.

'Time to put our big-boy trousers on,' says Jamie. 'Take the hill.'

My turn to lead, so I start climbing at a shallow angle, as steep as I can stand before zagging back the other way. Every step feels like I'm adding another couple of centimetres onto each Achilles tendon. My right heel is getting hotter from where the crampon frame is pinching it, but there is nothing I can do. There is no way I can get up this hill without crampons.

There are occasional icy patches where the sled clatters along, then it's back to wallowing through sand. Before I've done a hundred metres, I'm wondering whether it just wouldn't be easier to go back and walk around the crevasses. By 300 metres, I'm wondering if it just wouldn't be easier to jump into one of the crevasses.

The top that we see, tantalisingly close just above, isn't of course the top. It's the place that we can see the top from, tantalisingly close just above. As we inch up we start to go past grey rock bluffs. This is as close as we've been to the real bones of Antarctica and not just its icy hide. Oh brother, now excitement is seeing rocks. What have I become?

At last, by late afternoon, we reach the top — a broad snowy meadow. From our lofty position, we can turn around and look back to see the hill dropping away to the immense plain, framed by the rocky outcrops. In the far far distance, I think I can pick out one of the nunataks. It's a neat encapsulation of the last week's worth of work. How about that? We've actually come a *long* way.

We could make camp here, but perched on the ridge, between the two ramparts, we are right in the middle of the maximum wind funnelling effect. One little puff of wind from the south and we would be flipped back to Hercules Inlet. So we start to head down the other side.

In those parts of the world where the laws of physics apply, we would feel the hill taking up the weight of our sleds. We should be able to stand tall and walk easily as our sleds slide down by themselves. Perhaps, even, we could sit on them, lift up our feet and enjoy a wild toboggan ride. Not here, though. The soft snow and shallow slope conspire to make an incline out of the decline, leaving us struggling to pull our sleds. That doesn't seem fair. In Antarctica, even downhill is uphill.

I'm very woozy by the time we at last get to a spot flat enough to put up the tent. After dinner, before getting into my sleeping bag, I open up the zip of the fly. The white field of snow stretches for miles into the horizon. This is how it's going to be from now on. There is nothing between us and the Pole, except a few crevasses, 570 miles of wind-tortured ice and a 3000-metre-high hill. We have left the harbour now and are heading out on the open ice ocean.

DAY 8. IMPERFECT WHITEOUT

I WAKE UP WITH my ankle throbbing. I got a glimpse of it last night when I was changing socks. It didn't look pretty, but I was too exhausted to deal with it. Apparently denial hasn't been an effective treatment.

In the Atlantic, because each person was rowing the other, an injury only meant that one of us would go slower in their shift. Here each of us has to make all the distance, so we can only go the speed of the weakest link. I peel off my sock hoping that it won't be me.

Where the crampons have been pinching my boot around the heel, a series of enormous blisters have become so large that they have joined together, covering the side and back of my foot. What would Jon Ackland say? Fortunately it looks a lot worse than it is.

I slice them open with the Gerber, and it is satisfying to massage all the fluid out and see it stain the snow a festive pink. I cut a large piece of Elastoplast from the roll and warm it near the stove until the adhesive starts to work.

'How are your feet going?' I ask Jamie.

'My feet are OK. My boots aren't great, though. I can feel a split in the side of my right boot.'

'That sounds serious!'

'It's under the overboot, so I think it'll be all right.'

With the pressure released from the blister and the bandage on, my foot feels as good as new. I put on my socks, slide on my boots and stomp out for my morning constitutional.

Looking around, the hill has disappeared. The grey overcast sky merges flawlessly with the grey snow. Everywhere is apparently the same as everywhere else. There is plenty of light but it's impossible to distinguish which way it's coming from. There is no wind, though, and the thermometer reads a balmy -7° Celsius. This means that packing up the sleds is a lot more pleasant and considered, which is good because there is some serious consideration to be done. So far we have always been able to use landmarks to keep us going in the right direction but now there is absolutely nothing to see.

'So, ahh, which way to the Pole?'

'It's this way,' I suggest.

'No, it's a bit more that way, isn't it?'

'We both can't be right.'

We can't use a GPS continuously as the batteries would soon freeze. Instead, it's time for the waist compass. This is a kayak compass which sits in a holder on a band of plastic supported by a cord around the neck to keep it about 30 centimetres away from the body. Thus we can simultaneously ski and look at the compass.

The problem with using a compass in Antarctica is that it doesn't point south to the south geographic pole (the axis that the Earth spins on); it points south to the south *magnetic* pole. This is not a subtle point. It would be a bad idea to try to walk to the south magnetic pole. It's so far away from the South Pole that you have to sail there.

Dealing with deviation (magnetic) is what every Boy Scout learns. Only down here it is a whopping 40 degrees. And you don't want to make a mistake with that maths as you could end up walking almost at right angles to where you want to go. So we double-check with the GPS.

If you stand still, a GPS only tells you where you are, it doesn't give a direction to where you want to go because it doesn't know which way you're facing. To solve this confusion, both of our GPSs also have the latest whiz-bang electronic magnetic compasses inside them, which automatically do the calculations and show the correct direction. So Jamie and I take one each.

'It's this way.'

'Yep, right here.'

'Are you pointing over here?'

'No, I'm pointing over here to the other South Pole.'

This is a little disturbing, but no matter, there is still Plan C. I walk out into the gloom, watching the GPS and altering my course to find the direction that keeps the longitude number the same, but increases the latitude number. Jamie follows behind me with the compass waiting for my mark.

'That's it there.'

'OK, got it.' Jamie hands me the compass. 'Way you go, I'll follow you.'

I start to ski off, the compass needle wobbles one way then the other. I try to stay in the middle of the wobbles.

'You're pissed!' Jamie shouts from over my right shoulder.

'What are you doing over there? It's this way!'

'Don't worry, you'll be coming back soon.'

The good news is that my goggles are working in the heat; although now that I can see, there is nothing to see. Then the clouds start to break up and suddenly there is. I can use a ragged cloud edge as a heading, if only briefly, which provides some relief from not having to look down at the fickle compass needle.

Over on the western horizon there is a strange, angry rust-coloured gloom, the type of cloud that in science-fiction movies hides alien spaceships. No doubt, it's a storm of some sort. It can't be raining but doing whatever weird thing Antarctica does, dropping thunderbolts and frogs probably.

Above us the cloud melts away from the ground up, as if raising the curtains on an enormous stage, revealing that we're walking down a gigantic ramp that stretches out for some kilometres until it reaches a plateau of snow below — it's the back of a huge snow wave crashing on the cliffs behind us. As the clouds break up, great shafts of sun jab the plain below, creating bright pools of light in the greyness. It's epic grandeur. It's *March of the Penguins* without the penguins. I can imagine the scene from our documentary now. There is a long shot of two tiny figures pulling their sleds, silhouetted against the God rays and Morgan Freeman's bassy voice intoning, 'For millions of years, Man has needed to pit himself against the might of Mother Nature . . .'

Unlike yesterday, the slope really is taking some weight off the sleds. We can stride nearly upright; at times it feels like we're going almost at walking pace. Each break, when we sit on the back of our sleds having our snacks, we look up to see the peaks of the Independence Range slightly smaller in the distance. It's just like rowing away from the Canary Islands to cross the Atlantic.

On our last break, I turn to Jamie. 'You know, however shit this trip turns out, they can never take the second to last shift of Day 8 away from us.'

'Yeah. Let's hope it stays like this. Hey, we've got the first cache to put out tonight.'

'That's right. Imagine what our sleds are going to feel like tomorrow!'

'Like sports cars.'

The first cache! The sooner we drop off weight the faster we will go. We would drop weight off every hour if we could, leaving a trail of food like Hansel and Gretel going into the woods. The problem is that it takes time to make a cache, and even more time to find it, so you need to be far enough away from the last cache to put a worthwhile amount in it to justify the effort. So tonight, about a day's kiting away from Hercules Inlet, is the soonest it makes sense to leave out the first depot.

After we set up the camp, I start digging a hole until the intense cold sends me shivering inside.

I scramble into the tent. 'So how did we do today?'

'It should be warmed up, have a look.'

I tap away.

'10.7 miles!'

'10.7 miles?'

'Actually 10.72 miles and half a hole!'

To put things in perspective, the conditions had been close to perfect and yet we still hadn't pulled as much as the Schedule (which demanded 11 miles) and the Average, now up to 13.4 miles, is continuing to race away from us.

So we are still on track to face-plant well short of the Pole. But if this rate of improvement continued . . . we might not make complete dickheads of ourselves. The satellite phone texts had even better news — today we had actually pulled further than the other expeditions.

'Too early to say anything yet,' warns Jamie.

'Oh yes, we shouldn't count our chickens.'

'That's right, one swallow doesn't make a summer.'

'No. We don't want to over-egg the icing on the lily.'

In our euphoria we decide to adopt a new policy. We're going to do 11 miles each day no matter what.

When Scott's men reached our latitude, they built a cairn 15 feet high and called it the Mount Hooper Depot. Our depot isn't 15 feet high. In fact, it's decidedly flush to the ground. In the morning I drop 10 kilos worth of food and a little fuel into the hole. We mark it with a pole frozen into a 2-litre bottle of ice. Finally, we slip a bright day-glo yellow flag on top.

I'm worried. It might be two months before we return here. Will the wind scour away the snow? Will a blizzard bury it? We stand for a long time next to the flag with the GPSs making sure they stabilise and that we get a very clean fix.

We hitch on our sleds. Jamie's leading and he takes a few steps.

'Feel any lighter?' I ask.

'Lighter? Do you want to check if I'm still tied on?'

I start off. I can't tell any difference. It still feels like the sled is upside down. I look over my shoulder again and again at the flag until the yellow disappears into the distance, swallowed up by the sweeping white enormousness. It doesn't take long at all.

'What do you reckon that is?' I point to a patch in the distance, where the white snow has been churned into grey, as if in the shadow of a passing cloud.

'I don't know, let's try to go around it.'

As we get closer we see that there is no getting around it. The wind has furrowed away at the snow and ice, leaving it carved into knee-high drooping waves like egg whites whipped in a gale. So this is the sastrugi that every expedition complains about.

Our sleds now ride up and down. We weave, trying to avoid the worst stuff, but we have to jerk our hips to pull the sleds up over little ledges. Every break we look up from the back of the sleds and see the Ellsworth Mountains still hanging stubbornly on the northern horizon.

At the end of the six shifts, we stop and pull out the GPS. It's only 10.5 miles. Bugger. I'm running on empty, swaying side to side in the breeze.

'Another twenty minutes should do it,' says Jamie.

I'm in great danger. Whatever I do, I mustn't think of anything that smells, looks or sounds like the small globe song. You know what it's like, once that song gets into your head, trying to get rid of it is like trying to get sticky tape off your fingers.

My brain starts counting steps. No. No. No. OK. OK. OK. How about a compromise? I'm walking about a step a second, with twenty minutes to go, so let's try counting backwards from 1200, that way I can keep track of time, and keep tabs on the blood-sugar situation in my brain. So 1200, 1199, 1198, 1195 — no, hang on, start again, 1200, 1199, 1198 . . .

. . . 3, 2, 1. I look at my watch. Still a minute to go.

DAY 10. FIRST DEGREE DAY
THE ALARM RINGS AT 4am. My head feels very strange. I put a finger into an oddly doughy cheek. I grab the camera and take a self-portrait to see what is going on. I look puffy like I spent the whole night hanging upside down by my ankles. I look like forensic evidence. What's going on?

During the *Discovery* Expedition's southern march, when Wilson believed that he was seeing the signs of scurvy in Shackleton, he took Scott to one side and they had a whispered conversation, so as not to alarm the patient. One hundred years later, social mores have changed.

Jamie looks up from his muesli. 'Mate, you look crap.'

More importantly, we're less than 9 miles away from reaching the first degree.

'Hey, we could be partying tonight!'

It had been Jamie's job to buy the degree treats.

'So what have you got for us?'

'Oh, you just let that be a little surprise.'

It's cold and overcast with a cutting breeze from the southwest that has our hoods up and our heads down. There is a new vim in our steps, though, that lasts through the day until at last, ten hours later, I'm shovelling snow onto the tent flaps.

Finally I'm done and scamper in through the fly. Jamie is just about to pour the hot water onto the milk powder.

'You can do the honours,' he says, passing me a small Nalgene bottle containing the 42Below feijoa vodka. I unscrew the cap and inhale the wonderful aroma of ripening fruit, summers on sandy beaches with crimson-tipped pohutukawa branches shading the sand. The cold clear fluid pours out like oil onto my trembling spoon. I empty it into the milk, then one more for the other mug. I bring the hot, sticky, aromatic, milky sweetness under my nose. The warmth of the mug seeps in through my thin glove liners. The sun is shining on the back of the tent warming it up. Through the gap in the fly, left for the curling steam, I can see the Pirritt Hills, a blue shadow on the western horizon.

> *An occasional glass of wine or a tot of spirits were things that we all, without exception, were very glad of. The question of alcohol on Polar expeditions has often been discussed. Personally, I regard alcohol, used in moderation, as a medicine.*
>
> — Amundsen

'Hey, here's a present for you.' Jamie pulls out a small white package from the food bag.

'What is it?'

'It's our treat.'

'What is it?'

'I don't know exactly . . . maybe some kind of pudding.'

'What are the instructions?'

'I don't know, they were in Spanish, I chucked them away. Just add water or something to it.'

I carefully tear off a corner and pour some greyish powder into a bowl. It turns reassuringly brown when I mix it with water. I put it outside to set.

Half an hour later, I check the bowl. It's still runny. That's weird; you can throw boiling water into the air here and it turns to ice before it hits the ground.

'Did you get it from the dessert aisle or the automotive department?'

'I don't know — it looked like a pudding on the packet.'

'Too bad, let's have it anyway.'

So we do, and in fact it is delicious, chocolaty, syrupy goodness. I lie back almost drunk on the calories, enjoying the feeling of all the sugar silting into my system.

Ten days to do the first degree. Crazy. We need to average *five* days a degree and we have taken twice that. Still, we are at last holding our own with the Schedule.

'We'd be on track now if we had started at 80 degrees,' I say.

'That fricking Stefan.'

If we can just claw back those three days, then maybe, just maybe, we aren't on a death march to Nowheresville, Antarctica.

11. TO INFINITY AND BEYOND!

WARM, COMFORTABLE READER, I know you have been waiting patiently for your turn at the harness. Well, here is your chance! I will make myself invisible (and weightless) and tag along for the ride, while you walk in my boots for a day as a member of the Thermal Heart expedition. I hope you're a size 13.

Your freezing shoulder interrupts your sleep. You open your eyes, and through the fabric of the pulled-up neck warmer you can see the light coming through Jamie's side, the 'morning' side, of the tent. Free your wrist and uncover an eye to check the time. What, only 2.43am? Still seventeen minutes to go! That's plenty of time for more sleeping.

It's 3am. WAKE UP!! Funny how you were so wide awake a few minutes ago. That cheery tune you are listening to is 'Mambo No. 5'. It's coming from a cell phone hanging off the drying rack. You still can't see, so you need to flail in the direction of the sound until your hand connects, then press any button until it stops. I hadn't thought of throwing it, but I see now that that works too. Very good.

Let's check the weather. Can you hear the tent flapping? Yes? That's bad. Now pull down the neck warmer from your eyes. Is there bright light filtering through the double linings? Yes? That's good. No whiteout today.

You hear a rustle and the whiz of the vestibule zip opening. This means that Jamie is awake and about to get to work lighting the stove. I suggest that you at least unzip your sleeping bag, because the process is 90 per cent similar to making a bomb and a speedy evacuation may be required.

Our little MSR stove is very efficient but requires a certain knack to ignite. The theory is that after pumping pressure into the fuel bottle, you tweak the outlet knob very carefully and very briefly to let a teaspoon or two of the clear cold fuel wind its way through the coiled metal piping and trickle out onto a little dish at the bottom of the stove. Unfortunately, by the time you see it trickling and turn the knob off, it is often too late and the fuel has spilled over and blended into the snow. Now that you have a pressurised tank, hissing escaping gas, and puddles of raw fuel, what do you do? Introduce a naked flame, of course.

If your judgement has been wrong then one of several bad things can occur — there may be a flambé-style ball of flame which with a 'whumpf' leaves scorched eyebrows on your startled face. Or there may be a frantic beating out of rogue flames around your feet. Or it may be necessary to hold the kettle lid between the stove and the roof of the tent for a few seconds until the tower of flames dies down. On the *Discovery* Expedition, Scott gave his tent a new window doing this.

If, on the other hand, the amount of fuel is correct, and in the right place, then you will see a small orange flame gently warming the heating coils above, to the point where they are able to vaporise the liquid fuel passing through. You don't know exactly when this point is, so you have to guess. You tweak the fuel knob again and will either get a small but effective flamethrower, or more often, the hiss will swell into a very satisfying jet-engine roar. There it is now!

The day has started and every minute until you get into the tent tonight has already been allocated. No time to waste, you need to get dressed! Just don't sit up too quickly. Yes, the tent roof is lower than you think and now your head has knocked a night's worth of frozen exhalations onto your sleeping bag. You should brush them off before they melt.

Getting dressed is awkward as you are already dressed, just in different clothes. Because exposing yourself to the cold all at once might be fatal, temporary dressing clothes are required. So you need to get undressed one and a half times and dressed twice.

Out of the sleeping bag the cold hits with such a shock that you look at the stove to check that it is really going. You should try to start a conversation with Jamie to distract both of you from the cold. Anything will do. I see you thinking. Here it comes.

Have you ever noticed that at the end of Wanna Be Startin' Something *by Michael Jackson you hear the backing singers chant 'Sad about the sale of Microsoft' again and again? What's that about?*

OK, full marks for randomness and it worked great — you've got the polar-fleece jacket on. Now rummage through the drying rack to see how well yesterday's socks dried. Found a good pair? OK. First the down booties come off while the socks and vapour barrier liners are put on, then the booties go back on. Now the long-john pants are pulled on. Take your polar fleece off, pull the suspenders of the long johns over your shoulders and put the fleece back on. Then comes The North Face Gore-Tex jacket. Then the fleece hat — no, no, not the hat, the neck warmer. Take off the hat and put on the neck warmer, then put the hat back on. Well done!

Roll up the bivvy bag containing the two mattresses and your sleeping bag. Not so tight that the slippery nylon squirts out the end like toothpaste and not so loose that the bundle won't buckle up. Try again. Great! You can use it as a cushion.

You will have noticed that your lower abdominal region is spasming with a fierce urgency; it may be the laxative effects of the freeze-dri or the extra fibre that we added to the muesli, but you definitely gotta go. So put on some outdoor gloves, pull the neck warmer over your mouth and nose, and retreat into the fur-lined hood of your Gore-Tex jacket.

'Good luck,' says Jamie as you undo the zip and crawl out. Notice how the cold of the snow bites through your knees and cuts through your gloves. You're about to stand up for the first time in eleven hours so be careful, but *keep moving*. Stomp immediately to the sleds at the top of the tent, keeping your head down or the wind will blow back your hood. It's shocking how much heat you can lose in just a few seconds, isn't it? So quick, open up the back pocket of the sled and pull out the big orange down jacket — make sure your grip is firm because the wind wants to snatch it from you. With it on, you've bought yourself five minutes, so take a look around.

Today, there are only a few wispy clouds scampering for safety, while the invisible bulldozer is out attempting to move Antarctica from over there to over here and rocking you from side to side in the process. You see that overnight a magical transformation has taken place in the landscape. Yesterday you walked up a hill and struggled to find a flat spot among some rough sastrugi. Now you're definitely on the flat, and the ground is smooth. Go figure.

Back to business. You need to get the toilet paper — unless you want to use a handful of snow? OK, OK, grab that plastic bag there with the roll inside and head downwind, picking up the snow shovel as you pass by the tent entrance. You want to stay close enough to the tent to still be in its shelter and yet far enough away so as not to be stepping in any surprises when you're pulling it down.

Plunge in the spade to use as a kind of handle and drop the toilet paper bag behind it. This leaves both hands free to do the most unnatural thing in the world — expose your tenderest skin to the elements. Fortunately, your bowels sense the urgency and come to the party. Tidying up needs to be done very carefully, especially the placement of toilet paper and gloves while you're pulling your long johns up. You don't want to be running back towards Patriot Hills chasing a roll of toilet paper with your pants down around your ankles. Finish with a quick blur of shovel work.

Before you go back inside, just a couple more things. Heave the sleds back alongside the entrance to make them easier to pack into and start pulling out some ski poles and skis into position. You think you're cold now but everything you can do beforehand will speed things up a lot for later when you are packing up the tent and *really* cold.

What are those Nalgene bottles Jamie has just put outside? They are the pee bottles — for you to empty out. A word of warning, Jamie somehow manages to fill his right to the very, very top, and then cranks on the lid with a torque wrench. His bottle is sealed like a preserving jar, same golden colour, too, just needs the peaches. So somehow you have to get the lid off in such a way as to not cause a brief but spectacular explosion of pee. Whoops. Don't worry, that will soon turn to ice.

That's enough fun for five minutes. Pour yourself as fast as you can back into the tent, do the zip up behind you and, while you wait to stop shivering, enjoy the scene of domestic bliss. The kettle is boiling and there might be a mug of hot chocolate and a bottle filled with warm water to heat your hands. If you sit on your bedroll and stamp your down booties up and down, you will soon warm up.

Here comes breakfast, a large bowl of toasted muesli mixed with milk powder and sugar. Now pour a generous dollop of grapeseed oil on top. Why grapeseed oil? Because it's mostly tasteless and stays liquid when other oils freeze solid. It's also packed full of energy, so go crazy, you'll thank me later. Then add some boiling water to make a kind of hot, sweet, oily porridge. Dig in! This is the most fun you're going to have for the next twelve hours.

I can see you're mesmerised by the steam curling lazily from the kettle on the stove. It snakes up to the roof before wandering too close to the few centimetres of unzipped fly where it's abruptly snatched outside. Where you *should* be looking is the dark, icy abyss of the boots in front of you. That's what's coming next.

Scott sometimes took an hour and a half to shove his feet into his frozen boots. Luckily there are some advantages to living in the twenty-first century. You will find that the nylon vapour barrier liners over your socks mean that your feet slide in easily. It's cold yes, but not unbearable. The worst part is dealing to the icy laces with your bare fingers.

We are lucky if our foot gets half way into its rocky cover at the first attempt. We leave it at that for the moment, and proceed with the other; by the time it is in a similar position, an inch can be gained on the first, and so inch by inch these tiresome boots are pulled on. Meanwhile our feet have got alarmingly cold, and with a groan we are obliged to start up and stamp about.

— Scott

Jamie has turned off the stove, and before it has even been stowed in the kitchen box, you can feel the tent cooling noticeably. It's his turn to crawl out into the wind. In a few minutes you have to pass out everything so he can hand-deliver it into the sleds. The kitchen box, the bedrolls, the cameras, the clothes bags, water bottles, booties, the battery box and cameras.

The last thing to do is to sweep out the tent. The built-in groundsheet makes it snug but is also a trap for any blown-in snow. So get on your hands and knees and reach into the back of the tent with this little cut-down paintbrush, and whisk the snow fragments out. If you can find a way to do it without turning your knees into ice blocks and freezing both hands, let me know.

The time consumed in all these simple operations of camping puzzled us greatly at first. There was no particular delay anywhere; from start to finish one was busy, and there was every incentive to hurry. The secret lies in the fact that the simplest operation becomes complicated in intensely cold weather.

— Scott

As you back out of the tent, Jamie is already pulling some of the tent poles from their eyes and doing the complicated origami that transforms the tent into a long rolled sausage. Now you can help him pull the bag onto it and strap it to the top of one of the sleds. Last of all, the solar panel is stretched over the back of the other sled to charge during the day.

Can you believe it's been two hours since you woke up? Two hours of near continuous eating, dressing, cleaning, stuffing, tightening, strapping, stowing, shoving — it seems like you have always had something in one hand and something else in the other. Yet you've done nothing but have breakfast and pack up.

Finally both the sleds are ready to go. The skis are lying in front of the harnesses, with the ski poles stabbed into the snow on either side. Between one pair there is the yellow crescent of the waist compass harness. You're all set.

You meet Jamie at the back of the sleds.

'Ready?' he asks.

'Yep. Yep.'

You sound quite anxious and I don't blame you. For the last half hour, precious heat has been leaking from you like air from the stretched neck of a balloon, and your body is making that same anguished reedy cry. I'm afraid it's going to get worse before it gets better, because now you need to take off your down jacket. Yes, it does seem like a dumb idea. No, I'm not kidding. Careful with the safety pins.

It's funny how the cold grabs control of your mind and turns you into a zombie with one purpose only — *run*. You know, there's a type of wasp that lays its eggs inside caterpillars, which then takes over the mind of the caterpillar. Isn't that what it feels like the cold is doing to you? OK, OK. I'll shut up about the caterpillars.

Get back up to the skis, hook yourself on to the carabiner. Tap the snow off the toe of a boot and carefully put it into the binding of the cross-country ski. Again, this time tap off all the snow. Press down on that lever with your glove until it locks into place. Harder. The bindings are getting filled with ice and will need to be chipped out tonight. Now the other ski.

Jamie is going to lead the first shift this morning and seems to be having some problems with the waist compass, which buckles awkwardly behind his back. Don't be alarmed at the strength of the uncharitable thoughts you are having about the delay. It's just the cold — if you can ignore the monster for a moment and shuffle over to give Jamie a hand you will get under way that much sooner.

Jamie is looking down at the compass, swivelling his hips left and right until the timid needle wobbles in the right direction. Then checks his watch.

'It's 5.13, so 6.33?'

'Yep. Yep. Yep. Yep.'

At last Jamie leans forward, jerks the sled and starts marching off. You just need to wait until he goes by and then drop into his tracks. That's it, now pull. Maybe a little harder. Come on, put your back into it. There you go. Now you're moving.

Take a look over your shoulder. You see that the wind is already reclaiming the campsite. Soon there will be no sign that it ever existed. Makes you think of what is happening to the cache a hundred miles away, doesn't it?

Oh, I see that the exercise has begun too late; your left hand is frozen numb. So why don't you just let it freeze and rewarm it at the end of the day? I'll tell you why.

In theory, ever since refrigeration was invented there has been a sneaky way to immortality. Put yourself in a freezer until cellular activity stops, then have your descendants pop you in a microwave every ten years or so for an update on how scientists are solving the problem of ageing. It *should* work, right? Look at the twenty-thousand-year-old mammoths they dig out of the permafrost in Siberia — sure they come out looking mangled, but only a little bit.

Unfortunately it's not so simple. There's a reason why that leg of lamb doesn't come back to life after you take it out of the freezer. It's because water, which makes up a large part of the fluid inside and outside of your cells, expands when it freezes. The sharp-edged ice crystals pierce the cell linings and the contents of the cell leak out. And that is what will happen to your fingers if you don't do something about them. First, you need to relax your death grip on the ski poles. Holding them tight just restricts blood going to your fingers. In fact, forget about the poles, put them under your right arm. Now pull your fingers out of the glove (keep the glove on — just the fingers!), ball them up and swing your left arm like a soldier marching double-time to try to get some feeling back. Keep tensing and relaxing your hand to pump some blood into it. I know when it's this frozen you can't even feel what you're doing, but every bit helps. Ah, here it comes, now you can feel it.

OK, what about the rest of you? Feet warm? Good. Hopefully that wrinkle in your vapour barrier liner will flatten itself out before it creates a blister. Now back to the trail. If you can keep in Jamie's ski tracks then your sled should also keep in his sled tracks, and because it's not having to compact snow it slides just a little easier. It's better to get a run-up for some of the smaller sastrugi; you can get the sled's centre of gravity over the ridge before the momentum gives out and you get stuck.

The sun is almost directly behind you and has bleached the landscape into a near uniform white. It should be better later on, when the sun swinging around to the side creates some contrast. For the moment, all you can see is that you are in a shallow dish, with gently sloping sides about 300 metres away. This is almost always how it looks. And yes, the terrain does look smoother over there, but that is just Antarctica trying to seduce you. Believe me, when you get there it will look exactly like here.

Did you think the vastness would be overwhelming, like walking over salt flats? You see now it's not like that at all. Instead, the experience is very intimate; if your hood is up and your goggles start to ice over, as they are now, it can almost be claustrophobic.

Your goggles are definitely icing up on the inside. There is only the smallest smudge that is not opaque. Unfortunately I don't recommend stopping to wipe them, as it takes several minutes of hard walking to catch up and they will only ice up again. Just keep focusing on the jerking North Face sticker on the back of Jamie's sled and remind yourself again and again that there is nothing to see. Scott's men, when they were suffering from snow blindness, trudged for days without being able to see much of anything. With any luck, if you get warm enough the ice will start to melt from the inside.

The situation has stabilised, so it's time for the iPod. This is in a protective casing deep in your inner layers. To turn it on you will have to give yourself a stiff thump to the chest. Try again. And again. Now it's working. Today you've dropped into David Beckham's autobiography, which at least isn't a Spanish lesson or horror of horrors 'The Macarena'. Notice how the hauling takes care of itself when you are trying not to mess up a World Cup penalty shootout.

If that's not entertainment enough you can always watch the sastrugi. Aren't they carved into fantastic, streamlined and fluted shapes? You often see ones that look like anvils or cycle-pursuit helmets. Sometimes they form as long ridges, other times they are shapeless slugs, standing alone, and big enough to sit on.

The sastrugi as a rule aren't organised but occasionally they do come together in a huge formation, which I've started calling a 'fish school'. This is because from the side it looks like thousands of bulbous forms leaping out of the water from a single source, before fanning out downwind, for one or two hundred metres or more.

Most of the time you don't see the fish schools from the side. The first hint that something is up is that little ridges start forming on either side of you, subtly guiding you in. They grow larger and larger as the channel becomes narrower and narrower and you are funnelled towards the 'head'. At the end you might pop out, and suddenly find yourself coming down a short exciting chute ride back to the plain. Or there might be a small, but shriek-inducing, drop or, worst of all, a wall, and you are left trying to make an escape the best you can.

Look, you've done twenty minutes already! The first twenty tends to go quickly (more or less) because you are so fussy and distracted.

Just think — another twenty minutes you'll be halfway through your first shift! Then after another twenty minutes there'll only be twenty minutes to go. Now you've done twenty minutes and seven seconds. I would go back to asking out Posh Spice if I were you.

> *Sledging therefore is a sure test of a man's character, and daily calls for the highest qualities of which he is possessed.*
>
> — Scott

You've had your arm out in front of you like a maître d' with his napkin for the last two minutes looking at your watch. It finally clicks over to 6.33 — at last the shift is over. Oh no! Jamie is still going. The rule is you stop when the time is up. Not a *second* later. You stop where you are, then raise your poles over your head in a cross. Come on, that's twenty seconds over! Oh no, he's forgotten when we started. That's thirty seconds! Ah, now he stops. I bet he was trying to give himself a few extra metres to lay down a challenge for your shift. Don't forget to get him back.

In the meantime, I see that you are frantically preoccupied with undoing your fly. It must be the exercise, or that your midriff is being constantly massaged and squeezed by the harness, but you really need to pee. *Now.* You'll find that large loop attached to the zipper is very helpful.

Take off your skis and get your down on. Once zipped up, you can plop down on the bedroll at the back of the sled and reach down and pull out one of the water bottles in their little parkas. As it's just the first break the water might still be a little warm.

Now it's time for the snack bag. You're in luck; we opened a new four-day bag last night so its compartments are bulging with three heart attacks' worth of all the major polar food groups — high-fat pecan nuts, high-saturated-fat salami, fatty chocolate and some palate-cleansing butter.

Slow down! Don't eat it all! You have to spin it out for twenty breaks at least, and one-twentieth is just a square or two of chocolate, a tiny bite of meat, four or five nuts and a nibble of butter. It's an amount that could be passed discreetly in a handshake. If you let the salami thaw in your mouth for a bit before you bite into it there's less chance of chipping a tooth.

'You should try a bit of salami and butter, it's good!' suggests Jamie. By now old sock and butter would taste good and by the sixth shift your boots as well.

Check your watch — ten minutes is up already. Bottles back, jackets off, zip up.

'Ready?' asks Jamie.

'Yep.'

Now it's your turn to do the steering. You'll find the compass horribly fickle at first. You could get more direction out of a horoscope. One trick is to find a feature en route, as far ahead as possible, and use it as a guide. A scrap of cloud will do (briefly!) or an unusual sastrugi. For example, take that black speck over there . . . it seems to be moving around as you look at it. No, it can't be a midge; a midge would explode in the cold. But it might be a meteorite, or it might be a Martian, or you might be a Martian.

If there is any place in the world you are going to find meteorites, it's in Antarctica. They are easily seen against the white snow, and the flowing ice sheets tend to concentrate them together. Since the mid-1970s, when scientists first started looking here, more than twenty-five thousand have been found.

Most meteorites seem to come from the asteroid belt, between the orbits of Mars and Jupiter, but in 1984 a meteorite was found in Antarctica that likely came from Mars itself, and uniquely, from a time four billion years ago when Mars had liquid water on its surface — and possibly things swimming in it. When the meteorite was studied under an electron microscope it appeared to show fossilised bacteria-like life forms.

Some researchers have gone further, speculating that life down here began out there. That the ultimate ancestor of all life on Earth was a microbe-carrying meteorite splashing into the warm seas of a young Earth. You don't need to give it such a wide berth. I'm sure no one is going to jump out of it and say 'Take me to your leader'!

That's enough daydreaming. No slacking, keep the pace up! Try to push it a bit, try to beat Jamie for the biggest shift of the day.

As we pass through the day, I think you're appreciating how each shift has its own personality. The first shift is essentially for free; you are just starting out, mostly warm, and still digesting your breakfast. The second shift you're still being carried by the iPod. The third shift you're focused on nearly being halfway. Then it's the afternoon and you would either have led or been led for two out of the three shifts. So either you look forward to having a slightly easier afternoon or to the opportunity to pick up the pace. That's what you tell yourself anyway.

By the fourth shift the iPod has long given up the ghost and you're on your own. It's not the dubious pleasure of halfway; it's not the glorious last shift. It's not one shift to go. It's just another fricking shift. It drags, doesn't it? What you need is a tune to pass the time. May I suggest 'It's A Small World'? Ha! Got ya!

Then there's the fifth shift. At the break, the GPS showed you how much behind schedule you are. You only have two shifts to fix it. The fifth shift is a scamper and exhausting but now you can let yourself think that this time next shift you will almost be finished.

At the break of the end of the fifth shift your water is sludgy with ice. Don't drink it all, though, you need to keep some fluid to begin the ice melting later. You're out of energy, your legs are hollow. But now there's hope. Every minute is a minute closer to getting in the tent.

The last twenty minutes of the last shift is when time slows down still further. May I suggest counting backwards from 1200? You have looked at your watch so much you are developing a twitch.

Start to hope that there will be a convenient campsite when the time runs out. It *normally* isn't a problem, but what if it is today?

Here's a spot. Hang on — didn't we camp here last night? Next to that piece of sastrugi? Have you skied in a big circle? No, you can't have. Have you?

Get your down on quickly, you're so exhausted you'll cool down like smoke. Dr Kevin prescribes two squares of chocolate administered orally to get through the next half hour. Yes, Jamie does look funny with the stalactite hanging off his chin. But don't laugh too hard, you've got one too. Now, do not, repeat DO NOT, let the tent blow away. So you help Jamie drag the tent bag over to the chosen spot and kick in the two-foot snow stake.

Once the tent is up we can put in the kitchen box and the bedrolls. That's enough for Jamie to start with so he disappears inside. The faster he gets going the better, as the time we get for sleeping is determined by how long it takes to make dinner and melt enough snow for tomorrow.

So start guying out the tent, using every pole and ski to stick it to the snow. The wind is not so bad right now but you know that the day you don't do this, the wind will come along like a spatula, scrape you off the snow and flick you back to Punta Arenas.

It's time to put snow on the oversized flaps of the tent fly. Wait! Sometimes the snow is good and breaks off in big chunks. Today it is rock hard and jars the arm. When a bit is finally prised loose, it sits awkwardly and ineffectually like a little polystyrene boulder on the flaps. Other times it is more like dry sand and hard work to move, but still a nice change from sledging. Although by the sixth shift, hitting your eye with a stick would be a nice change to sledging.

It's almost time to go inside. The flaps are covered in snow, the tent is guyed out and is going nowhere, the sleds are in a V-shape, upwind of the tent so that the drifting snow can be directed around it. You're standing by the entrance ready to go inside. Why not take a few moments to enjoy the view. Take a deep, nostril-freezing sniff and reflect for just a second — *you're in Antarctica*!

Right, that's enough fun. You're cold; it's time to go in. What's this? The zip has opened from the inside and a large bright-yellow plastic bag is thrust out.

'Don't forget the snow bag,' shouts Jamie.

Bugger, I always forget the snow bag. We need to collect half a big rubbish bag of snow to make water for dinner, breakfast and the trail tomorrow. So stomp on the base while trying to pour enough snow into the flapping mouth — nice, small, pot-sized blocks of snow. None of the fluffy stuff.

Now it really is time to go inside. Take off your down jacket and stuff it in the sled. I find if you run towards the entrance shouting 'INCOMING!' with a real sense of urgency, Jamie might come to the party and undo the zip. Try not to garrotte yourself on the clothesline.

'Ready for your milk?' says Jamie.

He hands you a warm cup.

'And there's your hot-water bottle,' says Jamie.

'Where's the other one?' you ask.

'It's in your bootie already.'

'You're a legend.'

Oh no, don't lie back! I know that's what you want to do, more than almost anything — to lie back on the bag and enjoy the feeling of being warm and safe and still and alive. To let your mangled muscles hang off your bones for a change. But if you start stopping you won't stop. If you lie down you will go completely catatonic; you won't move until global warming forces you to swim out.

> *The march has been arranged to absorb the maximum portion of our energy, but there is not much present satisfaction in contemplating the limp condition that results.*
>
> — Scott

So start taking off a boot, peeling off the sock and vapour barrier liner. Now you see one of the most strange of all things in Antarctica — uncovered flesh. The skin of your foot has been slowly decomposing in its warm, wet bag during the day and now emerges white, wrinkled and tender, but at least warm. So take out the hot-water bottle from one of the down booties and slip your foot into it.

The down booties are a revelation. Regardless of how badly they have been treated during the day, they quickly spring back to shape. It doesn't matter if they have been sitting in a puddle in the bottom of the sled or digested and regurgitated by wolves, they still pop back up fluffy and inviting. To free a mangled foot from its boot and put it in a warm light bootie is an exquisite pleasure that requires a few moments of reflection.

Pull off the rest of your cold, stiff outerwear and replace it with the dry fleeces and down pants. Plug in the solar cell to the battery box and start charging all the cameras, cell phones, iPAQs. Get the satellite phone out of its bag and start the long process of sending photos back to the website. Start on repairs, like that ice that's threatening to jam the binding on the ski. You left it outside, didn't you? Are you going to get it or will you tell yourself it will be all right for another day?

Now the food starts to arrive, a conveyor belt of sweet and savoury calories. The highlight of the evening is the freeze-dri, perhaps spaghetti Bolognaise, or Thai chicken curry, served like everything else, swimming in grapeseed oil.

This is a moment to be lived for — one of the brief incidents of the day to which we can look forward with real pleasure. The hot food seems to give new life, its grateful warmth appears to run out to every limb, exhaustion vanishes, and gradually that demon within, which has gripped so tightly for the past hour or two, is appeased.

— Scott

Once finished there are still two hot drinks to go while Jamie replenishes the Nalgene containers. Then another hot chocolate while doing diaries and repairs, with two biscuits. Very carefully allotted.

On the *Discovery* Expedition, Scott had a copy of Darwin's *Voyage of the* Beagle to amuse himself with in the tent of an evening. Shackleton would read aloud from *The Merchant of Venice* during blizzards. Perhaps after a day of pulling 80 kilos, one can still rouse oneself to a little light academic reading, or engage in an amusing round of whist. But you'll agree after a day spent yanking 150 kilos or so, you're buggered to incapacitation.

Now it's time for journals. The pen ink has frozen, but if you suck on it for a bit you'll find it thaws out briefly. With the stove off, the bubble of heat quickly evaporates and the chill air soon invades and forces you to retreat to the citadel of the sleeping bag. Put in the earplugs to block out the noise of the flapping tent and the snow hitting the nylon. Pull a neck warmer over your eyes and screw the sheepskin balaclava backwards down on your head.

The sleeping bag works well. Scott's reindeer sleeping bags, whether three-man or singles, must have been excruciatingly uncomfortable. I have no doubt that if Captain Scott came as a thief into our camp he would sniff at our stoves, be confused by our apparently too-flimsy tent, frown at our stiff boots, then nick a sleeping bag and a tin of fuel, and bolt.

The sleeping bag is quite tight fitting, and it isn't possible to sleep on your front without squashing your nose, and on your back you feel too much like Count Dracula. So try sleeping on your side without letting any part of you touch the groundsheet.

You need to pee? No problem, you don't even need to get out of the sleeping bag. Use the pee bottle. It's all about angles and very careful listening — followed by very, very careful screwing on of the lid. If you make a mistake with this you can end up having a very fragrant and sloshy night. Now you have a little yellow friend to cuddle, because if it freezes you have a big problem. So tuck it in close and make sure it doesn't touch the ice.

Now get some sleep. It will all happen again in six hours!

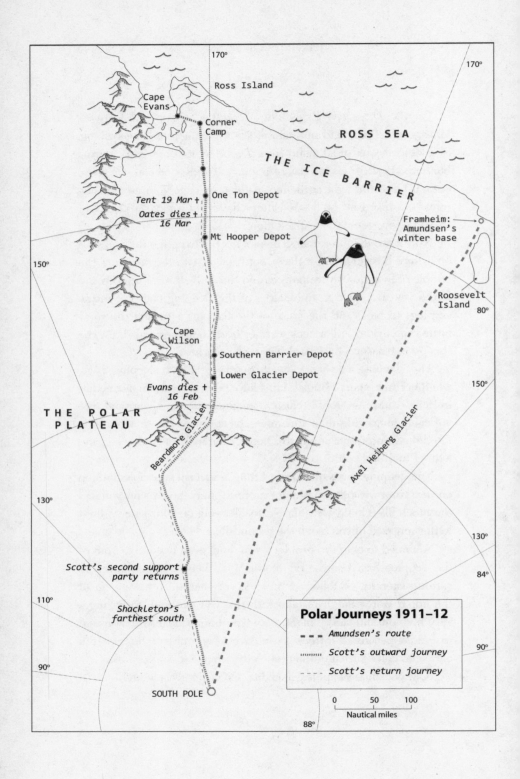

Polar Journeys 1911–12

170°
170°
Ross Island
Cape Evans
Corner Camp
ROSS SEA
THE ICE BARRIER
One Ton Depot
Tent 19 Mar †
Oates dies †
16 Mar
Mt Hooper Depot
Framheim:
Amundsen's
winter base
150°
Roosevelt
Island
80°
Cape
Wilson
Southern Barrier Depot
Lower Glacier Depot
150°
Evans dies †
16 Feb
THE POLAR
PLATEAU
Beardmore Glacier
Axel Heiberg Glacier
130°
130°
84°
Scott's second support
party returns
110°
Shackleton's
farthest south
90°
90°
SOUTH POLE
88°

Polar Journeys 1911–12

‐ ‐ ‐ *Amundsen's route*

········· *Scott's outward journey*

‐ ‐ ‐ *Scott's return journey*

0   50   100

Nautical miles

12. THE COLDEST DAY (SO FAR)

I'M JOLTED INTO LIFE by 'Mambo No. 5'. Only one eye opens. The eyelashes on the other side have frozen together. I pinch them with some bare fingers to thaw them out.

'Muh mowf mont mohpen!'

My mouth won't open either. Time for the knife! No, instead I prod my tongue between my lips until they pull apart. A cloud of vapour comes out, and turns into tiny white specks which fall to the ground. This is not a good sign. The light is uniformly gloomy. I can hear the sound of the tent flapping hard. No. This is not good at all.

'You up?' I ask.

'Yep.'

'Bloody cold.'

'You're not wrong.'

I hear the shloka shloka sound of the pump. It takes two goes and much forceful language from Jamie before the stove starts to roar.

Now it's time for ablutions. Do I really need to go? Yes, I do.

'Good luck,' says Jamie.

As soon as I step outside the cold attacks like a demented knife-wielding monkey. It cuts through my clothes in a dozen places before trying to snap off my nose and scrape off my beard. Without ever looking up, I pull on my down jacket and retrieve the toilet paper, only pausing to do a double-take at the sledge thermometer. It's reading ¯34° Celsius — it doesn't read lower than that. Instead, it helpfully flashes 'lo'.

An SAS medic, who had spent time in Antarctica, told me that when going to the loo on cold days, you've got ten seconds before you don't know if you are starting, stopping or what you're wiping. It's like that now. It's all I can do to take three shuffling steps back to the entrance, pulling up my trousers, and dive in — just in time to get hit by two full pee bottles coming the other way.

'Not today!' I shout.

No airlock on a spaceship has been shut faster than the zip behind me.

'What's it like out there?' asks Jamie.

'Jandals and togs, mate. Jandals and togs,' I say, rocking back and forth hugging my knees.

I've just finished sweeping up the tent when Jamie stumbles in. Breathing hard, he pulls off his goggles.

'You want to know something?'

'What?'

'It's pretty cold out there.'

'Do you want to know something?' I say, stabbing a finger at him.

'What?'

'Chuck Norris doesn't feel cold. Cold feels Chuck Norris.'

Jamie stiffens.

'That's right. Kids wear Superman pyjamas. Superman wears Chuck Norris pyjamas.'

'Exactly. Let's do it.'

There aren't too many problems that can't be solved by flight. Charging wild animals, bushfires, marriage. Cold is the same; the primeval part of my brain is demanding that I run with a specific and fierce urgency. But where? The equator presumably. Having nowhere *to* run makes me panicky, as the cold begins to invade from all sides.

My brain is screaming, *'Let's go, let's go, LET'S GO!'* Jamie looks at his watch, and we set off.

Some days you feel like a tiger and sometimes you're a little bunny. Some mornings you can swat away the cold monsters and other times they're ten feet tall, sabre-toothed and snacking on your widdle wabbit heart.

Maybe we underestimated the weather today. Maybe we should have started in our down jackets. Maybe we should be wearing our fleece tops. It's too late; we're committed. My hands are much too frozen to be any use changing clothes, now they're only good for clubbing seals or bashing in nails.

The sleds feel much heavier in the cold, and the snow is like sand. My head is firmly down as lifting it just a little would give the wind the chance it has been waiting for to yank my hood back, choke me on my drawstring cord and chisel the plaque from my teeth.

I pull my fleecy neck warmer over my mouth. Breathing in through the fabric helps to soften up the incoming air before it assaults the lungs. Eventually, though, the moisture in my exhaled breath turns it to ice and I have to give the cloth a tug to rotate it around a few centimetres to a new patch. Today I have left it too long. The ice has glued it to my beard. I contort my lips to blow warm air around my face before ripping it free. I keep plucking and turning the neck warmer, and by the end of the first shift I'm wearing a cold, heavy collar of ice. Some of that puffing has blown wet air into my goggles, which by now may as well be smeared with Vaseline.

Well, that last break was an almost complete waste of time. The seconds it takes to have a few gritty nibbles and a sip of freezing water is exactly the amount of time it takes to lose the last of the trail heat. After half an hour of panicky towing, I'm still wondering if I'm going to warm up.

Now leading, I can only see out of one quarter of one eye. I can just make out where the compass needle is pointing; luckily the sastrugi are behaving themselves and I'm not having to detour much.

I whack my chest to try to start the iPod up. Seldom is one blow enough; today it turns into a one-man boxing match. I'm doing a passable imitation of the chief gorilla defending his harem, complete with head-swivelling roar, before the entertainment begins. Then, less than a minute later, it stops. That's it. It's frozen.

At the next break, I pull the GPS out of its internal pocket and switch it on. Worried if it will even start, I pay close attention to the characters on the screen as it does its little diagnostic check. It gives the battery temperature — -16° Celsius. How could it be that cold pressed against my skin? Why isn't my skin freezing? Or is it? Are we doing the right thing carrying on? If there were a smart-bomb option in this game, I would push it now.

As we start off again both hands are painfully aching with cold. I read somewhere that when doctors want to measure your pain threshold they don't cut you or burn you or make you watch *American Idol*. The standard test is to put your hand in freezing water and time how long you can stand it. Cold equals pain. Pain equals cold. Any questions?

The most baffling thing about the cold is that we should be great at dealing with it. We should *thrive* on cold. Our species has been defined by its relationship with ice — without it we might not even be here.

Our earliest ancestors started using tools just over two million years ago, about the same time as the last Ice Age began. Since then, the Earth's climate has swung, often very abruptly, between short periods of relative warmth and much longer intervals of apocalyptic cold. During these times, gargantuan ice sheets inundated much of northern Europe and North America, crushing and gouging everything in their path, and burying the land under kilometres of snow, with only mountain peaks remaining.

It was probably a brief interglacial period, fifty or so thousand years ago, that enticed modern humans to leave Africa and spread throughout Europe. There our ancestors would have come across the ice sheets for the first time. It would have been a stunning sight — cliffs of ice up to 800 metres high, tumbling down to enormous plains of tundra continuously rustled by the cold dry wind pouring off the frozen cliffs.

As our forebears gaped at this giant wall of ice descending from the sky, how did they react? They shivered of course. Humans are tropical animals and lousy in the cold. We are, after all, one of the very few mammals that have no pelt. A naked human will start to feel cold if the temperature drops below a very balmy 25° Celsius.

If the hypothalamus detects too much heat it has a suite of sophisticated responses to draw from. For example it can activate, via the sympathetic nervous system, some or all of the 2.6 million sweat glands the average person has, and take advantage of the latent heat of evaporation to create an efficient cooling system. Or it may choose to replumb the blood supply to shunt more flow to capillaries near the skin's surface to effectively radiate heat out into the environment.

On the other hand, when it comes to cold, our scourge for the last fifty millennia, what is the best our bodies can do for us?

Goosebumps.

In the cold, your body has only one really effective strategy and that is to clamp off the blood supply and stop the flow of life-giving warmth and oxygen to the affected body part. At the first hint of trouble it shuts down, withdraws, capitulates, sacrifices. Long before the cold has won, while the rest of you can be quite warm, it quickly and cravenly abandons your fingers, toes and other dangly bits and leaves them defenceless. Your body might not *like* being too hot but it is terrified of the cold.

By the fourth shift slowly it becomes clear that things aren't getting worse; in fact, they might be slightly improving. With the hood up things seem under control, and it looks like we *are* on track to make 82 degrees. This degree only took us five days. That's what I'm talking about! We can even share some words at the end of the fifth shift while we wait for the GPS to find itself.

'End of a four-day bag today,' Jamie says.

'How's it looking for leftovers?'

'Oh, we won't be starving tonight.'

'So, what are we at?'

'81 degrees 57.9 minutes. If you can get us through 2.1 miles in this last shift then we can call it quits, eh?'

We haven't done a shift over 2 miles all day. But I really don't want to do a seventh shift. As Scott would say, 'Lets leg it.' I start out, trying to make the strides a little longer, and a little faster. Each ridge of sastrugi is met with a clenched jaw and a tight stomach to try to bust through.

The shift goes quickly. While I have my head down between my poles panting, Jamie checks the GPS.

'How did I do?'

'Not bad, only another hundred metres and we're there.'

Awesome! I had got us there.

Tonight I allow myself an extra sniff at the horizon before I get into the tent. Today could have gone either way. We could have stayed in the tent. We could have stopped at lunchtime. Instead, we got there. We kicked some serious ice.

In the tent the pot is chuckling on the stove and I'm soon thawing my fingers around a cup of feijoa-vodka-flavoured milk and ripping open a packet of Chilean Mystery Pudding with my teeth. I inhale deeply. Ahh, nothing but highly processed carbohydrate goodness!

'I think it's toffee!'

We had food. We had progress. We had survived.

'Do you want to see if there is any news on how the other teams are coping with this?'

Soon the satellite phone is beeping as texts arrive from Kate.

'Apparently the Marines are saying on their website that they are drawing on all their military and commando experience to get them through the suffering and anguish and personal demons they are facing,' I report.

'I know what they mean,' says Jamie. 'We're having to call on all of our telecommunication and banking experience to get through.'

It looks like we are only about two days behind the Jardines and the Marines, even though we had essentially given them a five- or six-day headstart. If we are not doing very well at least we have company.

For the first time in fifteen days we can feel slightly chuffed. Somehow we've staggered back up to our feet before the ten count. Ready for round two. Is that your best shot, Antarctica? Then bring it on! In fact — you know what? This calls for a celebration. I'm going to change my undies.

I go to pull down my long johns and see that on the top of my left thigh the wool fabric has matted from ooze that is coming up from the skin below. I pull it off slowly, wincing as the fabric rips away from the flesh. Jamie wrinkles his nose.

Those bruises from the first week weren't bruises. The top layer of skin has melted away and the tissue-thin membrane that is left is weeping a clear fluid.

Jamie wrinkles his nose. 'Mate, that's gross!'

'I know!'

'How did that happen?'

'I don't know. It must be the cold.'

The weird thing is I hadn't felt anything. Although, come to think of it, I do now remember other adventurers complaining about a 'rash' on their thighs. I had always thought that this was caused by friction. Instead maybe it's what I'm staring at now, some kind of cold-induced ulceration.

What kind of sick place melts away your skin without you even knowing it? Now I know what it's like to be a fly inside a Venus flytrap — immersed in corrosive fluid and having to watch your legs disappear. At least it doesn't seem infected. I peel the backing off two large waterproof bandages and carefully place them over the wounds. I do a close inspection of the rest of me to make sure that nothing else has fallen off without me noticing. Everything seems intact except for some red lumps on the skin of my nose and cheekbones, where the mask has been pressing ice against my face. Jamie has them too.

Jamie is also rubbing the back of his right leg.

'What's up?' I ask.

'I've got this funny tightness in my hamstring. Keeps feeling like it wants to cramp, but never does.'

'That's shit,' I say helpfully. 'Maybe you could take some Voltaren.'

Jamie doesn't look very happy about it. He hates swallowing pills whole and has to chew them first. Judging by the look on his face they don't taste that good.

I'm looking at the Schedule. Eleven nautical miles a day won't cut it any more. We need to be doing 12s without any excuses, and don't even think about complaining because that's a holiday before having to knock out 13s. Then we can start looking at the Average, which *already* is up to 13.7 miles.

'You know what we should do?' says Jamie.

'What?'

'We should just add another five minutes to each shift. Spread the work out a bit. We'll still have to do more work at the end of the day but hopefully not as much.'

'Great idea.'

After dinner it's straight into sleeping bags, and I pull my neck warmer up over my eyes. I'm too exhausted and too buzzed by sugar to sleep. It seems like a long long way to the Pole. I think of home and what we have there. All the things I've taken for granted. Warmth, food, beds. How precious the people we've left behind.

'What are you going to do when you get back?' I ask.

'Eat Punta back into the stone age.'

'Then what?'

'Marry Kate.'

Makes perfect sense to me.

13. CREVASSES, WHITE NINJAS, JAMIE TRYING TO KILL US AND OTHER IRRITATIONS

FOUR-WORD SENTENCES YOU DEFINITELY don't want to hear in Antarctica:

> 'Is that a crevasse?'
> 'I'm cutting the rope!'
> 'No more toilet paper.'
> 'That will thaw out.'

This morning, just like every other for the past three weeks, Adam the Radio Guy has breakfast in the mess tent at the Patriot Hills base camp and then takes his coffee mug a few steps to the snug white portacabin. There he kicks the snow off his boots, hangs up his jacket and sits down in front of the amber glowing dials of the big multiband transceivers and amplifiers that connect the camp to the outside world. He gives special attention to the Iridium phone because soon the sched calls will arrive from the expeditions out in the field.

The news the last few days had been alarming. The expeditions have been reporting that they've seen crevasses. This morning, one by one, the teams call in. The Jardines, Hannah, the Marines, the

RAF, each leaving brief messages.

At 3.15am NZ time, the Thermal Heart team should call. Nothing. 3.30am. Still nothing. Well, it could be anything: sunspots, the batteries may have got cold, it may have been too overcast for the solar cells to charge . . . or they could be dangling down a crevasse.

Adam notes it in his log. That makes twenty-four hours since their last contact. If there is no word from them by this time tomorrow, then Stefan will have to get in the Twin Otter and go hunt some Kiwis.

On a bright day we're weaving among great jumbled slabs of sastrugi, as if through the demolished remains of a giant cathedral. Then we crest a small ridge and the view pulls me up short. On the other side of the field in front of us is a gentle slope scarred with long horizontal stripes, a series of what looks like partly filled-in ditches.

Jamie comes up alongside, pushes up his mask and shakes his head. 'Crevasses. I hate crevasses.'

The last of Scott's ponies had been shot. The dog teams had been sent back. There were just three teams of four men pulling their sleds up the mighty Beardmore Glacier. A million acres of tortured fractured ice, hiding gaping maws deceptively concealed by a thin white lipstick of windblown snow. The men started to fall in.

One second, they would be trudging over a hard smooth surface and the next they were dangling by their harness lines over an inky abyss. 'The Lord only knows how deep these vast chasms go down, they seem to extend into blue black nothingness thousands of feet below,' explained Cherry-Garrard.

On some days the men were dropping in continually. One of them fell the full length of his harness eight times in twenty-five minutes.

'Little wonder he looked dazed,' reported Cherry-Garrard. At the end of a particularly bad day one man wrote in his diary:

> *We have today experienced what we none of us ever wants to*
> *be our lot again. I cannot describe the maze we got into and the*
> *hairbreadth escapes we have had to pass through today. Often*
> *and often we saw openings where it was possible to drop the*
> *biggest ship afloat and lose her.*

And the next day, simply: 'Worse than yesterday.'

It is a miracle that no one was killed. Perhaps the luckiest escape was by Frank Wild, who had been leading the last remaining pony, Socks, up the Beardmore in the earlier *Nimrod* Expedition. Shackleton heard a 'whoosh' and turned around to see the sled still on the surface and Wild clinging onto the edge of a freshly made pony-sized hole. After helping Wild out, they lay down on their stomachs and peered over the edge, but there was no sign of Socks. He had apparently dropped clean out of his harness and disappeared without so much as a whinny into the 'black, bottomless pit'.

As a fine judge of crevasses (having seen my first one half a minute ago), I would have to say that these particular ones don't look like the sled-gobbling kind. They are scarcely wider than the length of our skis and appear to be well bridged over.

We approach the first crevasse at a point where the snow looks the strongest.

'You go,' I suggest.

'No, no, after you,' says Gentleman Jamie.

I walk out into the middle and am ever so slightly disappointed when nothing dramatic happens. I bang my ski pole firmly down on the snow and it jars comfortingly. So I try a little harder and am startled when it pops clear through the crust and out the other side.

'Would you mind not doing that?' says an oddly high-pitched voice behind me.

Most of them could be seen by the strip of snow on the blue ice. They were often too wide to jump though, and the only thing was to plant your feet on the bridge and try not to tread heavily.
— Cherry-Garrard

After a few more ditches the slope starts to flatten out and I'm beginning to think that that is all the fun we are going to have. Until we come across a Very Big Hole. The closer we get, the more enormous it becomes. It is perhaps the size of a football field, but as we get closer we see that it is disappointingly not bottomless; it's simply as if the snow had slumped three or four storeys. If we could find a way down there it might not be a bad place to camp out of the wind.

It's nevertheless quite spectacular. What it needs is a bit of perspective to do it justice in a photo. I turn to Jamie. 'Stay here with the camera and I'll go around the other side and you can take a photo with me and the hole that really shows the size of this thing.'

'OK.'

'Which way? Left or right?'

'Try left.'

So I start to ski clockwise around the side of the hole, careful to give the lip itself a wide berth. Then a vivid indigo crack appears in the snow and opens underneath me, my skis cross over, and I pitch forward, falling head first into the fissure.

And fall . . .

And fall . . .

. . . stopping only when my arse hits the opening and wedges in firmly. A total of about a metre.

Oh. That's all right then.

My arms are out in front of me as if caught midway through a shallow dive. Fortunately my ski pole leashes had been looped over my wrists. I'm staring down at a rapidly narrowing ice-walled fissure that takes an abrupt turn about 2 metres away and so spares me the worst of the view. My skis are still on but have crossed awkwardly, leaving me jammed in the hole like Winnie the Pooh.

'Jamie!' I shout. Nothing.

'Jamie?' Still nothing.

I find I can use my elbows against the sides to get some purchase and with a little puffing and heaving I back myself slowly out. When I've finally extricated myself, Jamie is a few metres away, taking photos and trying not to laugh.

'Maybe going right would have been better. Anyway, good on ya mate — anyone with a skinnier arse would have fallen right through.'

I'm a little shaky as we trudge away, trying to come to terms with the fact that the ground can open up and swallow me whole pretty much whenever it wants to.

What if we were kiting back through here? Would we see a crevasse before we fell into it? What if my sled had fallen through? What if we had been in a whiteout? My imagination is only too happy to supply the answers to these earnest questions so I spend the afternoon being dropped down imaginary crevasses of various sizes. There is always a rustle of collapsing snow, followed by either a quick squeal, then a crunchy 'plop' or a long yell complete with Doppler shift as I ricochet down the blue glassy walls to a landfall thousands of metres below. This is a fiendish place. If it can't dissolve you slowly, it will gobble you quickly.

The next morning we finally get through to Adam.

'Crevasses? Well, that's good to know. I don't think anyone has ever been through that area. I'm marking them on the map now. We can call them the Kiwi Crevasses if you like?' he suggests helpfully.

At the end of the day I come into the tent. Jamie has the GPS out, checking the mileage of the last shift that I had been leading. '2.0. Don't worry, Henrietta, we can paint little flowers on your sled tomorrow if you like.'

I look at the other GPS. 'You mean 2.2.'

'No, 2.0. Have a look.'

We put the two GPSs together. They read differently by more than several hundred metres. That's too weird.

My glucose-starved brain struggles to make sense of what's going on. Clearly both of them can't be right, but what if both of them are wrong? Are we going to be able to find the caches? Umm, where exactly are we?

'Let's just use the one that gives us the biggest number,' suggests Jamie.

'Good idea. That way we can get there faster.'

As I sip on my hot milk drink it occurs to me that sledging in Antarctica is a lot like the sport of chess boxing I recently read about — a round of boxing followed by a round of chess. You're first bludgeoned by right hooks and uppercuts, and then have to sit in front of a chessboard and respond to a fierce Fried Liver Attack. I don't know how they move the pieces with their gloves on, but there you go.

Antarctica is like that. You first get softened up with a few hours of gruesome effort to make you dizzy with exhaustion. Then you make camp and have to solve why a fuel bottle won't hold pressure. Why the sched call won't go through. Why the battery box won't charge. Why the two GPSs are reading differently. There is always some bullet that has to be dodged *Matrix*-style.

I have started calling it the Daily Disaster, although it hasn't been a disaster (yet). It's an irritation, an erosion of our slim safety margins. It seems to come singularly so I'm always happiest when we get the Disaster over in the morning. That way we can relax. For example, a couple of days ago, Jamie didn't make a tight enough bundle of his bedroll, so the straps didn't quite meet. He gave it such a huge yank that the buckle broke. It's not a big deal, he just has to tie it up instead. Disaster managed, and the rest of the day went fine.

Yesterday nothing happened all day. I couldn't bear the tension. When Jamie's neck warmer dropped off the drying rack to get briefly toasted on the stove before being plucked away, we both agreed it was a relief.

Now there is nothing we can do about the GPSs. Fortunately we're going to one of the two places in the world where it doesn't matter where you start from, or what kind of mistakes you made in your course yesterday: as long as you keep heading south you will arrive at the Pole. The GPSs don't seem to be arguing about that.

The next morning when Jamie returns from having his constitutional, he becomes caught in the drying line where my goggles are hanging. By the time he disentangles himself and sits down, they are lying broken on the floor.

'Shit, sorry mate.'

It's nothing a safety pin can't fix. But as I look at them, and run through our recent breakages and misfortunes, a certain pattern begins to appear.

The fuel-bottle lid screwed on so tightly it munted the washer — Jamie.

The hole in the tent roof from trying to use a ballpoint pen to mark our progress — Jamie.

Dropping his neck warmer into the stove — Jamie.

Sitting on my goggles — Jamie.

I'm not saying anything. It's probably just coincidence. A few minutes pass in tense silence. Then Jamie asks me a question. Of all the things that you don't want to hear in Antarctica, one of the worst is: 'You seen the lighter?'

The stove is already going so Jamie must have had the lighter in his hand until quite recently. So what begins with a tepid poking of kitchen utensils ends up fifteen minutes later with us sitting breathless, with everything in the tent turned upside down or inside out or emptied. No lighter.

We do have a spare, and even a piece of flint as last resort. But still, to lose a third of the stove-lighting tools is to start a very disturbing trend.

'It's got to turn up,' says Jamie.

I go back to fixing my goggles.

'Oh, here it is.'

I turn around to see that he has just lifted the lid of the pot. Bubbling away in the water is the lighter.

I chew on my lip while a conversation I had with Scotty, the guy who had walked unresupplied to the North Pole, floats into my head.

'If you ever have a problem with anyone during the day — then wait until after you get into the tent at night before saying anything.'

'Right. Wait until you're out of the cold then blast him.'

'No. Wait until after you've had something to eat.'

'Yeah! Do it on a full stomach.'

'No, wait until after you've had a sleep.'

'Yep. Hit them with it first thing in the morning.'

'No. Then wait until you've had breakfast. If it's still a problem then raise it then. Only if it's still a problem. Nine times out of ten it won't be.'

He's right, after breakfast the next morning I'm over it.

I'm backing out of the tent when Jamie, as has been his recent habit, picks it up and gives it a violent shake to remove the last of the snow. Today, after a couple of shakes, the dome collapses in his hands and I find myself wearing the tent as a hat.

'I think a pole has broken,' Jamie shouts.

Maybe I'm not over it.

We carefully work out the pieces of aluminium, trying not to rip the tent sleeves, which is not as much fun as it sounds when the wind is trying to wrap the tent around your legs and the metal sears through all layers of gloves and precious sledging time is being wasted and there is the real threat of having to sleep in your sled if you screw up.

We have spare pole segments, but oddly they now turn out to have slightly different diameters, as if imperial versus metric. So by the time the pole is taken out, we have removed the bungy that connects it and created a rigid pole of more or less the right length, at least 50 per cent of the expedition has concluded that they are very cold and grumpy — and there is something else that is bothering me and I can't quite put my finger on it. Oh yeah, that's it.

Jamie is trying to kill us.

He may be a gazelle in the snow, but he's a rhino in the tent. He must be stopped before he snaps, grinds, scatters and skewers all of our gear.

During the second shift my left hand is freezing, refusing to come back to life. At the break I decide to change to the North Face mountain mitts. The wind sees its chance and flings one of the gloves onto the snow where it starts tumbling away.

Jamie hurls himself after it, lying sprawled but getting up triumphantly with a face full of snow and the glove in his hand.

'Ta,' I say tersely. My gratitude tempered by the sure knowledge that he'll probably set fire to it tomorrow.

The next day is worryingly cold. I had turned on the iPod before leaving the tent, but something about the way it's sitting means that the volume starts fluctuating, first so quietly that I can barely hear it and then deafeningly loud. For the next hour and a half, I'm tortured by David Beckham whispering and then shouting in my ear as my goggles ice up.

By the time I get to the first break, I'm blind and deaf. I angrily yank up the headphone cord to get at the iPod and feel it lift up out of its pocket inside my thermal top before becoming stuck on something. I pull harder, and then, with a click, the plug pops out and the iPod slithers down inside my long johns until it hits the top of my boot. Bugger. Well, there is nowhere it can go now. It can stay there until I rescue it in the tent tonight.

After setting up camp, I get into the tent and sit down and pat my legs feeling for the familiar rectangle. Nothing. I pull off my long johns. Nothing. I shake out my boots. The iPod isn't there. Having gone through Denial, I quickly cycle through Anger and Bargaining, before I arrive at Depression. I sit staring at the empty leg of my trousers, trying to come to terms with my colossal stupidity. It must have fallen out onto the snow when I was having my little tanty. How could I not have seen it? What was I thinking taking a *white* iPod to Antarctica?

This is a heavy blow. The iPod is one of the most precious pieces of equipment that we have. The headphone ear buds have been two little white plugs stopping my sanity dribbling out of my ears. Two sponge lozenges that have faithfully provided a drip feed of distraction to stop my brain dissolving in doubt.

For half the day, sometimes longer, I had been whisked away to cheerful distracting places. I had listened to *A Short History of Nearly Everything*, conquered Abyssinia with Flashman, got married to a Spice Girl. It had provided a reminder of happier times at home that made this mad, endless ploughing expedition seem normal. If I had had to leave the burning tent with my hair on fire, I would have stopped to get the iPod.

Now it's gone.

'Don't worry, mate. We can share mine.'

'Serious?'

'Sure.'

I'm staggered, this is really something.

'You don't have to.'

'Yeah no, it's no problem.'

I'm dazed into speechlessness. A big slab of humble pie has knocked me off my high horse. I don't deserve this. I'm not the one that breaks or loses things, *Jamie* is. He *has* been careless, he *has* broken all those things — but now I see that I was completely missing the point. The problem isn't what Jamie is doing, it's my death grip on wanting to be right. His mistakes aren't the problem, my anger is. Now his generosity has completely exposed me as a self-righteous fraud.

Shackleton forced upon me his one breakfast biscuit . . . I do not suppose that anyone else in the world can thoroughly realise how much generosity and sympathy was shown by this; I DO, and BY GOD I shall never forget.

— Wild

For better or worse, we are in this together, our fates aren't separable. Instead of nursing my resentment, I could have talked to him about it, had a laugh, and worked together to do something about his problem, and mine. Right now my brain is unhelpfully pointing out all the things that I have broken over the last few weeks (not through any carelessness on my part of course, but through unlikely accidents and manufacturing defects).

Dinner is eaten in a chastened silence. It's not until later on when my fleece hat falls into the stove, and I finally beat the flames out, that we both have a good laugh.

Is this what marriage is going to be like?

I had thought that I would come to Antarctica to find out about a country a long way away that I hardly knew anything about. Instead, I'm finding out more about someone who I thought I knew well and who I see every day.

We have an allowance of a few precious minutes each night to use the satellite phone. Jamie always has someone to talk to. I look on curiously as he works his way through a long list of numbers. He somehow draws strength from his network of friends, whereas I find it hard to talk when the spectre of colossal, headline-grabbing, craptacular failure is still hanging over us, and the flitting back between the carefree barbecue season in New Zealand and our gloomy life in the freezer does my head in.

One person who we do hear from nearly every night is Kate, who's updating us by text with news from the other expeditions' websites and reading out the streams of well-wishes that are coming into our own website from all over the country. Jamie has told her everything about our plans.

I had adopted a different policy with HPG. Before leaving, I had tried hard not to alarm her about the dangers of sledging in Antarctica. Perhaps that's why our calls now are so difficult. She doesn't seem to know what to say. She seems caught up in her day-to-day life, planning her upcoming move to a hospital in Whangarei. I feel like I'm talking to a stranger. I'm sure at some level she resents what I'm putting her through; I know I wouldn't like it if the situation were reversed. I feel like she's drifting away.

So tonight after listening to Jamie having another robust conversation with Kate about upcoming weather conditions and progress, I decide to call HPG and try again.

Soon she asks, 'What are these sastrugi you keep talking about?'

I'm stunned.

She continues, 'Why don't you just walk around them?'

'Because they're *everywhere.*'

Then the moving truck is there, friends have arrived, the conversation ends in a muddle of cold goodbyes and warm hellos.

I still have a few minutes left of my daily allotment. I decide to call Mum.

'Hello dear! How's it going?' She is always so cheerful.

'Oh yeah, not too bad. I lost my iPod the other day.'

'Oh, don't worry, just keep an eye out for it on the way back!'

I love Mum.

DAY 24. INSIDE A PING-PONG BALL

TODAY WE CAN MAKE 84 degrees south. It's not a snappy symmetrical milestone like 'a third' of the way, but a sturdy respectable one nevertheless. If we can get to 84 degrees south, then we are within striking distance of halfway. My subconscious shows me crevasses — I show it chocolate pudding.

Recently we have had encouraging signs that we are getting

faster. Our worst day the previous week was 12.4 (the day I fell into the crevasse), but mostly we had made 13s. Though this hasn't been quite enough to arrest the upward creep of the Average. Now 84 degrees was only 12.7 miles away. If we could just get there in six shifts we would not only earn some Chilean Mystery Pudding, and a fat tablespoon of feijoa vodka, but we could also get some sleep. Hallelujah.

I look at the battery box. There is a row of LED lights that measures how much sun is hitting the solar panel outside, a good indicator of the type of day that we are going to have. They may as well have labelled the lights accordingly. Today there are no solid green lights at all. Just one flashing: 'You're screwed'.

'It doesn't look good does it?'

'No, it doesn't.'

I open the fly and look out. Just white. My eyes bulge and strain, like a seeking auto-focus on a digital camera. It's a whiteout again, but this one is positively mathematical in its perfection.

You know the scene in *The Matrix* where Neo and Morpheus first go to the white space that is Nothing, then the racks of guns arrive? This is like that — without the guns. What a soundproof room is to the ears, this is to the eyes. It is whiteness that is as impenetrable and concealing as darkness. My eyes are open but I'm blind — at least to shades of white. Anything in colours, like the sled, appears bright and normal, but hangs in the air as if cut out and stuck to a white backdrop with white glue.

I step outside but standing up is precarious as there is nothing to reference. My legs unfold, but all they erect is a very wobbly tower. I look up and down trying to find the right spot to place my first step until gravity takes over and I stumble forwards.

The sun has been diffused perfectly. The sky and ground is uniquely and consistently white. I am inside a light bulb. I have no shadow at all. None. The sastrugi have vanished. I fall over again on the way back to the tent. No, they are still there. Just impossible to see.

Two hours later the tent is packed and we are hooking on to the sleds. I'm going to lead the first shift.

I turn to Jamie. 'Ready?'

'Yep.'

I turn my hips until the compass is pointing the right way, shuffle forwards until the traces are tight, and stamp the poles in. Thirteen miles to get today — 2.17 in each shift. No excuses. No time to waste if I want to get my snout into that big bowl of hot chocolaty nirvana that floats in front of me.

I slide my left ski forward, put my right ski pole into nothingness and topple over. Bugger, I must have been on the lip of something. I wobble back to my feet.

'Are you right?' says Jamie.

'Yep, yep.' OK. This time. Here we go. I get the compass reoriented, take two steps and fall over again. This time I flail around, while a speech bubble filled with hashes, ampersands, exclamation marks and percentage signs appears over my head. Finally I untangle myself and stagger upright.

A few steps later, I hit the ground with yet another thump. This time I hypothesise, as I stare up (or is it down?) at the sky (or snow?), that perhaps some forcible cathartic discourse may ameliorate the growing sense of injustice and indignation, particularly if I accompany it with a little unsynchronised limb thrashing.

Nope. It doesn't help. It just disturbs Jamie.

'Mate. Take it easy!'

I take off my goggles. It doesn't make any difference at all. I could close my eyes and it wouldn't make any difference. I don't need eyes, I need sonar. I need echo location. Dolphins would be great out here (no legs, though).

I try waving my ski pole out in front of me like an ant's antennae, tapping and stabbing to feel anything. It kind of works but it's far too slow. No, I'll just have to stride out and take the knocks.

A few minutes later I hear 'Whoa!' and look around to see the curious sight of my sled levitated about a metre and a half in the air. Having taken its own path up the side of an invisible slope, it is now threatening to topple over. Jamie comes alongside and with some difficulty pulls it down to safety.

A few minutes later he shouts, 'Wait up!' I turn around to see that I'm towing my sled quite happily along on its side. How long has it been like that? What about the fuel cans! I can imagine the fuel gurgling out of a not-quite-screwed-on lid, spreading its greasy, stinking poison through the food.

I sigh. Here we are, more than three weeks into the trip and our sleds are still so heavy that whether they are upright and being pulled over a small lip, or on their sides, the effort feels the same.

Jamie comes up to my sled and tries to turn it while still in his skis but the sled is too heavy and the angles aren't right. So he bends down, unclips from his bindings, steps out and then walks around and pushes the sled over. Then trudges back to his skis, clips in again and shouts, 'OK.'

I take three steps and I hear, 'Yeah, nah.' The sled is over again.

Sometimes I start to feel a gentle ramping, and a waved ski pole reveals the sides are getting closer and closer as we start to be drawn into one of the fish schools. Often the tips of my skis bump into a wall and I have to shout out a warning to Jamie, then very awkwardly back up in our skis, shove the sleds around and retrace our steps, losing precious minutes.

Or more often the white-gloved white ninjas will just come out of the whiteness, and push me over and trip me up for no reason. There is nothing that I can do about it except get madder, madder and madder.

I'm never going to be fooled again by earnest documentaries with names like 'Antarctica: The Threatened Wilderness' and 'Antarctica's Fragile Beauty' and yadayadayada. Because you know what? Antarctica kicks puppies. Antarctica never calls its Mum. Antarctica parks in the handicapped spots. It throws its McDonald's wrappers out the car window and flicks cigarette butts into drains that run to the sea. Antarctica is mean. And if Antarctica thinks that you are on a tight schedule then it organises a squad of white assassins to give you a good smiting, just for giggles. When I get home I'm going to buy the biggest SUV I can find, convert it to run on dirty brown coal and leave it idling in the driveway with the exhaust pointed due fricking south.

At the end of the first shift, the GPS (if you can believe it) is unforgiving — 1.2 lousy miles. There's no way we are going to get to 84 degrees today. The pecans are cold little stones in my mouth.

Following is easier. Jamie provides a reference point and the lead sled throws a little contrast out to either side, revealing something of the snow. Funny how light is no good without shadow. It's not very taxing work as there are frequent pauses while Jamie does the route finding/falling over.

My main job then is to call out when it's clear he's going wrong. Like now. I'm watching mesmerised as Jamie's sled magically floats up and to the side, takes on a dangerous lean before toppling over and rolling to a stop upside down. Jamie, oblivious, keeps pulling.

'Whoa! Your sled's tipped over,' I shout.

Jamie turns around. 'Yours has too!'

I look around. Yes, it has. I thought it felt a bit harder to pull than usual.

Third shift and Calamity Kev is again at the helm. In twenty minutes we travel only a hundred metres. Our sleds are over nearly every minute. More than once we have both sleds over at the same time. By lunchtime we've done only 4.9 miles. We'd be going faster if we rolled our sleds to the pole end over end. It looks like we'll be lucky if we finish the day only 3 miles short.

Jamie is eating nuts and not saying anything. The way his jaw muscles are bulging, he looks like he wouldn't have noticed if they were in their shells. He then takes off and strides out. Whatever he is going to hit, he is going to hit it hard.

Yet he doesn't hit anything. He keeps going. I struggle to keep up and I can see and he can't. I'm not going to ask him to slow down, I'm going to just hang in there.

Where has the rubble gone? Where are the fish schools? How can he see where he is going? Frick this is fast. I'm not going to ask him to slow down. I'm not.

At the break we find we went 2.4 miles. A new record for a shift.

'You're a monster,' I gasp.

'I'm going to get that pudding if it kills me,' he says hoarsely.

So now it's my turn to step up. The trick is not to care what you are about to run into or fall over. After all, it scarcely makes a difference if you hit something at 1 or 1.5 miles an hour. I don't have quite the luck with obstacles, but it's still a solid run. By the time Jamie finishes the sixth shift, we are only 1.3 nautical miles off the degree. So we put another hour in. Finally there is only a ninth of a mile left to go, then an eighteenth. It's 84 degrees or it doesn't count. The GPS finally, reluctantly, agrees we are there.

Three quarters of an hour later I'm very happily occupied inside the tent. Jamie watches closely as I dispense a single, quivering, bulging tablespoon of clear, fragrant, oily vodka into each cup. No chemical titration has been done more carefully.

I'm very proud. Eleven hours on the trail. One of the hardest days of the expedition so far. So much of it had seemed so bleak and hopeless but we had stuck it out and got there. We lie on our sleeping bags, carefully sucking on chocolate-chip cookies and enjoying the very simple pleasures of the trail. My heart is pounding, either from the workout or from the sudden unfamiliar bombardment of sugars.

'One more degree and we are halfway.'

'Quarter way, you mean,' says Jamie.

'Mambo No. 5!'

There is a groan from the other side of the tent.

'Too much partying last night.'

'It's not what we're drinking, it's where we're drinking.'

'It's what we're doing in between the drinking.'

Is that sun coming through the nylon? I pull my booties on and roll out of the tent — not since Peter Pan has someone been so happy to find his shadow. Somehow we dodged some very nasty stuff on our way in. It's like we've been helicoptered onto the only flat spot in what is otherwise a graveyard of jumbled ice slabs.

Today, after only ten minutes on the march, it's so hot we have to stop to take off our jackets. But still the sun bakes us, and without any wind to whisk away the heat we get hotter still. As a last resort, we undo the arse flaps on our long johns. Hopefully I don't look as funny as Jamie.

The thermometer on the sled reads ⁻5° Celsius. No wonder we're hot. It's practically Florida; any hotter and we could grow oranges.

By the end of the third shift I get out the GPS and rest it on my knee while it starts up, enjoying how the shift breaks have been transformed from desperate, urgent struggles to gentlemanly stops.

Then it gives the distance.

'Wow! You won't believe this: 6.8 miles.'

'Cool.'

'We might be able to make . . .'

'WOAH! NUP NUP NUP!'

'What?'

'Were you going to say how far you thought we could go today?'

'Yep, what's wrong with that?'

'You'll "Murray Mexted" it.'

'Eh?'

'You know when you're watching a test and Murray Mexted says "The All Blacks have it in the bag", or "He never misses from here"?'

'Yeah.'

'Then what happens?'

'The opposite.'

'That's what I'm saying. Don't Murray Mexted it.'

'Yeah yeah, you're right . . . lucky if we make 8 miles for the day then?'

'If we don't fall down a hole and break a leg first.'

A few minutes later Jamie is checking texts.

'Do you know what this one is about?' he asks.

'What does it say?'

'Peace talks stalled in Washington. Ten-foot snake found in bathtub. Giant iceberg off the coast of Dunedin. Wheldon.'

'Oh yeah, I've asked some friends to send us the news headlines. I thought it might be fun to keep up with what's going on.'

'Is he making them up? Do you really think there is an iceberg off Dunedin?'

Antarctica is continually shedding ice. The Ross Ice Shelf advances 2 to 3 metres a day and that ice has to calve off, mostly in small icebergs, sometimes in massive chunks. The largest recorded iceberg, B15, was about the size of Jamaica when it broke away in March 2000.

For the next five years, B15 bounced around the west coast of the Ross Sea, changing maps, blocking resupply ships and upsetting wildlife. Eventually it ran aground off Cape Adare at the end of 2005 and began to break up and drift away. Some of the fragments, still very sizeable chunks of ice many football fields in size, took a detour past the bottom of the South Island. The most surprising thing about these icebergs was not that they were the first to be seen from the mainland in seventy years, but the fact that they might have had Norwegian tents on them.

You will recall that Amundsen staked his life and the lives of his men on the assumption that the ice they camped on in the Bay of Whales was safely parked on land. B15 was the iceberg that proved him wrong. The bit that parted company with the Ice Shelf was where Amundsen had his compound.

Can you imagine skiing along the Ice Shelf and have that crack open up between your skis? If only you knew when it was going to happen and which way the iceberg was going to go. What an incredible way to travel! In theory, you could pitch your tent in the middle and float up nearly to New Zealand. Even the largest waves would scarcely cause a wobble. That is — until they did. As icebergs get older they become unstable and develop a disconcerting habit of turning upside down; then you'd wake up with 300 metres of iceberg on top of you.

The question is — is all this ice floating away being replaced? Is the ice floating past New Zealand the start of a disturbing new trend? Is it the tip of the iceberg? Do we need to start moving up to the attic?

Not yet. *Most* of Antarctica is being spared from *most* of the effects of global warming by a very unlikely ally — our friend the ozone hole. It had to happen eventually, one man-made global screw-up fixing another. Still it's very bizarre. It's like finding out that dumping nuclear waste in the ocean brings dodos back to life. Or that drift-net fishing cures cancer and stops acid rain.

The ozone hole cools the stratosphere over the Pole, intensifying the winds that spiral clockwise around Antarctica. These air currents effectively isolate the continent from the weather of the rest of the planet. The main casualty is the Antarctic Peninsula, as it sticks out into their flow and is most affected by the warmer wet sea air they bring. Weather stations in the Peninsula have reported astonishing temperature increases of 2 to 5 degrees in the past fifty years. Of the 244 glaciers in the area, 212 are in retreat. Meanwhile the South Pole itself, if anything, is getting colder.

Eventually the ozone hole will heal, the winds will slow and the Antarctic ice cap will start to warm — but not to melt. At least not most of it. At least not in this century. When one of Scott's men first saw the deep, rich soil of the Dry Valleys and the clear meltwater flowing down from the glaciers, he remarked, 'What a splendid place for growing spuds!'

Hopefully it's going to be a few years before he's right.

14. 'SHALL I COMPARE THEE TO A HAMBURGER?'

*We are gradually passing from the hungry to the ravenous; we
cannot drag our thoughts from food, and we talk of little else . . .
one sometimes gets almost a sickly feeling from want of food, and
the others declare that they have an actual gnawing sensation. At
night one wakes with the most distressing feeling of emptiness,
and then to reflect that there are probably four or five hours more
before breakfast is positively dreadful. We have all proved the
efficacy of pulling our belts quite tight before we go to sleep . . .*

— Scott

POLITE SOCIETY IS A little squeamish about cannibalism. While
tolerated under certain circumstances, such as aeroplane crashes
in the Andes, it's otherwise generally frowned upon. Not so in
Antarctica. In fact, for unsupported expeditions it's practically a
requirement. Admittedly it's not the picking-your-friend's-thigh-out-
of-your-teeth type of cannibalism, but make no mistake, human flesh
is being devoured — yours.

This is because of a nasty catch-22 that every unresupplied

expedition finds itself in. If you take the amount of food that you actually need, say 8000–10,000 calories per day, multiplied by the amount of days estimated to reach the destination, the total is a very heavy sled. So heavy in fact that you decide it will definitely take longer than your first estimate. So now you have to take more food for the longer trip and so on until your sled weighs three and a half tons and is going nowhere.

To escape this escalating weight dilemma you try cutting your toothbrush in half, separating your two-ply toilet paper, sandpapering the paint off your ski poles, but it's not nearly enough.

Then one day you catch sight of yourself in the mirror — and there you see all the weight you need. If only you could bite on those plump buttocks? Lap up all those luscious lipids? If only you could serve yourself up as sashimi or steak tartare?

Of course you can, it's easy. All you have to do is be very very hungry and your body will do the rest. But how much less can you get away with? Every unresupplied team has to weigh up (literally) how far they are planning to travel, how much weight they can pull, how large their own fat reserves are, and then choose a point on the weight-versus-calories curve. We had chosen two, and split our food into four-day bags, consisting of 6500 calories per day for four days, and two-day bags of 4300 calories a day for two days. The plan was to use the latter when closer to the Pole and for the kite trip back, when our energy requirements should be much less.

We knew we were going to go hungry, so for months before the trek no plate had been turned away and no food was too sweet or too creamy. As a result we had both packed on many kilos of excess blubber, but out on the trail the reality of starving, while gorging on food, is something quite strange.

In everyday life, 6500 calories is an amount of food that would leave you staggering as if hit by a medicine ball. In the normal world an average person eating our diet would gain about 4 kilograms a week. So twice a day, in the morning and evening, for at least a few minutes, we can't help but feel full. But even before we have finished licking our plates, that feeling has evaporated and we are trying not to gnaw on the plastic. Which leaves the other twenty-three hours and fifty-five minutes to obsess about food.

Lunch has become almost an insult in its insufficiency; it is gone in a twinkling, and we gaze at the provision bag, frown at the cook, and wonder if he has not cut our allowance too fine with a misplaced ardour for saving . . .

— Scott

One break, Jamie turns around with a face frozen in alarm. 'Wait! Wait! Don't move!'

'What?'

'There's a nut around here somewhere.'

We lift up our limbs, one after the other, very carefully, until a single pecan drops onto the snow.

'There it is!'

Phew. That was close.

In the tent another night, I'm quizzing Jamie. 'Tell me, where do the steaks come from in a cow?'

'It depends on the type of steak.'

'How many steaks could you get from a seal? Or is a seal just one big sausage?'

Still another time, Jamie is looking through the medical dry bag for some more Voltaren for his hamstrings. I hear an 'Aha!' and look up.

Jamie is holding up a foil packet with the look of a new Lotto winner. He takes a breath and attempts to compose his face. 'Now I'm going to ask you a question. I want you to think about it carefully. Are Strepsils food?'

'Oh, I think they are!'

'Well then, we deserve some lollies.'

He pushes one out of the foil and hands it over. I suck on it thoughtfully. There's definitely sugar, or something that tastes like sugar. Or something that makes you think you are tasting something like sugar. It's certainly plenty better than the grinding emptiness.

One remembers declining a particularly succulent dish; what an extraordinary thing to do! What a different being one must have been in those days!

— Scott

It's the fifth shift break at the end of the last day of the four-day bag. It is the Break of Reckoning, for now the world can see exactly how well you've resisted temptation the last twenty or so snacks. There is nowhere to hide from the consequences of your gluttony. It takes a lot of self-control to manage a four-day snack bag. When it comes to food, your mind has a mind of its own. How did that piece of chocolate get in your hand! No! Put it back.

Perhaps you let your guard down two days ago. Perhaps it was an afternoon in the middle of a whiteout, when you convinced yourself that a little extra nibble would help get you through. At the time it was just a little brown bump, there were plenty more. Surely it wouldn't matter?

Or maybe it was the perpetual temptation of the salami, which is not always cut into little chunks. Instead you have to nip a twenty-fourth off a lump. How much is a twenty-fourth? You should have thought of that before you put it in your mouth because now, when your salivary glands are squirting, it's easy to convince yourself that it's almost certainly a bit more. But those giddy days when I had options are over. Today it is the last shift and I get what's left. There is barely anything. Judgement time has come and I have been found wanting.

Wait! My frantic ferreting has been rewarded. I reach down and pull out a particularly large piece of chocolate. It doesn't need dusting off but I dust it anyway. I hold it up to ensure that my colleague can see my wealth, the fruit of iron self-control. (In fact, mysteriously found in a fold of the snack bag but he will never know.) My eyebrows make a tent while I consider out loud, whether it would be better to have this piece 'neat', or to have it with a little butter, of which coincidentally there appears to be a dab, to give myself a particularly memorable mouthful. Ah, nothing like a piece of chocolate and butter washed down with a big cup of gloat!

My companion forcibly suggests plenty of other things that I can do with my chocolate while he wails and gnashes his teeth. It is seldom this way around. More often, I'm left licking the nylon walls of the snack bag, while Jamie burps loudly and lovingly taps his apparently full stomach with the back of his closed fist.

Every four days the food bag is exhausted and we need to take another from the least light sled and put it in the kitchen box. The breakfasts and dinners are already separated out but to shorten an already laborious job we didn't split the snacks in Punta. That's OK, doing this couldn't be better entertainment if *America's Next Top Model* guest-starred on *Top Gear*.

The salami and butter are produced and quickly halved and dispatched, using the traditional I-cut-you-choose method. Next, the pecan nut bag is split open and the brown, aromatic seeds are revealed. Each person is given a turn to choose a single nut and put it in their snack bag. Since a nut is a nut with little variation, this is speedily done. So far everything is just a curtain-raiser for the real show — the Chocolate.

We have developed a ritual. First, the assigned Grand Chocolate Poobah reaches into the master food bag, rummages for a bit, then rummages some more turning his face towards you with an exaggerated look of horror. You know he is going to do it, yet you feel your innards pinch as if an internal drawstring has been pulled. Did we leave the chocolate out of this bag? It's not possible, surely? How will we survive four days without chocolate? But no! There it is. Ha ha! (Bastard.) The bag is presented with great ceremony and delight, and passed over so you can heft it in one hand to appreciate its extraordinary weight, and stare through the translucent double-bagging at the hazy outlines of all the exquisite jostling morsels.

After carefully rationing out our chocolate over the past four days, seeing our meagre supplies disappear, and finally licking our snack bags clean in the last shift, here is the mother lode. Lo! The amazingness of so much chocolate in one place.

The top of the bag is carefully untied. Oh smell that! Inhale the pungent, dry, sweet, carbohydrate bliss. Smell the loamy soils of an equatorial jungle, see the gurgling waterfall in the chocolate factory, hear the Oompa Loompas singing.

Now the chocolate is tipped onto the lid of the kitchen box. A tumbling cascade of deep brown nuggets: Jamaica Dark, Dark Cacao, Black Forest, Ghana, Fruit and Nut. Firstly, all the good and true squares are selected, turned about and carefully secreted into our snack bags. When this is done its time to play chocolate jigsaw. Each of us takes a turn examining the remaining fragments and then pulls out two, or more, pieces that form more or less the volume equivalent of a square, holding it up for inspection and an approving nod. Creating more than a square is met with a slightly raised eyebrow and the production of a reciprocally oversized square.

And so on, until there are only chocolate shards left. A pile is made of these and split down the middle. Now there is only chocolate dust, which is coaxed from the bag and also divided. Finally the bag itself is split in half and handed out so that the chocolate molecules can be licked from the inside. (I note that once again there is slightly more chocolate staining in Jamie's side of the bag but it would be poor form to complain.) Finally the clean plastic sheets are now folded and kept for homeopathic and spiritual purposes. They once held chocolate and are therefore sacred by association.

We're writing in our diaries one night in the eighty-fourth degree, when Jamie looks up.

'We haven't got many more four-day bags left, have we?'

No, we don't. Our plan that smaller ration sizes would be sufficient closer to the Pole is now looking very unlikely to be the case.

'I think we should try alternating two-day and four-day bags. Average it out a bit,' Jamie suggests.

'That's really ugly.'

'There's not much of an alternative, is there?'

No. At the moment, we have been arriving at the campsite each night barely able to function. If we were to go only onto two-day bags we will risk becoming completely ineffective.

A few days later, we're dividing up the snacks from the first two-day bag.

'Are you sure there isn't any more?'

I've seen more calories in a tea stain. It is absurdly meagre. I poke at the few bits of chocolate with my finger. When I put the food into the snack bag it scarcely bulges. I go to lift up my replenished bag.

'Watch your back,' warns Jamie.

I do finger curls with it.

We exchange mournful looks.

'It's only for two days,' says Jamie.

The next morning there is a whole new level of scrutiny on the divvying of the cereal. Shackleton invented a three-person method used in the *Discovery* Expedition. After the bowls were filled he would look away, then Scott would point at a bowl and say 'This one?' and Shackleton would say one of their names to allocate it.

Our system is less sophisticated. We pour the muesli more or less equally out into the two bowls and then look at them very closely. If a person thinks they are of different size then he picks up say two nuts and shifts them from one bowl to the other. Then we look at them again. The other person might pick up one nut and take it back. More staring, until we are both satisfied.

Today, as soon as I leave the tent, I'm obsessed with food. Fortunately the surface is good for skiing — unusually hard, but rutted and carved as if a greedy giant had raked his fingers over cold ice-cream. There are some small sastrugi — like the flicks on top of a meringue. The sky is clear, and blue like the tangy bits in blue cheese, with bits of tantalising white candyfloss racing over it.

Antarctica could use a few signposts. Don't get me wrong, I mean there's definitely a place for pristine unspoilt wilderness. It's just that every so often it would be nice to come across something man-made. I'm not saying a concrete toilet block or a car park. Just a single signpost, every three hundred miles or so, might be an amusing diversion and interesting counterpoint to the otherwise sapping desolation, and supply some much-needed perspective.

So I'm very happy when we take the last few steps up a rise and the horizon accelerates away and we're treated with a rare distraction — off to the right-hand side, rearing up out of the snowy mantle, are the shadowy grey blobs of Thiel Mountains.

They vanish and reappear over the next few hours until they grow into a permanent fixture on the horizon, providing a welcome visual anchor to stop the landscape from doing its Alice in Wonderland shenanigans and something to admire as the light plays across them during the day. Best of all they are a signpost, for they are conveniently located at 85 degrees south — exactly halfway to the Pole.

We have slowly accumulated enough miles from our last cache to make it worthwhile to put out another. But where to put it? We certainly don't want to leave it anywhere near the crevasses that we had come across. We are starting to approach the answer.

At the base of Thiels, ALE maintains a small fuel depot to top up the Twin Otters as they go to and from the Pole. At the start and end of the season, ALE use a Sno-Cat, a direct descendant of Shackleton's polarised car and Scott's motorised sledges, to drag out some drums of fuel. A couple of weeks ago they had driven up a longitude line to the west of us and then done a right-angle turn and cut across at about 85 degrees latitude. This means that we should, at some point on our southward course, cross the tracks. If they are still there then they might provide an excellent guide to locate our cache on the way back — giving us another navigational marker in case the

GPSs were really bonkers.

So, with the promise of reaching the milestone of halfway, and of having lighter sleds, our spirits rise in proportion to the size of the cliffs floating up from the snow.

Which is just as well as the breaks offer little comfort. The miserable amounts that are allowed for our ration quickly turn expectation into dismay into impatience; there's no point sitting around staring at a near-empty bag. At least the lack of choice saves time.

HPG starts her new job at the hospital in Whangarei in a couple of days, and I thought it would be nice if I could organise sending her some flowers and perhaps even a little poem to try to reconnect and show that I'm thinking of her.

This is proving very difficult. I'm not a natural poet and there is only a short window after each break before my brain turns to sludge. After that, I can't think of rhymes any more, and in any case all my rhymes have a similar theme. I mean, what goes with 'snow'? Chocolate? No. Cake? No. Biscuits? No. Cow? Maybe! Let's try.

> *I wandered lonely as a flake of snow*
> *That floats on high o'er vales and fields*
> *When all at once I saw a cow.*
> *That I could eat in a single meal.*

It's not quite right. Hmmm. You know my problem? This isn't a love poem — it's a poem about a cow. Let me try again.

> *Shall I compare thee to a hamburger?*
> *Your buns are more pert and symmetrical.*

That's as far as I get before I run out of brain juice and my attention drifts away to my current favourite fantasy: having a picnic with HPG.

There is a little pathway at the northern end of Waihi Beach on the Coromandel Peninsula, which winds in and out of the bush and around the cliff tops. HPG and I walk side by side, led by fantails flitting in the sun and the shady gullies, the noise of the surf vanishes and we stop to hear the liquid warbles of tui. After a few minutes the path curves around a headland and we look down onto a perfect white crescent of sand lapped by ultraviolet water, and backed by bush leading up into the hills. Feeling like Captain (and Mrs) Cook we descend down the hill to Orokawa Bay.

And there, under the branch of a shady pohutukawa tree, I lay out a blanket. HPG flings herself down and lies there, eyes closed, wearing her white strapless cotton dress. I reach out and gently grab . . . the picnic hamper.

Inside, the plump ripe tomatoes are jostling in their container. The eggs are melting through the greaseproof paper. Oh look, the balsamic vinegar bottle has leaked! I have to lick the black sweetness off my fingers. I take everything out of the hamper, spread it out on the blanket and try each of the delicacies one by one. I unpeel one of the boiled eggs; it's slippery in my hand and I break it open to reveal the golden yolk. I lick the damp ham and bring it to my nose before nibbling a small piece and letting it melt in my mouth. I cut a tomato, salt it and bite into its firm yet compliant skin. But after my feast something is missing. I can't put my finger on it.

In the tent at night, after the satisfaction of dinner has evaporated, my thoughts again turn to food.

'Jamie, I need something for the picnic in Waihi.'

'What have you got so far?'

'Nothing special really: a little freshly baked ciabatta, ham on the bone, smoked salmon, tomatoes, kalamata olives, boiled free-range eggs, Picual olive oil, home-made lemonade. Maybe a rosé and a sav. Grapes. Butter. Pâté. Gherkins. A little salad, feta, onions, rocket, balsamic . . .'

Jamie nods as each item is mentioned, then as I come to the end he nods quickly, 'And . . . !'

'Um, salt and pepper?'

'What? No chutney? No relish? Mustard? Where's the cheese board?'

'Oh, of course! Thanks.'

'No problem.'

A few minutes later, Jamie wrinkles his nose.

'Do you smell roast beef?'

'I wish.'

'No, really.'

I sniff. He's right. I sniff around. Normally (and thankfully) very little cuts through our frozen olfactory sensors. But there is a smell of meat from somewhere. Hang on, it's from me. It's coming from my leg. It's from the bandages on the top of my leg.

'That's gross.'

How hungry are you when your own wounds start to smell delicious?

DAY 29. HALFWAY

BEFORE LEAVING THE TENT I make a quick note in my journal.

```
I called Dr John this morning about my cold injury.
He was quite distressed by it and said I must at
all costs avoid re-chilling it. He said that he
wished he could send me a photo of what happens
if they get repeatedly cold. So I've started
wearing my fleecy pants under my long johns.
```

At the end of the second shift, I pull out the GPS.

'Hey! We're over halfway!'

'Quarter way,' corrects Jamie.

He's right; all we need to do is all that again and again and again.

By the afternoon sessions there isn't enough glucose to sustain my daydreams. My conscious thoughts fade away and my brain becomes a vacuum that must be filled. It needs something to amuse and distract it, anything. Then my sledge runners give a long howl as I painfully haul the sled over a ridge of firm ice. It sounds uncannily like Paul McCartney when he gets loose in the long fade-out of 'Hey Jude':

Nah nah nah, na na na naaah (WAAAAAA AAAAAAAAAA!)

For the next hour or so, my now cheerful subconscious sings me this chorus about twenty or thirty . . . thousand times.

With miraculous timing, right at the end of the sixth shift we come to faint but unmistakeable corrugations, directly across our path, heading straight for Thiels. We spend half an hour building a cache, and doing radio interviews with back home. Now we know we can find the stash again. Dodgy GPSs or not.

What with making the cache, splitting up another four-day bag, sipping on vodka-flavoured milk and feasting on a banquet that includes a precious sachet of Hannah's pork crackling and the vanilla creaminess of some sort of sweet stuff from a white packet, we don't get to bed until 8pm.

Oh well, tomorrow we will have full stomachs and lighter sleds and more snacks, and, best of all, because we finished the day at 85° 9.8' we might get another Degree Day in just four days' time.

When Scott was passing eighty-five degrees, he was nearing the top of the Beardmore Glacier and about to swap the dangers of crevasses for the thin air and brutal cold of the Antarctic Plateau. Of the twelve men that made the climb, only eight were needed for the next stage. It was time to choose the first team of four who would go back. Cherry-Garrard describes how he was told the news.

> *Scott came up to me, and said that he was afraid he had rather a blow for me. Of course I knew what he was going to say, but could hardly grasp that I was going back, tomorrow night . . .*

I said I hoped I had not disappointed him, and he caught hold
of me and said 'No no no,' so if that is the case all is well. Wilson
told me it was a toss up whether Oates or I should go on.

But first there was one more big day of man-hauling to get out of them.

DAY 30. THE BIG DAY

ANOTHER BREEZY AND FREEZING pack-up, but the cold is soon
forgotten with the excitement of hitching up to the new lean sleds,
which lasts until I take a few steps. It feels almost the same. Damn.
Soon I'm leading through a washing machine of sastrugi and it's hard
to get into a rhythm, and what pace I do have is very much the speed
of previous days.

At the end of the first shift the results are disappointing.

'Only 2.0. I think we've trained our legs to go slow,' I suggest lamely.

Jamie raises an eyebrow, and starts eating chocolate, staring
straight out in front.

I spend the next hour and a half wishing I had kept my big fat
mouth shut and trying not to get dropped off the back of Jamie's
sled. When we finally reconvene at the next break we've done a new
record: 2.56 miles.

'Well, that should have blown the cobwebs out,' Jamie suggests
dryly.

And so I then had to go and pull out a 2.5 myself.

Scott was fairly wound up, and he went on and on. Every rise
topped seemed to fire him with a desire to top the next, and every
rise had another beyond and above it.

— Cherry-Garrard

Later in the day the plain begins to pitch upwards, but still we keep up our manic pace. It's my turn with Jamie's iPod, which has somehow stayed alive. I'm listening to the Ten Tenors wailing. Going up some of the tougher slopes I become the eleventh.

The last twenty minutes of the day is dragging. I try a new idea. There are only twenty days left (with any luck) so I imagine that each minute is one of the last remaining days of the trip and play the shifts at high speed in my head. Here we are at Christmas Day, now Boxing Day. By the time we've come to a likely-looking campsite, and the dying strains of 'Nessun Dorma' swell and fade, I've reached the Pole.

We have done our biggest day yet, 15.3 miles in six standard shifts, and beaten our previous record by a solid geographic mile. This has been a good day to do a big day, just after halfway when the weight of the trip is heaviest. If today was a taste of things to come, then we're in good shape.

I pause as usual before getting into the tent to look out at the now impressively large snow-webbed cliffs of the Thiels, leaping out of the ice and into the low clouds. It's a real pinch-myself-I'm-in-Antarctica moment.

After Kev said that we had trained our legs to
go slow I pulled out the three biggest shifts
of the campaign. Great for morale, but not so
good for legs. Hammies were starting to hurt
by the end of the day and very sore now.

After accompanying the others for one last day, it was time for the first party to return to Cape Evans. Scott wrote a note for them to take back.

We are struggling, on considering all things, against odds. The weather is a constant anxiety, otherwise arrangements are working exactly as planned. So here we are practically on the summit and up to date in the provision line. We ought to get through.

Over the last few days we had at last been doing enough distance to stop the Average from increasing. If we can keep up 14 miles a day, then we can get to the Pole on time. If you're prepared to say that we aren't going to have a blizzard day then we could even claim to be up to date on the Schedule. We can finally breathe through both nostrils. It's not over until the fat lady counts our unhatched glittering chickens, but it is starting to look like we ought to get through.

15. PLATEAUED

All we have done is to show the immensity of this vast plain. The
scene about is the same as we have seen for many a day, and
shall see for many a day to come — a scene so wildly and awfully
desolate that it cannot fail to impress one with gloomy thoughts.
— Scott on the Antarctic Plateau

YOU'VE PROBABLY ALWAYS SUSPECTED that you haven't been
told the truth about the interior of Antarctica. After all, why is every
image of Antarctica you can think of — slabs of ice calving off the
Barrier face, marching penguins, flopping seals, bobbing orcas —
taken from around the *coast*. Why are you never shown what it's like
in the middle? What are they hiding?

I'm afraid that I'm not authorised to disclose that. However, what
I can now reveal for the first time is that every expedition heading into
the interior gets met by a black helicopter and after a brief exchange,
the grateful and relieved trekkers are taken to McMurdo Base and
then onto an enormous hangar at Area 51, Nevada. Each day they
spend a few minutes in the large dome-shaped studio that mocks

up Antarctica to allow them to shoot a little video and file in their reports to the world. The rest of the time is spent playing foosball and hanging out in the Apollo 11 model next door.

Except for us. Somehow for us, the protocols have changed. They seem to have got us into the hangar without letting us know. I have only figured out what's going on because being in a movie studio is the only way to explain why it seems like we are always skiing in a slight saucer, why the horizon always looks three hundred metres away, why the weather is so extraordinarily fickle as if levers are being thrown by a bored, and slightly sadistic, teenaged technician. It can be fine one minu . . . no, wait, it's cloudy. The temperature fluctuates by 20 degrees and the wind switches on and off. And why the hill that we parked our tent on has disappeared by the morning.

Another week of heaving and crashing has seen us through the eighty-fifth degree and almost out the other side of the eighty-sixth degree.

Often it occurs to me that this is not terrain that lends itself to carefree kiting, rather a landscape that is good for smashing legs and bashing brains out. And if that happens, it looks too rough for Stefan to do anything other than wave his sympathies from the window of the plane.

At least the weather had been mostly good; only one day in the last week had been spent wrestling with the ninjas in the whiteout room, and the rest had been more or less windless.

We had mostly kept up our 14 miles — sometimes a little more, sometimes a little less. But it wasn't getting easier; if anything it was getting harder. I'm setting the alarm earlier and earlier (Jamie doesn't need to know) to try to get out of the tent before 5am. The seventh shift is now nearly always compulsory.

This is strange because the sleds must be getting lighter. We've dropped off about 15 kilograms each at the caches. We eat more than a kilo each day, plus burn a few hundred grams of fuel. Thirty-six days into the trip the sleds have *got* to weigh significantly less. Somehow they don't feel as if they do.

The GPS provides the answer. The reason it's getting harder is because we're climbing. Not every shift, but in fits and starts; we're leaving the icing sugar and making our way up egg-white crust to get to the top of the Big Pavlova.

We are now some 2000 metres high and starting to feel the subtle effects of the altitude. There is a certain breathlessness, a dizziness and light-headedness when I bend down to undo my bindings. There's always a bladder-bursting need to pee at the end of each shift as our kidneys suck out water from our blood to try to concentrate the red blood cells. The hot chocolate feels a little cooler as the boiling temperature reduces.

> *Thin air, low pressure and oxygen deficiency reach a point, at about ten thousand feet, above which even well-fed, fit humans will be affected by altitude 'sickness'. It is best not to exert yourself but, if you must, you find every movement is an effort.*
>
> — Wilson

It's only going to get worse. The South Pole is at a physical altitude of some 2800 metres. But as usual, Antarctica has an extra little kicker — the intense cold reduces the air pressure still further, creating an altitude (at least as far as your heart and lungs are concerned) of between 3500 and 3600 metres at the Pole and up to 5000 metres elsewhere on the plateau.

The same lack of oxygen that makes our stove difficult to start and yellows its flame means that we're metabolising our food less efficiently. So the knife of hunger wedged in our guts just got another tweak.

DAY 37. REACHING 87 DEGREES SOUTH

BREAKFAST TIME IS QUIET as we consider our position. Thirteen miles away lies a new degree and another cup of feijoa-vodka-flavoured milk.

Jamie puts his muesli bowl on top of the kitchen box while he pulls on a boot. His elbow knocks the bowl and I watch in horrified slow motion as a big dollop of hot, precious muesli lurches, like bulging oil in a lava lamp, out of the side of the bowl and splats on the tent floor.

Jamie's face falls. Then he's in a blur of action, spooning up the puddle, and when that doesn't get all of it he drops down and starts licking the rest off the nylon. Then his head stops moving.

'Ay!'

'What?'

'My dungs tuck!'

'What's that? Your tongue's stuck to the floor?'

'Arrrh!'

'OK, OK. Stay there. I'll get the knife!'

Jamie sits back upright, smiling. 'Just kidding, it's pretty cold though.'

Tonight Shackleton upset the hoosh pot. There was an awful moment when we thought some of it was going to run away on to the snow; luckily it all remained on our waterproof floorcloth, and by the time we had done scraping I do not think that any was wasted.

— Scott

A family of fat snow goblins are hitching a ride on the sleds on the first shift. There's a Carnivale load of hip jerking just to get a few centimetres out of the sled at a time. It's as if we are back in the first week.

Last night it snowed, and the ground is coated with several centimetres of fluff, which Scott would call 'woolly'. Jamie is having a very difficult time breaking trail. His hamstrings seem to be slowing him up. But that can't explain all the problems; we must be going uphill again as well.

By the break we've only made 1.7 miles. As a consolation prize, the GPS says that we have climbed 60 metres — a twenty-storey building.

We try swapping the lead sled to see if it makes it easier. Maybe a bit, but not enough. This day definitely won't be over in six shifts. That's a pity. There is a kind of symmetry about six shifts. Seven makes for a long afternoon.

Time to bury myself in a daydream. The smorgasbord picnic at Orokawa Bay has become too complicated — there is now so much food in the picnic hamper that I'm doing as much work pushing the wheelbarrow around the cliff path as I'm doing pulling the sledge. So I begin another, more simple, daydream.

I'm at my grandma's bach at Waihi Beach. I shut the door so as not to wake HPG sleeping inside. The sun has just risen and the sky is filled with a soft golden light. I breathe a deep silky lungful of cool, freshly ionised salt air.

The pavement is comfortably solid and predictable, slapping beneath my bare feet as I walk (relaxed and upright!) down to the shops. Soon I'm coming back, carrying a loaf of white bread, still warm, in a brown paper bag, trying not to grab pieces of its warm, yeasty softness. I walk up the drive to the house, careful to put my feet on the big round stones. In the kitchen, I put the kettle on, while I get out the breadboard. I cut a slab off the loaf, resisting the temptation to cut it too thick or it won't fit in the toaster. The soft bread squishes and the cut piece comes out uneven. I hate it when that happens. I cut another piece too fat and it won't fit in the toaster.

Finally two pieces are in the toaster and while it's browning, I rinse the tea kettle and put in the leaves and smell the tangy, slightly salty aroma. While it's drawing, I carefully take out a piece of toast and press a slab of golden yellow butter across its surface, which quickly disappears into the pores of the toast. Now the honey — should it be creamed or manuka or the runny kind? I think creamed. I look in the fridge; there isn't any. I'll have to go back down to the shops. Anyway, I'll have the tea before I go. I turn the pot three times, and now I'm pouring it into a mug. Hang on, did I turn the pot clockwise or anti-clockwise? It has to be anti-clockwise. How do I unwind the tea? This isn't working out. No problem, I'll just start again. I shut the door behind me and step out into the dawn. The sun has just risen. I inhale the cool, tingling air . . .

The effort to take a step cuts through my eighteenth piece of toast. Just when I feel like I can't take any more, we crest the hill. For the first time in days here is somewhere a plane could land. In fact you could land a jumbo jet here. It's even quite warm. Flat and warm — this is strangely generous of Antarctica. Then the clouds mass and pounce and we are left crawling through an oppressive featureless gloom. That's more like it.

Jamie apparently hasn't noticed and bolts off like he has radar. I'm working hard just to keep up. Stuffed full with toast and honey, I struggle hard to get a new daydream going — the best I can come up with is buying and riding an electric bicycle, which doesn't really work for me. So at the next break I ask Jamie what he was thinking about.

'What have you got?'

'I'm planning my stag do.'

'Great idea. Mind if I use that one?'

'Be my guest.'

After my turn in the lead, trying to push the pace, I'm wild-eyed and raving and eat large chunks of my snack bag, including a very precious sachet of Hannah's pork crackling. It doesn't help. I'm shuffling like a geriatric. There aren't enough calories to stop my brain from floating away. I'm starting to get spacey. Outer spacey. My pole swivelling in the snow groans and growls, making sounds *exactly* like Chewbacca from Star Wars. Suddenly I am escaping from the Death Star, Obi-Wan urges me to go on, while he holds off a black-robed, black-helmeted, raspy-breathing character. My subconscious is sending me a message via a mental videogram.

VADER: I've been waiting for you, Obi-Wan. We meet again, at last.

Why this scene? There's no Chewbacca in this scene.

VADER: The circle is complete. When I left you, I was but the learner; now I am the master.
OBI-WAN: Only a master of evil, Darth.
VADER: Your powers are weak, old man.

Oh ha ha, very good.

Your powers are weak, old man.

Yes, I've got that. Message received.

Your powers are weak, old man.

OK. That's enough. Over and out.

Your powers are weak, old man.

Bugger. OK. This calls for the big guns. I'm in Disneyland. I go to the Small World ride. I get into the little cart and as I go around I hear, 'It's a . . .'

Six shifts, then one final shift, then just another half hour, then twenty minutes to finish, then one final ten minutes to bring it home. Then another. Twelve hours on the trail and we've finally made it. Bagging another milestone makes everything worthwhile.

Soon I'm in the tent happily trying to make head or tails of a sweet colourless powder that glows red like a traffic light when water is added. For a special treat, we turn on a second stove and bring them both into the sleeping area, and for a few minutes completely drive the cold out.

A whole new degree. Every degree has its own character. I wonder what this one has in store. Unfortunately nothing good by the sounds of it. There are strange text messages from the other teams complaining of monster overhead sastrugi and steep climbs further south. I wonder what they're talking about.

If we can keep up 13.7 miles a day, then we can get to the Pole on time, in thirteen days.

Scott was also confident as he passed into 87 degrees south. It was time to prune the party down to the three others who would accompany him on the Pole attempt. Instead he chose four.

First choice was Wilson, his good friend, artist, doctor and veteran of the *Discovery* Expedition. Then Bowers, who seemed immune to cold and injury. As Scott put it, he possessed 'untiring energy and the astonishing physique which enables him to continue to work under conditions which are absolutely paralysing to others. Never was such a sturdy, active, undefeatable little man.'

Taff Evans was by far the largest and strongest man (although not necessarily the brightest). He had won Scott's admiration when they had first sledged together across the Plateau during the *Discovery* Expedition. This had included on one occasion dangling down a crevasse with him. Scott described him as 'a man of Herculean strength, very long in the arm and with splendidly developed muscles. He had been a gymnastics instructor in the Navy, and had always been an easy winner in all our sports which involved tests of strength.'

Finally there was the grumpy Lawrence 'Titus' Oates, the cavalry officer, who had become much better company now the horses, which had been his responsibility, had all been shot.

The next day, the B team — Lieutenant Teddy Evans and seamen Lashly and Crean — walked beside the polar party for an hour making sure that everything was OK. Then it was time for a hasty goodbye in the intense cold. Lashly describes their poignant parting on the desolate plain.

*There was no more need for us to go on farther; so we stopped
and did all the talking we could in a short time . . . so the time
came for the last handshake and goodbye. I think we all felt it
very much. They then wished us a speedy return and safe, and
then they moved off. We gave them three cheers, and watched
them for a while until we began to feel cold. Then we turned and
started for home. We soon lost sight of each other.*

They had no reason to linger in the cold, nor was there any need for
sentimentality. Scott was only 150 miles from the Pole and everything
was going according to plan. Scott wrote a note to go back with the
group.

*A last note from a hopeful position. I think it's going to be all
right. We have a fine party going forward and arrangements are
all going well.*

Their bodies were found ten months later.

Scott may not have made such a hopeful assessment if he had known
about the injuries the team members were hiding from him: a nasty
cut on Evans' hand and Oates' frost-damaged toes — the start of a
frostbite that was to fatally delay the rest of the party.

So with three degrees to go, it's time for a health check. I start
by taking off my boot and socks. All of my toenails are black — not
from frostbite, just from stubbing them inside the boots. (If only I
had made that clearer in the blog, then I would have avoided an
awkward conversation with an alarmed HPG!) It is entirely cosmetic.
They only look a little gothic against my white feet when I change
my socks.

My fingers, on the other hand, are slowly worsening. The tips look healthy and pink enough at the ends, and if squeezed, refill with blood, but are quite wooden almost up to the first knuckle. When taking socks from the drying rack I have to place them against my cheek to detect if they are wet or dry as my fingers can no longer tell.

I take a photo of my face and examine it on the screen. It certainly isn't puffy any more — instead my hairy cheeks hang puckered under my cheekbones. The hard red lumps where the goggles press against my skin remain, but at least the skin hasn't broken down. However, the tip of my nose crumples alarmingly when pressed.

As for the rash on my leg, I had put a bandage on it for protection, but now, as I check on it, I find my thermals are sticking to the wound. It is an exquisitely delicate operation pulling the wool away millimetre by millimetre to reveal what's going on.

The bandage is bulging and fluid is leaking out of it. Around it, the skin has further melted away as if the plaster has aggravated it. I see now that using a waterproof plaster was a very bad idea.

I wince as I slowly, slowly pull off the plaster. I would pull it off quickly but I'm worried about taking a chunk of skin with it.

'Now that is gross,' says Jamie wrinkling his nose.

By the time I've replaced the dressing with a more absorbent and breathable one, I'm feeling cold and shivery as if I have a fever. I get inside my sleeping bag and hold a hot Nalgene bottle until I stop trembling.

Jamie's fingertips are badly split, and he has to reapply superglue frequently. Also split is his right boot. At the widest point the leather has given way and his socked foot is protected only by the thin insulation of the external overboot. Yet his skin seems not to be worse for wear.

But none of these compare in seriousness to Jamie's hamstrings. He has been stretching every night and often during breaks, but the inflammation is worsening and his stride during the day gets increasingly hobbled. Today's efforts haven't helped, and he winces as he tries to stretch it out.

'I think I might have to call Dr John tomorrow, eh.'

Our ailments seem complementary; between the two of us you could almost put a single decent sledger together.

DAY 38. THE VALLEY OF EVIL SASTRUGI

AFTER THE MORNING SCHED, Jamie talks to Dr John. They have a short conversation, then he pushes the 'off' button and starts unscrewing the antennae and packing up the phone.

'How did it go?' I ask.

'He said if nothing else was working I should rest.'

'What? More than ten minutes every hour and a half?'

'Apparently.'

The fourth shift has just started when Jamie stops at the top of a little rise and signals to me to join him. I pull up alongside.

'Holy moley.'

We are standing at a line of ditches or storm drains that are angling across our path. Normally, the sastrugi go more or less in the right direction, or with a slight angle, so that you can at a pinch follow the grain until it mellows enough for you to break free and resume going directly south. There is no chance here — the terrain has been raked at right angles to our route with the devil's plough. We'll just have to wriggle and weave and crash our way through.

Jamie leads off, but he isn't moving with his usual efficiency. There are plenty of stoppages and although he doesn't say it, it's clear his hamstrings are troubling him. As always, with slow progress the tension starts to increase. At this rate we're not going to make 14 miles today. Not even in twelve hours. What should we do?

So how bad would it be to not get 14? Here's the thing. We *have* to get to the Pole by the end of day 50. Once there, we will have only ten days' worth of food to get back to the cache at 85 degrees. If anything, it is going to be harder than we had thought, judging by the roughness of the sastrugi. We are going to need all of those ten days, not nine days, not eight days. Ten days.

If we can't get 14 today, can we make it up tomorrow? So far, for the whole trip, we *have* bet more on going further tomorrow. Somehow we've always managed it. A month ago achieving 11 miles was an extraordinary feat. Then before we got used to doing that we started doing 12s. Now inconceivable 14s have become the norm. Maybe in a week, when our sleds are even lighter, we might be pulling out 15s and 16s. But I don't think so.

The thing is that we have achieved our greater distances not by walking faster but by walking for more hours each day — and you can only play that game for so long. There is a point where you can't cook your food, melt all the water you need, do repairs and all the other obligatory work and still get enough sleep to sustain the effort. The last few days we have been hauling for eleven to twelve hours, going to sleep at 8pm and getting up just after 2.30am to be on the road by 5am. We're waking up wrecked and our performance is suffering. We simply can't do with much less sleep. If there is any way out of this it's by going faster. I'm going to tell Jamie at the break. No, I'm not going to tell Jamie. We're both feeling beaten up. I'm just going to go faster.

So at the end of the fourth shift I get out the GPS.

'1.5,' I say. Addition and division say the rest. We've done only 7.3 miles so far. Only three shifts left and we have to get 2.2 in all of them.

'You know what,' says Jamie. 'I'm not going to get stressed by it. What happens happens.'

I'm taken aback. 'I was just thinking exactly the opposite. We've got to make 14 today or we're stuffed.'

Jamie doesn't say anything as we hitch back up.

I remove my Gore-Tex jacket and lead off. There's a ridge to the south that I suspect marks the end of the sastrugi, so I bolt for it, putting the hammer down and barging through like Jamie had done yesterday. I have to move fast; I'm freezing without my jacket on.

Half an hour later, the view from the ridge reveals only another heavily furrowed field with yet another ridge on the other side.

Perhaps it will be better when we get there.

No, it isn't. Nor from the next ridge, nor the one after that, nor after that. I lurch and haul over the rutted ground trying to stay viable. My arms never warm up and I'm tired — but I end up pulling out a 2.3.

Jamie's quiet during the break, which means he's pissed off with something. But when he leads, the pace mostly keeps up although the conditions worsen. We finish the day at 13.2. I'm very proud. I had stopped the rot and turned it round.

Later, inside the tent, very little is said.

Eventually Jamie offers, 'I think your attitude was negative.' Then he closes up.

Diary entries are much longer tonight as we scribble angrily at each other, trading dark glances over our notebooks.

```
Tough day with going uphill and
against the grain of the sastrugi, not
nice. Slow progress. After a few shifts
Kevin and I aired different views on
our progress and this left me with a
bad mood for the rest of the day.
```

```
              My negative attitude? I don't see what
           Jamie is complaining about. Often it's him
              who salvages the situation! But I don't
              think it's me he's pissed off with. His
              hamstrings are giving him a lot of pain,
           they seem to be getting worse and worse and
           he hates not being the one to set the pace.
```

16. THE BEGINNING OF THE END

DAY 41. COLD, FUNNY LEGS AND KITING

JAMIE EXPLODES BACK INTO the tent from his morning poo, looking horrified. I zip up the fly behind him.

'Cold, eh?'

'Mate, it froze before it hit the ground!'

Forget what you think about temperature; here is how it feels in Antarctica. If it's sunny and there's no wind then the temperature doesn't really matter because you can feel warm. If it's windy, though, then:

-10° Celsius and above = 'I'm surprised how warm I am given how cold it is.'

-20° Celsius to -10° Celsius = 'It's cold but if I keep moving I can stay warm.'

-20° Celsius to -30° Celsius = 'This is very cold, if I stop I'll freeze.'

Below -30° Celsius = 'Do I really want to be doing this?'

Today as I flash by the sled I see the thermometer has defaulted to

-34° Celsius again. I'm scared. Any part of me gets cold in weather like this and it will stay cold. If I don't pay constant attention I could easily get an injury — particularly my hands. I still haven't found the glove combination that reliably keeps my hands warm throughout the day without a huge amount of conscious effort.

As we pack up I have a fiddly problem with the straps on a sled that can only be fixed by taking off my gloves. Instead I ask Jamie if he would mind doing it. I feel a crock, but his hands don't seem to feel the cold so much, at least that's what I tell myself.

Normally it is necessary to have a zip or two open somewhere on your jacket to let the heat out; not today. Today every chink is blocked up against the drilling wind. Heads are buried in the backs of hoods, which are pulled tight to reduce the world to a furry tunnel. The ski-pole handles, now wrapped with foam as fat as Coke cans, still seem to be sucking heat out of my hands.

The conditions are marginal — if it gets any colder then perhaps we should just walk in our down and have no breaks. Our pace is noticeably slower today but for once I'm not obsessing about progress, I'm more concerned about not getting frostbitten, and mentally scanning all parts of my body to make sure that they are still sending in reports.

Shortly into the second shift, Jamie is down to a slow shuffle. I would tell him to go faster except I'm having trouble keeping up. My quads scarcely fire. Once again I'm having to lift my hips to swing my legs. I'm walking like the Tin Man before a service.

There are times, say at the end of a long running race, when you could go faster if you were sufficiently motivated — like if you found you were being chased by a lion. Then there are times like this when you are completely disconnected from the Hinged Ambulatory Extensions below your waist. If chased by that lion now, I could only turn and make a wobbly last stand.

At the second break I ask, 'How are your legs feeling?'

'Stuffed. Yours?'

'Same.'

This is strange. We've suffered from heavy legs before but not so early in the day. Could it be lack of food? But we've just had breakfast (well, four hours ago). Maybe it's the altitude?

The wind is picking up, but it's not from dead ahead. Exactly where, it's hard to tell with the hoods up, but it appears to be *nearly* on the shoulder, or maybe coming in from two o'clock.

At the next break Jamie says, 'What about trying the kites?'

'I really don't know.'

If they don't work, we waste a lot of time and we will get very cold. And the wind isn't quite far enough around for us to be able to head to the Pole, and maybe not quite strong enough. On the other hand, the sastrugi around here *are* lower than usual . . .

'Come on. Let's just try it.'

'OK, you go first.'

So I help Jamie set up a 5-metre kite and put on the kite boots. A half hour later, the kite leaps into the air and yanks him one way then the other as he tries to stay upright. The sled refuses to budge. It's not clear why it's not working — not enough wind? Thick snow? Our still too heavy sleds?

By the time we're packed up again I'm freezing and we've lost a whole precious hour from our day. Bugger. If it had worked, we could have been gliding along, catching up with the Schedule, instead we're worse off. As we march, I explain all my problems to my slowly sawing skis.

Stop! I slowly look up. I'm teetering on the edge of an enormous bluff. In front of us, the ground drops away with the gradient of a steep sand dune for several hundred feet down to a vast plain. Jaw-droppingly, uncomfortably vast. It's African Rift Valley in its immensity. It's like the scene from *The Lion King* where Mufasa gives Simba the 'All this will be yours' speech. There are no animals singing the chorus but the grey shadows of the clouds file in lines like elephants in a row.

Jamie comes up alongside.

'Wow,' he says.

This is where I would have my glass dome. To be able to sit here and enjoy the view from a sofa with cookies and hot chocolate. We must be able to see all the way to 88 degrees, and it looks so flat!

The drop is not so steep that we can't ski down nearly directly with our sleds, and for a few blissful minutes we are actually going downhill with our sleds weightless behind us. We can even tow side by side.

'So this is what an 80-kilo sled feels like!' says Jamie.

Soon after we get to the bottom, sastrugi start to sprout out of the snow, turning into enormous, tortured, jumbled, sinewy swirls.

For one whole shift I'm heading for a formation that starts out looking about the size and shape of a soccer ball. As I get closer it gets bigger and larger until it's about 3 metres high, whereupon it morphs into the prow of a boat. Then for the next shift we weave towards a perfect camembert, the size of a band rotunda, complete with a wedge missing.

Then it's as if we are ants walking through the licks and piping of some crazy baroque wedding cake. We are at one stage spiralling down the side of a sastrugi as if on a frozen water slide. At other times we are trudging through fields of giant meringues. What is this?

We slog up to a crest of a hill to see a huge field as rough as if it had just snowed on top of a junkyard, with another ridge at the end. I tell myself that from the ridge we will see views of smooth plains. It's a slim hope but it gives something to cling to. We put our heads down and pull for half an hour to the ridge and look out. No, it's just another rough snow field with a taunting ridgeline at the end, offering a glimpse of hope . . . until we get there. Then again. Then again. It starts to get personal. When I come up another ridge to view yet another field of saw-toothed sastrugi, I sob. I feel broken. It's just too big. I feel like a TV dinner — cooked, frozen, thawed, digested, discarded.

By the time we find a spot flat enough to put up the tent, we've been on the trail for eleven and a half hours and we have only made 12.3 miles. There's no talk of valiant last stands. There's nothing left. We didn't make 14 today. That leaves a stench. We failed. Oh sure, we're still alive and no frostbite, but that's not winning, that's a certificate for participation.

Just as I have done the last forty nights, I plug the solar panel into the battery box. Only this time there is a 'pop' and that distinctive electrical sizzle and a sharp smell of burning rubber. As grey smoke starts streaming out I yank the cable off, open the lid and pluck out all the wires I can until the noise stops. I undo the zip of the fly to let the smoke out.

'That didn't sound very good,' says Jamie.

I sigh and get out the screwdriver and start checking all the pieces and putting them back together. Somehow the little motorcycle battery has short-circuited; it's probably stuffed.

Yesterday Jamie asked me if tonight I wouldn't mind taking care of the last of the snow melting and hot-chocolate making. He has been saving the battery on the iPod all day so he can watch a bit of a movie. He wants to escape for an hour; I can't blame him.

After a few minutes I hear a loud sigh.

'What happened?'

'Ran out of juice.'

'Bum,' I say sympathetically.

'So what do you think is harder, rowing the Atlantic, or Antarctica?'

'Antartica. This time on the Atlantic we had finished and remember how much food we had?'

'We could live for a week on what we rinsed off the deck.'

'And it was warm.'

'Yeah, a bit too warm.'

'You know, being warm is uncomfortable, being cold hurts.'

'Yeah. This is harder by far.'

DAY 42. THE SMELTING FACTORY

JUST BEFORE I LEAVE the tent I review the little vox pop I had made. The video shows a haggard man, blowing out his cheeks and shaking his head in disbelief.

```
It's one of those mornings, it's about 4.30am.
It's minus 20 outside, it's blowing about
20 knots. It's a bit of a whiteout. It's
cold and miserable. We're at 87° 55'.
Getting out of the tent is hard work.
```

Two resolutions. If I ever get out of this mess:
1. I'm never going to complain about getting out of bed ever again.
2. I will hold HPG in my arms until the world ends.

As soon as we start pulling, the weather begins to deteriorate further. The rushing clouds start to expand and grow. But these aren't the mountains of fluffy white mashed potatoes like you might see in a Constable painting. These swirl and heave as they reach upwards to cloak the sun, and look brown and venomous, as if they are being pumped out from some Eastern-bloc, state-run, lignite-fuelled, heavy-metal smelting factory.

The sunlight popping briefly through gaps in the fast-moving clouds lights up the scene like a magnesium flash, revealing row after row of ghostly bone-white fish-hook-shaped sastrugi, silhouetted against the seething dark sky. It's like I imagine a diorama of the North Sea in winter, bleak and horrible.

As the wind picks up speed, the snow begins boiling around us. Jamie appears only periodically in the murk. What if I lose him? What is the plan? There is no plan. Hang on — I have the tent on my sled. He better have a plan. So we plough on into the gloom, through the dark curling drapes of blown snow. Eighty-seven degrees is very reluctant to let us go. I can't wait to see the back of this shitty degree.

At some point on the third shift we cross into 88 degrees. I don't know what I thought was going to happen. Each degree has its personality, so I was hoping that the sun would put its hat on, the sastrugi would iron themselves out and gumdrops would fall from the sky. Instead, nothing changes. Only that the sleds suddenly start overturning as we walk through the sastrugi as if we are upsetting jackin-the-boxes buried in the snow. I get a fright as I tumble down a small drop and roll upside down.

During the sixth shift I have nothing left in the tank. Once again I'm picking up my body and swinging my legs. My quads have all the tension of overcooked pasta. My left leg, the tendons damaged in an old motorcycle accident, is now doing a little semi-circle sideways flail on its own as it comes forward. I have the skiing gait of a poorly made Thunderbirds puppet. I have never felt such exhaustion. Not at least since yesterday.

We only make 12.3 miles. That's two days in a row we haven't made the Average. The situation has turned so quickly! A week ago we were pulling like bulls, doing 14s and 15s in normal time. Now we are right on the edge of not making it. How could things go wrong so fast? What's going wrong with our legs? For the last three days they've been particularly and mysteriously pathetic.

In the tent, I take off my long johns and see that my thermals underneath have lost their elasticity. I suppose that's not surprising after six weeks of continuous use.

Hang on, no. They haven't got baggy; my legs have shrunk. I pull down my thermals and see all of my legs for the first time in weeks. They look skinny. I put my knees together. I can see clear through my legs. I haven't been able to do that since I was ten. Where have my thigh muscles gone?

'Hey Jamie, take a look at your legs.'

Jamie quickly de-trousers and puts his thumb and forefingers like callipers around his legs, then looks up, eyes wide in wonder. We laugh, a little manically. No wonder I didn't have any strength in my legs — I've eaten them.

Jamie pulls up his shirt. His ribs are sticking out of his skin like bony judder bars. Every muscle of his stomach is clearly defined. He flexes his abs.

'How's that! Ripped, eh?!'

'Mate, I think I can see your liver.'

So this explains why our beds were feeling so much bonier, why

I was now having to wear two thermal tops all the time. I wonder why we haven't noticed this before. I suppose because we have been sponging ourselves with our shirts on. Because our hair and beards have been growing and we look like Grizzly Adams from the neck up, we have assumed that we have his robust heartiness. Now with shirts off we look like cotton buds. Or Wolverine on a vegan diet.

We've been slowly eating ourselves inside out. Not even slowly. I'm guessing we've lost 20 kilos each. That's half a kilo a day. Forget the South Beach Diet. Try the South Pole Diet. Jamie looks up from counting his ribs. 'What's going to happen if we keep losing weight like this?'

I suppose the law of subtraction will mean that we will eventually float away. We're not the first ones who've gone through this. What happened to Scott?

As Scott, Bowers, Wilson and Oates neared the Pole their hopes started to rise. Every day that they didn't see Norwegian tracks made it more likely that they were going to get to the Pole first. Then on 16 January, just 18 miles from the Pole, Bowers spied a speck on the horizon, which eventually became a black flag on an abandoned Norwegian sledge. Tracks continuing on in the direction of the Pole and the multitude of paw prints told the whole story.

> *The worst has happened, or nearly the worst . . . The*
> *Norwegians have forestalled us and are first at the Pole. It is*
> *a terrible disappointment, and I am very sorry for my loyal*
> *companions. Many thoughts come and much discussion have we*
> *had. To-morrow we must march on to the Pole and then hasten*
> *home with all the speed we can compass. All the day dreams*
> *must go; it will be a wearisome return.*

All had been for nothing — except if Amundsen and friends fell into a crevasse on their return. Unlikely, but you can always hope.

So after reaching the Pole the next day, they turned around and began the dash back over the Plateau to the top of Beardmore Glacier and down to the safety of the warmth and thicker air of the Barrier. At least now the wind was at their backs, they could use their tent floorcloth as a makeshift sail. For several days they 'fairly slithered along before a fresh breeze'.

Only a week from the Pole, Scott first noted, 'There is no doubt Evans is a good deal run down.' Then with bewildering speed Evans began to unravel. His nose became badly frostbitten and turned rotten. The cut on his hand became infected with pus and his fingernails started to fall out. Then he got a large blister on his foot.

They reached the top of the Beardmore Glacier, and began fumbling down through the maze of crevasses, desperately trying to stay out of the gaping voids and in touch with their trail of caches.

Each day Evans became more and more befuddled. On 16 February, Scott wrote, 'Evans has nearly broken down in brain we think. He is absolutely changed from his normal self reliant self.'

Oates was less sympathetic, angrily writing in his diary, 'He has lost his guts and behaves like an old woman or worse.'

The next day tensions were ramped up as they found themselves behind schedule, and so on short rations as they struggled towards the Lower Glacier Depot only a few miles away. They had to stop the sledge when one of Evans' ski shoes came off. Then it happened again and then again. Finally an exasperated Scott told him to unhitch, get his bindings right and catch up.

After the lunch break, Evans still hadn't caught up so they went back to look for him. Scott described the scene: 'He was on his knees with clothing disarranged, hands uncovered and frostbitten, and a wild look in his eyes. Asked what was the matter, he replied with a slow speech that he didn't know.'

Emaciated, frostbitten, hypothermic, Evans was pulled into the tent and put in a sleeping bag. Now what to do? Do they stay with him and starve? Or abandon him to certain death? Fortunately, as Scott put it, 'Providence mercifully removed him at this critical moment.' Two hours later they were back marching.

What was the cause of this sudden collapse? Cherry-Garrard lays the blame squarely on Evans' size.

> *He was the biggest, heaviest and most muscular man in the party. I do not believe that this is a life for such men, who are expected to pull their weight and to support and drive a larger machine than their companions, and at the same time to eat no extra food.*

By this time we're continuously on our diet of 4300 kilojoules, about the same as Scott's team. So what did the 'biggest, heaviest and most muscular man' of their party weigh? A dainty 80 kilograms. Scott himself only weighed close to 70 kilos. Compared with modern-day physiques, Scott's men were hobbits. Alternatively, back in 1912, Jamie and I would be circus exhibits as the two of us weighed as much as any three of them.

So how long did we have? From 11 December, when Scott and his team started man-hauling, until 17 February, the day Evans died, was 67 days. Adjust that for our difference in weight and, if we had been on his ration the whole time, Scott would be leaving us to adjust our bindings about now.

Of course we hadn't been on his ration the whole time. We knew we were going to be cutting it fine, but not *this* fine. Would it all come down to a couple of handfuls of chocolate?

On 1 March 1912, during a warm and sunny lunch break, Scott took a moment to assess their situation. He was cautiously optimistic. In the two weeks since Evans had died, they had been picking up their depots more or less on schedule. At each they had found food for five men — and they were four. They had also dug up pony meat, and so were having some of the best hooshes of the trip, noticeably improving their physical condition.

The increase of ration has had an enormously beneficial result.

— Scott

To get home required making on average a very modest 9 or 10 miles a day. Definitely achievable. After all, they had been making 15 miles a day in the anaemic air of the Plateau. It gets better. Scott had ordered the dog teams to come out at least as far as One Ton Depot to bolster the supplies there, and then 'come as far as you can', which meant that the dogs should have at least been to the depot at Mount Hooper. In fact, it was quite possible that they were waiting there now, ready to whisk them back to the coast.

They were tired, their clothes were threadbare; after all, they had been on the march for an astonishing 120 days, and man-hauling for the last 81. But on 1 March 1912 it looked like they would make it.

Just twenty-four hours later it definitely looked like they wouldn't. They had been hit by three blows in quick succession.

Overnight, it was as if the Antarctic winter had arrived. The fine, still weather vanished and the temperature plunged to ⁻40° Celsius. In the cold, the snow had turned into harsh sharp crystals grabbing and slowing their sled runners. The effort to move the sled increased enormously.

They had reached Middle Barrier Depot to find it strangely short of fuel. This meant pulling in damp and freezing clothes, eating lukewarm food, and constant thirst from a shortage of water. Worst of all, Oates now revealed that his feet were badly frostbitten.

Taken together they were, as Scott put it, 'in a very queer street'. They were grievously wounded, but not dead yet. They stubbornly set out for the Mount Hooper depot and on 9 March they finally saw the fifteen-foot-high cairn in the distance. There they would find ample food and fuel to warm feet and dry clothes, and possibly also the happy yelps of the dogs. With any luck they could be roasting marshmallows at Hut Point in ten days.

Then they arrived. They found only *just* their allocated food, and nowhere near their share of fuel. The dogs weren't there. The dogs hadn't been there. What had gone wrong?

With little choice, they began trudging grimly towards One Ton Depot. Could they make it? There was food and *just* enough fuel if they got there quickly. *Let's go!*

Three of them could walk well enough, but not Oates. Oates was slowing them down in the morning as he took hours to ease his boots over his grotesquely swollen and frostbitten feet. Oates was slowing them down during the day as he hobbled alongside the sled. Oates with his useless frostbitten hands who could no longer help in setting up camp.

Scott showed enormous sympathy towards him. 'He is wonderfully plucky,' he wrote. 'He does his utmost and suffers much.' This was very generous; in their extreme circumstances, Scott would have been well within his rights to gently nudge his plucking arse into a crevasse.

As much as Scott admired Oates, he was also practical. On 11 March he ordered Wilson to open the medical case and give each man his share of the opium inside. Thirty tablets each. Now each could do as his conscience dictated.

Still Oates persisted, suffering horrible agonies as he dragged his frostbitten feet. Finally, on 16 March, Oates had had enough. Scott described his last minutes.

He did not — would not — give up hope to the very end. He was a brave soul. This was the end. He slept through the night

248

. . . hoping not to wake; but he woke in the morning . . . It was blowing a blizzard. He said, 'I am just going outside and may be some time.' He went out into the blizzard and we have not seen him since.

He wasn't planning to go far, he left his boots behind. It was his thirty-second birthday.

We aren't dead yet. Tomorrow is Day 43. Counting Day 50, we have eight full days to get the 113 miles to the Pole. We need to make 14.13 miles each day. So we decide that tomorrow we will only do six shifts, but we have to get 2.35 each shift, and we don't stop until we do. Hopefully this will be psychologically easier than having a very long end of day, and the sapping feeling of finding out you are behind schedule.

This really is our last chance; if this doesn't work then it will be time to dispense the opium tablets.

17. LIVE DONKEYS

DAY 43. CHRISTMAS EVE

THE SUN SHINING THROUGH a thin mist is creating a kind of white disc, like a compass rose. There are large bright spots at each of the cardinal points, so where the ring touches the horizon it's as if another sun is about to rise. The effect is uncannily like a giant eye. Under its unblinking stare we are trudging through soft snow and an endless succession of ridge-topped judder bars.

At the end of the first shift we don't unhook; I just wait, breathing hard, leaning on the poles, while Jamie gets out the GPS.

'How did we go?'

'Not even close, we're going to have to give it another thirty minutes.'

I'll go back to singing Christmas carols to myself then. The 4/4 beat makes them great songs for marching, and my subconscious comedian is loving the fresh material.

Dashing through the snow, on a one-horse open sleigh,
Dashing through the snow.
Dashing

Dashing [repeat]

I like 88 degrees. Compared to the hostility and turmoil of 87 degrees, it feels gentle and benign and the sastrugi are small. Today I'm only focusing on the positive. We can only do what we can. There's only so fast our legs can go. I'm just happy to be making any forward motion at all. There are only so many hours that we can walk and after all it's Christmas tomorrow.

> *Our sledge weight was reduced almost to a minimum and we*
> *ourselves were inured to hard marching if ever three persons*
> *were, yet by our utmost exertion we could barely exceed a pace*
> *of a mile an hour.*
>
> — Scott on the Plateau

At the end of the day I've finished setting up the camp and I'm about to come in to the tent when Jamie calls out through the nylon. 'Do you mind hanging on? I just need to do some stretches.'

'Sure.'

It's a good night to get a photo of the tent, so I start walking away from camp. Without skis, the snow is surprisingly deep, each step punches through the crust up to my ankle.

After a minute or two I look over my shoulder; already the tent looks so small, a few more steps and it would be lost over the horizon. I'm feeling a little unnerved being so tenuously connected to it. I slowly turn around. Except for the tent and the sun, every direction looks like every other. The plain is not exactly featureless but the minor corrugations are indistinguishable from each other. This is just the way the End of the World should be, everything fading out to flat white snow, cobalt-blue sky and interplanetary coldness.

What would it be like to keep walking, Oates-like, out into the perfect whiteness? It's creepy enough on a beautiful day; it's easy to imagine the horror of walking out into a howling blizzard. He may just as well have jumped off a moving ship in the night as find his way back. Did he lose his nerve and flail around disorientated and despairing, or did he peacefully drown in the cold? From what I know of cold, the latter seems unlikely. After the blizzard was over, Scott and the others looked for his body; they couldn't find it so he must have made some distance. With a shiver, I follow my footsteps back.

There is not much being said in the tent. The writing's on the wall or, in our case, on the roof. We're scribbling in journals and looking up at the latitude marks that Jamie drew on the ceiling a few million years ago and the dashed line that marks our progress that now runs from before 80 degrees up into 88 degrees.

```
We only made 12 nautical miles. Our legs
are still very heavy and we are going as
slow as we have ever been — just for longer.
The new system is just arranging deck
chairs. Fourteen miles into twelve hours
won't go. We are 2 miles short today, can
we make them up? It's looking improbable.
One more bad day and it's impossible. We
are reaching the point of no return.
```

```
              I had a great chat to Kate, Mum at Whiri
                  and Dad and Moira too. They are all so
              supportive that it makes me want to do well,
                  but magically appear in NZ now. I want the
                  next 7 days to disappear ASAP so we can get
                  to the Pole. This trip has been an enormous
                      challenge for me; emotionally, physically
                  and everything else. 103nm to go.
```

The satellite phone beeps. Jamie pulls it out of the drying rack, looks at it and blows a soundless whistle. 'Hey, there's a text from Kate —

the RAF are pulling out.'

'Really? What happened?'

'Apparently there's a mention on their website of frostbite on their privates.'

'I didn't think they had privates in the air force?'

'I don't think it's those sort of privates.'

'Ouch!'

'I wonder if they'll have to have any cut off?'

'You'd hope not.'

The RAF are only just in front of us. Over the last few days they had been slowing up a little, but they were nearly there. That is cruel.

DAY 44. CHRISTMAS DAY

IT'S A BEAUTIFUL SUNNY day. We're once again out on the trail, flattening sastrugi. Endless, endless sastrugi. Not dramatic, just endless, upsetting the rhythm, adding strain onto legs, a thousand pauses, a thousand heaves.

Jamie is limping noticeably. He called Dr John in the morning and was told again that if the drugs and the massages weren't working, then the only solution was to rest before they became unusable. So we agreed that we would think about our options during the day and talk about it tomorrow. Today we are going to give ourselves a mental holiday.

We open up the Jardines' Christmas present on the trail. It's a little slab of green fudge! That's so thoughtful of them! It tingles as it melts on my tongue and soothes my mummified brain.

Our other Christmas present is to pass a hundred miles to the Pole. This is the furthest south that Shackleton made on the *Nimrod* Expedition. At this point he decided he had to turn around. It doesn't seem like a hundred years ago.

Jamie asks me to stay outside again while he does some stretches in the tent. After a few minutes he shouts out, 'OK, you can come in!'

I unzip the fly. What's this? There are balloons and even a cheery Father Christmas ornament dangling from the drying lines. Jamie is wearing a Santa hat.

'Ho ho ho! Merry Christmas!'

'Wow!' I'm staggered. 'You planned this two months ago?'

'Yep!' says Jamie, beaming.

With the back of the tent toward the wind, and the vestibule facing the sun, we are completely sheltered from the breeze and can even have the flap wide open. A more perfect veranda on the world is hard to imagine. Happiness is sitting 90 miles from the Pole in a little cup of sunshine, looking out on the fields of pristine and ancient snow, a bowl of delicious rehydrated spaghetti Bolognaise with extra oil on my lap, a stained plastic mug of lukewarm hot chocolate in my hand and a jaunty plastic Santa banging into my nose. For a few minutes, we forget our concerns and just enjoy being in a very special place, and laughing at the text messages and dropping in by phone to the Christmas dinners of our family and friends.

DAY 45. BOXING DAY

FOR WEEKS THE SASTRUGI had been affecting us, causing us to bang and crash and swerve. For nearly 600 miles the snow ridges have upturned our sleds, barked our shins, yanked on our sleds and made our life hell.

Now they melt away.

We have suffered the Time of Trials and at last we have been admitted into the Promised Land. We are walking through vast, rolling meadows of brilliant white icing sugar, Tellytubby-like in its surreal perfection. There are no more shadows; there are no more Martian meteorites. There are no distinguishing lumps of anything. All is a sinuous, billowing sheet under a dome of flawless Kodachrome blue. We plough on slowly and blessedly smoothly, the runners hissing quietly through the gently undulating swells.

My usual daydreams have been interrupted. I'm now having conversations with everyone I've ever had a disagreement with, apologising, reaching a compromise or explaining the misunderstanding. (*Chantelle, it's nothing personal. It's the way your fluff clogs the vacuum cleaner.*) Isn't this what dying people do? Am I preparing for passing over? Hang on, everything already is white. I'm walking towards a white light. Am I already in heaven? Where is everyone? The standard must be higher than I thought.

Unfortunately this heavenly terrain has come too late. My legs have been amputated and replaced with wooden pegs. I move with a Frankenstein-fresh-off-the-slab twitching, rolling lurch. Jamie is worse, trudging slowly and wincing with every step.

Now I finally understand Scott not being able to strike out for the last 11 miles to the depot, because now I know exactly how far 11 miles can be. Eleven miles can be the moon. It didn't matter how much food there was at One Ton Depot; there could have been a giant circus tent filled with soft-drink fountains, chocolate waterfalls, dancing girls in jelly-bean bikinis, swimming pools filled with warm M&Ms. It might have been a hundred metres away; it wouldn't have mattered. There comes a point your legs just don't go.

Oates did a noble thing — pity he did it so late. For the three days after his death, Scott, Wilson and Bowers made good gains until, on 19 March, they were only 11 miles away from One Ton Depot. Then they were hit by a blizzard, so they put up the tent and waited.

Two days later the fuel ran out, but still the blizzard blew on. Bowers and Wilson wrote in their letters of a plan to make a dash for the depot and return for Scott, now lame with a frostbitten foot — it came to nothing. For them, the blizzard never ended. They each succumbed to cold, dehydration and hunger.

On 29 March Scott was somehow still alive, and still turning out clear prose. On that date he wrote to his wife:

Every day we have been ready to start for our depot 11 miles away, but outside the door of our tent it remains a scene of whirling drift. I do not think we can hope for any better things now. We shall stick it out to the end, but we are getting weaker, of course, and the end cannot be far . . .

With hindsight, knowing what we know about how his men and the weather were going to deteriorate, Scott could only have survived if he had turned around a few days short of the Pole. By the time Scott was confined to his tent, he didn't have any choices left. We still do.

We should, Jamie's hamstrings permitting, get to the Pole. Arriving not on the fiftieth day, but sometime on the morning of the fifty-second. That means that we will have only eight and a half days to get back to the cache at the Thiels. It's just possible, but it will require the conditions to be kiteable on nearly all of those days. We will be throwing ourselves on the mercy of Antarctic weather and there are too many bodies buried under the ice to be happy about that idea.

Even if the wind did blow, it would be a risky proposition. Kiting wasn't going to be any easier on Jamie's hamstrings than pulling a sled, and we would still have to pull the sled through long stretches of sastrugi too rough to kite through. If Jamie's hamstrings worsened and we became incapacitated, then we would be relying on outside help. We would be like Scott hoping for the dogs (in our case, Otters) to come get us and that might work just as well for us as it did for him. We might be stuck, out of food, in our tent, waiting for a week for the weather to be fine enough for a plane to land. Or if it was too rough the plane might not be able to land.

I had promised HPG sincerely that I wouldn't kill myself and would come back safe and sound. It was an easy promise to make because I never thought that I was putting myself in harm's way. For me, the hours pass slowly and mostly uneventfully; for her, I'm always just a step away from a crevasse. Now we are going to take on a new level of risk and I find myself imagining the return trip back, and realise what it will be like for her and what I'll be putting her through. How bad it would be for her if something happened to me.

I certainly didn't want to end up like Scott, frantically writing a letter to his wife as the blizzard roared outside, trying to cram in years of fatherhood and advice about raising their young son.

> *Make the boy interested in natural history if you can . . . Above all, he must guard and you must guard him against indolence. Make him a strenuous man. I had to force myself into being strenuous as you know — had always an inclination to be idle.*

There was another role model. Someone else who had to make a tough decision at almost exactly the same latitude as we were. Someone else who was thinking of his wife.

Back in January 1909, just after crossing into 88 degrees, Shackleton's party held a council of war. Over the last two months they had discovered and named a new mountain chain, discovered and climbed one of the largest glaciers in the world, and had gone further south by hundreds of miles than any other human being. They were now the closest to a pole, north or south, than anyone had ever been.

They were very unhappy.

Despite the extraordinary efforts they had made, and the miracles that they had accomplished on a few handfuls of pemmican biscuits, they were now desperately short of food. They could get to the Pole or they could make it back alive — they probably couldn't do both. There was a vote and they decided to live. Shackleton was bitterly disappointed, but facts were facts.

With a savvy awareness of media sound bites, they switched to a new goal — to get within one hundred miles of the Pole. So on their last day they left the tent behind, and with just the biscuits and chocolate in their pockets, made one final out-and-back dash. When they returned to their tent that night, they estimated that they had turned around just 97 miles from the Pole.

Shackleton later explained his decision to his wife, 'I thought you'd rather have a live donkey than a dead lion.'

Shackleton made the right choice turning around when he did. He had so many extremely narrow escapes on the journey back to the coast that he might well have died if he had pushed on even a couple of hours further. Instead he lived to outrageously cheat death again in the *Endurance* Expedition and see his three children grow up.

On the other hand, a live donkey is still a donkey.

We wouldn't be doing what we said we would do. Would people be disappointed? Would some people say 'I told you so', and that our plans had been too ambitious? Are we letting our sponsors down — and all the other people who had offered us so much help?

When I was training for the trans-Atlantic race, I had several conversations with Jon Ackland about winning. He was keen to impress upon me that winning is the most important thing. Winning is EVERYTHING.

But winning can't be everything, I had argued. What if you win the Olympic marathon because your main rival gets hit by a meteorite a metre from the finish? What if you lose the Tour de France because you swerve to avoid a small orphan? What if you score the winning try in the final of the Rugby World Cup, but the referee disallows it? Does that make you a failure?

Jon had sighed and leaned forward as he reluctantly revealed the darkest secret of his profession. 'Of course winning isn't everything.

But you TELL YOURSELF it's everything! You make yourself believe it's everything because THAT'S the way you get the MOST OUT OF YOURSELF.'

Which is, in the end, how Shackleton justified his decision. He had been striving to get to the Pole for years. He had very nearly lost his life on the first attempt. He had brought himself, and his family, to the brink of bankruptcy, and had just endured months of gruesome sledging. He had every reason to be consumed by bitterness. Yet, just two days later, the ever-buoyant Shackleton had reconciled himself with these simple words written emphatically in his journal. 'Whatever regrets we have done our best. Amen.'

Would I spend the rest of my life wondering if we had done the right thing?

No. We had done our best.

We flop and lurch through our six shifts, then an extra hour, and then another half hour, just to get 12 lousy miles.

'It's not happening, is it?' says Jamie.

'No, it isn't.'

DAY 46. DECISION MADE

MIKE SHARP IS NOW down at Patriot Hills so we can talk to him directly. He is very understanding and the logistics are quickly arranged. One of the Twin Otters had just dropped off a small team who will be walking the last degree. The plane will return in about a week. If we get ourselves to the Pole it will take us back.

The Twin Otter had also dropped off kiting gear for the Marines who had arrived that day at the Pole, and would be starting back as soon as the winds allowed. Hannah was due tomorrow. She's right on track for breaking the record, after averaging an extraordinary 15 miles a day for nearly forty days.

It is a sombre day of trudging. I'm feeling a little woebegone.

'You know what?' says Jamie at a break.

'What?'

'I'm not going to make Scott's mistake.'

'What's that?'

'Getting all the way to the Pole only to let myself be disappointed. We have to focus on what we have achieved rather than what we haven't. We've done one of the longest, heaviest drags in Antarctica. Very few people have pulled so much weight for so long . . .'

'. . . for so little.'

'We're still going to be the first New Zealanders to have trekked unsupported to the South Pole.'

He's right. Slowly the heaviness lifts and some pride starts to return.

That night we take a deep breath and start calling sponsors to talk to them about our decision to return. We needn't have worried — the APL guys in particular have been 100 per cent behind us the whole way and now are very supportive and understanding. They have been living through all of this too.

DAY 48. THE LAST CACHE

DR JOHN COMES ON to the sched this morning and suggests, then asks, then insists that we leave all of our excess weight, all our kiting gear and everything we don't need for the next few days, because the plane heading to the Pole can easily pick it up.

It makes perfect sense. The sledging will be easier, we will speed up, and the strain threatening to sever Jamie's hamstrings will be reduced. And I don't want to do it. We've dragged our kites and skis and boots all this way; let's finish the job. We can still be one of the handful of teams who have reached the Pole with at least some of the capability to get back to the coast. Let's have it mean something.

As soon as I think it, I realise that this is exactly what Scott felt — *this has to mean something*. That's why they spent precious time fossicking for rocks on the way back — because although they hadn't got to the Pole first, they could still hope to achieve something worthwhile. Amundsen wasn't collecting geological specimens. He was riding his doggy railroad as fast as he could back to the coast to catch his boat and tell the world about getting to the Pole first. So if Scott could bring some geological specimens back that might shed light on the origins of Antarctica, well then, all their hard work would not have been completely wasted. This is why, even after they had left all other equipment behind, they were found with 35 pounds of rock samples on their sled. I get it now.

It might have made sense for Scott but it would be madness and vanity for us. So I work with Jamie to pull everything out of our sleds and lay out our biggest cache yet.

There is a lot of anticipation as we hook on. Now our sleds are only going to be 50 or 60 kilograms — surely we must feel that difference. We start off, and after a few steps we look at each other and giggle like little girls.

'This must be what the other expeditions have been feeling like nearly the whole trip,' says Jamie.

Yet as light as the sleds are, they don't seem to let us go any faster. Our legs only oscillate at the same clockwork pace. And every mile still has to be hauled.

The reconciliation fantasies have passed and I'm back to the usual daydreams. Except they're different; now I know they are going to happen, so they are almost hallucinatory in their vividness. I have buffed and polished the formula of the toast-and-honey fantasy until it glows.

I can feel the bite of the knife as it hits the breadboard. I can smell the distinctive sour, slightly salty aroma of the tea brewing in the battered aluminium kettle. I can feel the skin on my fingers sizzle a little as they hold down the edges of the hot toast. I can see the yellow butter frictionlessly spread and melt. As I bring it to my mouth, I feel the dry crunch yielding to the soft butter then to the tangy sweetness of the honey.

In the tent that night the mood is upbeat as we go about our chores. While I fix the fly on my long johns I turn to Jamie. 'It's hard to believe that in a few days we might be back on Earth.'

'On Earth?'

'You know, the real world.'

'Yeah, that's going to be weird.'

'Can you remember what dark is like?'

'It's like having your eyes open and not being able to see anything.'

'You mean like a whiteout?'

'. . . but it's black.'

Jamie is reading the information we have about arriving at the Pole. Apparently the degree of hospitality you get from the Americans at the Amundsen-Scott base at the Pole varies with management from year to year. Some years, expeditions get met with stiff formality and are left on the doorstep, in other years . . .

'Hey hey hey! It says here that you may get invited in for a cup of tea and a biscuit.'

'A biscuit!'

'Do you think that means *a* biscuit or a *plate* of biscuits?'

'They couldn't give us just one . . . could they?'

As the end of March neared, the men at Hut Point expected Scott and the others to appear at any moment. One morning the dogs started howling, their usual welcome for teams returning from the Barrier. But no one came.

A few nights later there was a distinct knocking on the window. They woke up and rushed to light a candle and put on the kettle, but when they threw open the door there was no one there. It had only been a dog's tail tapping on the glass.

On 27 March, the only remaining officer, Edward Atkinson, took another man and went out onto the Barrier to try to reach Scott's party and help them in. For three and a half days they pushed out into the thick weather, with temperatures below ⁻40° Celsius, before the severity of the conditions turned them back. 'At this date,' Atkinson wrote, 'in my own mind I was morally certain that the party had perished.'

Hopefully he was right. Only a day before, Scott was very much alive and writing his last note in the cold and dark, with only the frozen corpses of his friends for company.

Over the long winter the thirteen remaining members of the *Terra Nova* Expedition debated about what had happened to Scott, Evans, Wilson, Bowers and Oates. The consensus was that the five men had probably burst through a snow crust on the Beardmore and they now lay smashed at the bottom of one of the bottomless abysses.

And there was another tragedy that had to be addressed. During the summer a group of six men had been dropped off 230 miles up to the west, on a rocky outcrop so bleak and comfortless it was named Inexpressible Island, to carry out surveying and geological work. A few weeks later, the *Terra Nova* went to pick them up, but so much sea ice had filled the approaches to the bay that, despite huge efforts, the ship had not been able to get in, or even come close enough to signal that they were there. The *Terra Nova* had to reluctantly abandon the six men to what was in all probability a lingering, painful death by hunger and cold. There was a small chance, though, that they had holed up in a snow cave with enough seal meat to last the winter. They may even now be fighting for their lives in some blubbery, dark, icy hole.

What then should be the first journey of the spring? Do they try and mount a rescue of the potentially living or search for the graves of the certain dead? A secret ballot was taken, the result was unanimous — to search for Scott.

Was there a sense of guilt that needed to be expunged? If Scott had died on the Barrier, and not fallen down a crevasse, then questions might well be asked of the other men. As Cherry-Garrard put it in his diary, 'It would be too terrible to find that, though one knew that we had done all that we could, if we had done something different we could have saved them.'

As soon as the weather improved, at the end of October 1912, they set out. Two weeks later, after passing One Ton Depot, they saw a strange lump in the snow off to the side of their track. When brushed, it revealed itself to be the flap at the top of Scott's tent, nearly covered by the winter snows.

They dug the tent out and looked inside. Lit up by the eerie green glow of light penetrating the canvas, they saw the last moments of their friends' lives frozen in time.

Bowers and Wilson were sleeping in their bags. Scott had thrown back the flaps of his bag at the end. His left hand was stretched over Wilson, his lifelong friend.

Captain Scott's face and his hands looked like old alabaster, his face was very pinched and his hands terribly frostbitten . . . their suffering must have been terrible.

As Atkinson searched in Scott's sleeping bag for his journal, those outside heard a crack. It was the sound of Scott's arm breaking.

That night they pitched their own tents a hundred yards away. Hour after hour, Atkinson read the diary out to them, and so they found out what happened to Scott, Bowers and Wilson in their last days.

They were horrified by what they had heard — none more so then Cherry-Garrard. It was he who had been given the job of taking the dog teams out to resupply One Ton Depot. He waited there for a week before returning to the coast. Now he had just learned that the day he had left One Ton, Scott, Wilson and Bowers had been only 60 miles away. He wrote in his diary, 'It is all too horrible — I am almost afraid to go to sleep now.' The realisation that he might *just* have been able to save them tormented Cherry-Garrard for the rest of his life.

Finally it was time to go. They took the bamboo poles from the tent, collapsing it over the bodies of their friends. On top they built a giant snow cairn, crowned with a cross made of skis.

I do not know how long we were there but when all was finished it was midnight of some day. The sun was dipping low above the Pole, the Barrier was almost in shadow. And the sky was blazing — sheets and sheets of iridescent clouds. The cairn and Cross stood dark against a glory of burnished gold . . . It is a grave which kings must envy.

Back at the hut, they developed the film from Scott's camera. In the fixing bath they saw the ghostly images of their friends appear one last time: Scott, Wilson, Bowers, Oates and Evans, standing in line at the Pole, cold and exhausted.

They are still out on the Barrier, in their tombs of snow, moving a little closer to home every year.

18. KNOCKING THE BASTARD OFF

DAY 51. NORWEGIANS?

JAMIE STOPS AND POINTS. There are several parallel indentations in the snow. Clearly the tracks of several sleds.

'Norwegians?' I ask.

Tracker Jamie bends down and picks up a little snow and watches it carefully as it falls out of his hand. He shakes his head firmly.

'English. Four women.'

It has been seven weeks on the trail and Jamie's senses are no doubt highly attuned, but still this is impressive.

'How can you tell?'

'Adam said on the sched this morning.'

They are disturbingly going in a slightly different direction than us. Confident that we're heading the right way, we let them veer off. They must be going to a different pole.

Soon we're rewarded with a dot on the horizon.

'No, it isn't,' says Jamie.

'Yeah it is, have another look.'

'Oh yeah. Is that a fuel drum — or a building?'

'It might be either.'

'It's still 10 miles to go so it can't be the polar station. Maybe it's some kind of outpost.'

Antarctica hasn't lost its sense of irony. Now that we have dropped off our kiting gear, a gentle wind has started blowing from behind us. At the breaks we turn our featherweight sleds completely around so we can sit with our backs against the wind and look at where the Pole will be.

The last few days neither of us has wanted to use the iPod. The pulling has become a kind of meditation that words and music intrude upon. The frantic internal chatter has given way to a kind of serenity.

Our time here is nearly over, and although I'm very much looking forward to seeing the end of all the effort, there are some things that are very appealing about our Antarctic lives. There's a refreshing simplicity and clarity. We have achieved so much over the last seven weeks; we have made an unbroken furrow more than 1100 kilometres long, just by sliding one ski tip in front of the other. Each day we have only had to get out of our sleeping bags and haul; it isn't always easy to get started but it's not like there's much else to do. It's not like we can watch Sky. At home I make hundreds of decisions every day, and with every one of them I feel the pain of the option not taken. To have crunchy cornflakes is not to have warm porridge. To have a good night's sleep is to miss David Letterman. Down here, I only make a handful of decisions, and so I don't miss anything. It's been a pleasure to be so single-minded, so cut off from other options. So much more gets done and hardly a moment is wasted. I feel as guilty about spending half a minute here admiring the glossy sheen of a pecan nut, as I would about watching half an hour of TV back home.

Trail life is so uncluttered. At home I have a house full of mostly junk. Here I can fit my whole life, everything I need and want, into a con-tainer the size of a small bathtub. What did I need all that other stuff for?

There is nothing like a bit of deprivation to sharpen the senses as well. All these weeks of starving and cold deadness have made me much more aware of my own mortality and more appreciative of the moment. I'm never going to rush past a sunset, a smile, time with family and friends, or a piece of toast and honey ever again.

I wonder what the next adventure is going to be. Hang on. Teamwork, commitment, purpose, appreciation, slow accumulation of milestones — is this what marriage is going to be like?

At the next break I get Jamie's take.

'What do you think you've learned doing this?'

'Take more carbohydrate on polar sledging journeys.'

'Seriously.'

'I think it's going to be a very long time before anything seems hard again.'

The world, at least as far as our senses can make out, is flat or maybe a cube. It's not often you get a sense of the Earth as an astronomical object, as a globe tumbling through space. But now, with the sun doing almost perfect circles around our heads, there is a real feeling of coming closer to the giant spindle of it all.

By the end of six shifts we are 5 miles away from the Pole. The Amundsen-Scott base runs, like us, on New Zealand time, so that means by happy coincidence we should arrive tomorrow at exactly morning cookie break.

In the tent we try to peel off some of our bandages and clean ourselves up a bit for our re-entry into soapy society.

```
I have quite the hair do. Magnificent.
You'd pay a lot of money for that downtown.
I took off my bandages and I hadn't
realised how bad some of the skin is on my
face. My nose is a bit artificial there
at the end. We'll see what the doctors
say about that. Otherwise I'm mostly OK.
It's going to be a great day tomorrow

            I'm going to put some moleskin on my nose
            because man it's looking heinous. Just like
```

```
Kev, I'm sporting a pretty funkarama do with a
nice little chooky bird happening at the front.
     But we're going to get cleaned up and we're
going to walk these last few miles like kings.
```

DAY 52. POLE DAY

WE WAKE UP AT normal time. We are only held together by routine at the moment. If we start to give ourselves a little bit of slack then we might completely unravel. So we pack up the tent the same way we always have, and set off at our usual time. There is no sense of occasion in the weather; it's not even a whiteout, more of a greyout, the sky hanging over our head like a giant brillo pad. It is intensely bitingly cold and my hands switch off almost immediately; I have to spend the next hour trying hard to keep them attached.

I'm leading at the end of the second shift when out of the gloom appears a lamp post. Aha! So we've been in Narnia the whole time; what's next — talking badgers, fauns in waistcoats?

But no, it's not exactly a lamp post, it's more like a telegraph pole with a wire that's strung off through the murkiness to the shadowy outline of another post. This is the VLF antenna that lines the long snow runway, at the end of which is the South Pole. So we turn and follow the wires. Slowly the gloom lifts and we can start to see a strange complex of buildings in the distance. Even more startling is seeing people. Real people, going to and fro between the buildings.

The snow is flat and we can walk side by side, like Butch and Sundance riding into town. Just before arriving in Barbados, after rowing across the Atlantic, I asked Jamie what the next adventure would be. His answer was, 'I don't know mate, but it's not going to be long and it's not going to be hot.' So I ask him the same question now.

'I don't know mate,' he says, 'but it's not going to be long and it's not going to be cold.'

'What's your daydream at the moment?'

'I'm just sitting at home, on the sofa, with a cup of tea.'

> *My greatest desire now seems to be to sit on the hearth-rug at*
> *Mother's feet and be petted, I feel so tired and hungry . . .*
>
> — Frank Wild

We're nearly at the buildings now and there, a hundred metres away, we see the circle of flags. It's just like any other hundred metres, that is to say more or less endless. Then we are walking through the flags. Then we stop, right in front of a red and white striped pole, about a metre high, with a mirror ball on top. It's the South Pole. I reach out and touch it.

Right. So that's that then.

I rest my head on the ski poles. Suddenly I feel a swelling in my chest and I'm blinking back tears. Two years of risk and uncertainty and doubt and all those lonely hours training, all the proposal writing and hundreds of fruitless phone calls. Then the emotional roller-coaster ride of the last fifty-two days, back and forth between satisfaction and despair. It's finally over. We did it. We had made it.

```
As I walked through the flags the emotions hit me
more than I thought. No tears. No hugs. Just a
deep breath and an overwhelming belief that Kevin
and I had earned this moment. Every single step.
```

A silver-haired man in a red jacket, who has been standing to one side, now comes forward, smiling, and puts out his hand. 'Hi, I'm Andy. I'm the station manager. Welcome to the South Pole.'

A few minutes later we at last make the phone call home that we have been waiting so long to make. The one that I had so often thought we might not ever make.

'Hello, it's Jamie Fitzgerald on day 52 for the Thermal Heart Antarctic Expedition. Our position is 90 degrees 0 minutes and 0 seconds south!'

19. 'CAN YOU TAKE A PHOTO OF US IN OUR BIKINIS?'

It seemed as if our voyage and all its labours were at an end and nothing now remained for us but to return home and be happy for the rest of our lives.

— James Clark Ross

AS ANDY LEFT, HE said that when we were done putting up our tent, we should come in for a hot chocolate and a cookie.

'Now you definitely heard the word "cookie", too, didn't you?' I check with Jamie as we frantically pull the tent bag off the sled and unzip it.

'You bet I did,' says Jamie.

'I mean, he didn't say "chocolate-chip wookie"?'

'No. But I could eat a wookie.'

With an invitation like that a tent is never going to be erected entirely in accordance with manufacturer's specifications, but what we lack in attention to detail we make up for in speed. In just a few minutes we're wobbling as fast as our spaghetti legs can carry us to the entrance of a building that looks mostly like a giant multi-storeyed ski lodge on stilts.

Andy meets us at a heavy steel door. Inside is a metal spiral staircase. Andy bounds up while Jamie and I laugh as we pluck at our pants to lift our feet to the next step. I suppose for the last seven weeks we've always shuffled along with both feet on the ground and some muscles have atrophied.

At the top is another large heavily insulated door that looks exactly like the entrance to an industrial fridge — or in this case the exit. Andy pulls it open to let us in and quickly slams it shut behind us. In two steps we have been transported from the middle of a wild and hostile continent to a safe and familiar-looking locker area.

'Hang up your things,' says Andy, 'then come into the canteen when you're done.'

I whisper to Jamie in amazement, 'Hey, it's warm!'

We laugh at that too. There seems to be a lot to laugh about. Inside the canteen there is a group of women dressed in ski gear sitting at a long table. They are the English team led by Fiona Thornewell, which has also just arrived after walking the last degree, and they seem to be laughing a lot as well. I find myself peering at them like they are aliens. Quite attractive aliens. They ask us questions about our trek and we try to answer.

We find out that after spending a week recuperating and waiting for the wind to start blowing, the Marines had left that very morning to try kiting back. Hannah did break the record for the fastest unsupported trek to the Pole and was picked up and flown back a few days ago. The Jardines are making steady progress, but are still about a week away.

Andy soon comes back and joins us with a tray of mugs and a large plate.

'Help yourself to a hot chocolate and have a cookie — they're freshly baked.'

In the ensuing mêlée, I may have eaten a finger.

The Amundsen-Scott base is an extraordinary complex. It's one part science lab, two parts workshop and five parts space station.

After a brief tour of the small but incredibly well-equipped medical rooms, we go to the neutrino lab. There a scientist explains that neutrinos are tiny, nearly massless subatomic particles travelling at nearly the speed of light which get poured out in vast quantities by the sun. A hundred billion fly through your fingernail every second. Almost nothing stops them; they waft through the Earth on their way to infinity like a sledger to a cookie. The South Pole is one of the best places in the world to have a neutrino telescope and I'm afraid I can't tell you why because at this point I start to feel woozy and light-headed. I'm uncomfortably hot and the colour starts to drain from my vision. When I come to, I'm lying on the floor and everyone is gathered around.

'What happened?' I ask.

'You passed out. Just stay there, the gurney is coming.'

'I'm fine.' And I am, but then the bed arrives and I'm wheeled back to the doctor's rooms while the others continue with the tour.

The doctor takes a history and runs some tests. The scales show that I weigh 87 kilograms.

'What did you weigh at the start?' he asks.

'One hundred and ten.'

'And how long have you been out there?'

'Fifty-two days.'

He does the maths and shakes his head. 'Twenty-three kilos in fifty-two days. That's about a pound a day.' He unhooks his stethoscope. 'Look. You're fine. You could just use a rest and something to eat.'

'Can I have that as a prescription?'

The doctor drops me off at the canteen, putting me in front of another plate of cookies. I try to eat only one a minute to drag them out. I gape at the view through the picture windows that stretch down one whole wall.

For weeks I had seen Antarctica mostly either exhausted through frosted goggles, or in glimpses through the fly of the tent. Now it could be gawked at in leisure. This is the glass dome I had daydreamed about. I'm three storeys high, warm and well fed. The weather outside has fined up considerably and it's now a bright and sunny day. From my elevated position I can look down on the circle of flags and the Pole, then out over a white pillowy surface to a crisp, inviting horizon, perhaps 20 miles away.

So far we had been walking in Scott's footprints metaphorically, but not literally. Until now. Scott stood right at this spot, in weather like we had this morning, disappointed, cold and cookie-less.

> *The Pole. Yes, but under very different circumstances from those*
> *expected. The wind is blowing hard, and there is that curious*
> *damp, cold feeling in the air which chills one to the bone . . .*
> *Great God! This is an awful place.*

Perhaps the most tragic thing about the race to the Pole is that it all took place just a few years too soon. The airship and the aeroplane were developing rapidly. If he had waited for just another dozen years, Scott could have flown to the Pole in warmth and comfort. In 1926, Amundsen himself became the first person to fly over the North Pole in an airship.

Soon Jamie is back. 'How are you feeling?'

'Ahhh.'

'What are you eating?'

'Nuffingh.'

'It's cookies! Where did you get them from?'

I wave towards the end of the canteen, swallow my mouthful, grab his sleeve and stare up at him fiercely. 'There's *trays* of them! They *keep making them*!'

Jamie laughs. 'Come on, we have to get on the phone.'

There is a 55-degree temperature difference between inside and outside. As soon as the cold hits me, I feel much better and snap back into full, perky consciousness.

We have the tent set up with its back to the wind and the vestibule facing the Pole, which is only metres away. We soon have one phone running hot sending back video and images of our arrival, while with the other phone Jamie and I alternate calls back home.

Except I don't have any luck getting hold of people. HPG's phone goes straight to voicemail, no one picks up at Mum's. This is frustrating when I'm so keen to share the fun.

At last I manage to get hold of Shamus the inventor on his mobile. Normally I wouldn't start by asking if it's a good time to call but I figure I'll cut to the chase. 'Hey, you'll never guess where I'm calling from!'

'The South Pole?'

'Yeah, that's right!'

'Kevin, congratulations, that's fantastic news. Hey, I'm out on my boat on the Hauraki Gulf and the engine's stopped working. We're just about to be washed into some rocks and the coastguard have pulled up alongside.'

'I'll call back later then.'

'If you wouldn't mind. Hey and well done. See ya, bye.'

The rest of the day and night disappeared. We had some dinner, took more interviews and at the moment I'm just lying on my sleeping bag inside our tent simply smiling. I don't know if this came from being proud of myself, or because we wouldn't be dragging the sleds tomorrow.

The tent is set up only metres from the bottom of the earth, metres from the spot we worked so hard for.

At some point we decided to call Adam, to get our 'sched call' out of the way. Bad news for the South Pole holiday — he says a plane will be arriving in about six or seven hours to take us back to Patriot Hills. Damn. We need to take loads of photos for sponsors, pack up, and get some sleep!

I finally get hold of HPG. She doesn't seem at all upset about us not doing the return trip. Her words come tumbling out in a rush. 'Oh honey, well done! I'm so amazingly proud of you. I'm so glad you're OK. I'm so looking forward to seeing you again!'

I can't wait to get home. I'm going to get married!

Just at that moment a very pretty female face pops into our tent. 'Sorry to bother you guys. You know we've been doing this trek for breast cancer? Anyway we need some publicity photos. Would you mind taking pictures of us in our bikinis at the South Pole?'

Jamie looks at me. 'I don't know, Kev. What do you think?'

'Well, I suppose so. Maybe just this once.'

'Great! Shall we meet you at the Pole in a few minutes, then? We'll get changed and be right back out.'

The ladies have cunningly moved their tent so it is just outside the circle of flags. I can hear the roar of the stoves going inside. Shortly after we arrive, a voice shouts out through the nylon, 'Are you ready, because this is going to be bloody quick!'

With much shrieking, a flurry of girls rushes out, wearing just bikinis, pink feather boas, ugg boots and goosebumps. They pause long enough only to have a few quick snaps fired off before they run screeching back to the tent. It's ⁻32° Celsius.

Jamie comes back from our tent.

'Hey Kev, can you get a picture of me and the South Pole and this?'

It's a sign that says 'Please say yes'.

'I'll get the photo blown up and use it when I propose to Kate.'

'And after that you can use it when you want to go on fishing trips,' I suggest.

With the phone calls and taking photos for sponsors, and repeated trips to the canteen to warm up, it feels like hardly any time has passed (so only about two and a half kilos of cookies) before the Twin Otter taxis around the corner, right up to the camp.

It's not Stefan, but another pilot, and in the back he already has the bags of kite gear and food that he picked up from our last cache. Soon we are scooting along, just a few hundred metres in the air while the great white ocean slowly passes beneath us.

I turn to Jamie. 'I've got us a treat for the flight!'

I carefully unwrap a paper towel to reveal a couple of cookies.

He laughs. 'I've got a surprise too.' And lifts up a bulging white bag filled with them.

'How did you get those?'

'I just asked!'

During the next four happy hours I'm talking and laughing with Jamie and the girls in the brilliant sunshine, or else my nose is pressed against the glass window, as I watch our journey of the past seven weeks slowly rewind below.

It is such a long, long way.

When the Twin Otter swoops around the end of the Patriot Hills we can see that the base camp has blossomed like a goldrush town into neat rows of tents. After we glide to a stop, Mike Sharp, on a skidoo, is the first of a small and enthusiastically supportive crowd to arrive at the side of the plane and pull open the door. There's Adam the Radio Guy all smiles, and a grizzled Dr John, and a considerably svelter Hannah beaming. Mike invites us into the mess tent and we eat at a table for the first time in nearly two months and have them laughing as we tell our stories and hear about Hannah's astonishing trek.

It's now high summer, and with the temperature at ⁻9° Celsius the air feels warm and soft. There is no difference between night and day, and without our trekking routine, time stops having any meaning. We sleep when we want to sleep, eat when we want to eat, but most of the time we want to hang out in one of the big tents, drink hot chocolate by the gallon and talk to the Mount Vinson climbers and have a laugh with Hannah, Fiona and the girls while we wait for the wind to drop enough for the Ilyushin to land. Given that there are only four flyable days a month, it might be a while. That's fine by me, I doubt if there is enough time to hear everyone's stories. I talk to a guy who was a safari guide in South Africa about being chased by an elephant. Another is trying to convince me that with a paraglider and a private jet, it's possible to climb the highest summits on all seven continents in a week. Another that you could do the first crossing of the Empty Quarter of Arabia if you took enough camels to carry water for the camels carrying water for you.

A few days later the Ilyushin drops out of a blue, but not cloudless, sky. Grey clouds are massing on the horizon adding a sense of urgency to the boarding. Jamie, still limping, and I are the last of the passengers shuffling down to meet it on the iceway. Mike relays us to the plane on the back of a snowmobile and waves us off with a smile.

A few hours later we touch down in Punta Arenas in the dawn of a beautiful summer's day. We taxi to a halt, the engines cut and the back ramp slowly drops down. Warmth, smells, moistness and glimpses of green flood in. Life again.

20. HITCHED

*I have had the world lie beneath my clumsy boots and seen the red
sun slip over the horizon after the dark Antarctic winter. I have
been given more than my share of excitement, beauty, laughter
and friendship . . .*

*For me the most rewarding moments have not always been the
great moments — for what can surpass a tear on your departure,
joy on your return, or a trusting hand in yours?*

— Sir Edmund Hillary

SIR ED SENT HIS apologies to the celebrations we had for our return;
he wasn't well enough to attend. I didn't see him again before he died
so I didn't get to thank him in person. I have to do it standing in front
of his casket, in the cathedral, early one morning, while queues of
people, each one feeling the same as me, go out the door, along the
street, around the corner and well down the road.

The Marines made it back kiting, although they had a torrid time,
dealing with the sastrugi and the fluky winds. It took them eleven

days to get to 85 degrees south. At about this point one of them was yanked into the air the length of the 12-foot lines to his sled, and may well have kept going upwards had he not pulled the quick release and jettisoned the kite. He fell so hard that for an hour it wasn't clear whether or not he had dislocated his shoulder. They arrived at Patriot Hills camp in twenty-one days.

Ray and Jenny Jardine got to the Pole too late to attempt to kite back. So with a little spare time on his hands, Ray climbed Mount Vinson, and then for good luck bagged Mount Aconcagua, the highest peak in the Americas, on the way home.

I shut the door so as not to wake HPG sleeping inside. The sun has just risen over Waihi Beach and the sky is filled with a soft golden light. I breathe in a deep silky lungful of cool, freshly ionised salt air.

It's all very close to how I imagined it. The pavement is a little colder. I hadn't realised how much heat would come off the bread tucked under my arm, or how much the paper bag rustles. I had the franticness of the boiling jug and the awkwardness of trying to turn a full teapot three times anti-clockwise on the breadboard *exactly* right.

I stop with my hand on the pot. For a second I'm back in Antarctica during one of those long cold hours where I imagined this moment so vividly. Then, with a shiver, the moment passes.

When HPG comes in I'm sitting in the sun on the sofa, a piece of honeyed toast in one hand and a cup of tea in the other, and a look of complete and utter bliss on my face.

I'm sitting in the front pew of the little church taking deep breaths and glancing over my shoulder as it fills up with guests. Jamie and Kate catch my eye and wave. There are two beads of sweat on my forehead. Partly because my morning suit is uncomfortably warm. Mostly because the bride is not on time, then fashionably late, then probably-on-her-way-to-Sydney late. Jamie comes up to console me.

'Don't worry, Kev. If you're nervous and you're getting married to *her* — imagine how she must feel!'

Another mate sidles alongside, looks left and right, and speaks without moving his lips, 'There's a car out the back, the engine's running. Just say the word.'

Then there's a flash of sleek polished paintwork outside, a glimpse of white silk and a few moments later the organ starts to play the wedding march. The crowd's hubbub quietens and heads turn, necks crane. I see the silhouette of HPG, framed in the archway against the bright sun, on her father's arm. She steps down the aisle beaming left and right at the guests and then, last of all, she smiles shyly at me.

She is so beautiful.

My reverie is interrupted by the voice of The Professor.

'Kevin, this is my treasure that I am now passing to you,' he says, and gives me her hand.

I take off her veil and there she is: happy, smiling, trusting.

A few minutes later the priest is saying, 'I now pronounce you man and wife.'

To the clapping and cheering of the crowd, I gently kiss the bride. Then I'm holding the most wonderful, special woman, and I'm the luckiest guy in the world.

My wife is lovely, charming and delicious. When I come home to our house she runs down to the door and leaps two-footed into my arms, peppering my face with kisses.

We snuggle on the sofa as we watch DVDs together in front of the fire. We exchange smiles as we work in the study at night. I cook her dinners while she's swotting for her final surgical exams. She opens the window to let the smoke out. Now we're laughing as we cycle down the road on our new bikes. Now she gives me a wan smile as I sit by her hospital bed holding her hand as she recovers from breaking her leg after riding into the kerb.

So *this* is what marriage feels like.

One night Jamie asked Kate if she wanted to come along to hear him speak at the local surf life-saving club.

'What are you talking about?' she asks.

'Partnership.'

Jamie seems to be taking the long way, a road that winds between the beach and the cliffs of Wellington's south coast. Then the car stops. Kate's heart starts to pound as she realises that she is outside The Keep, a little B&B romantically fashioned after a castle. He opens the door to flickering tea lights leading up the stairs to the first-floor room. There are more tea lights, flowers everywhere, special chocolates on the bed, plates of Kate's favourite food and a spectacular sweeping view of the starry night sky and the crashing waves of Cook Strait.

Jamie is giving a speech, which Kate doesn't really hear. Then he brings out a large photo of the South Pole with him holding a sign. She peers at it closely.

'Hell yes!' she shouts.

A few months later, on a warm summer afternoon, HPG and I are standing outside with other guests on a grass lawn in the Wairarapa countryside. Sheep munch in the field next door while the guests sip bubbles and listen to a string trio. Jamie is doing an excellent job of appearing nonchalant and unflappable.

Soon Kate walks up the aisle looking gorgeous. They exchange vows and kiss while we all hoot and holler.

Later in the evening, while the guests are dancing, Jamie and I escape to a quieter corner to enjoy a couple of glasses of wine.

'You know what scares me most?' I say.

'What?'

'What we're going to come up with for the next adventure.'

Jamie laughs.

'Yeah, I've been thinking. I'd like to help other people to feel what it's like to get to the end of a big challenge.'

'Sounds great. What's the plan?'

'It's . . .'

He pauses and looks up. I follow his gaze. In another corner Kate and HPG are looking over at us and laughing together. There seems to be a lot of nodding and agreement.

'Uh oh. That looks like trouble. What do you think they are talking about?' says Jamie.

'I think the expedition team just got two more members.'

EPILOGUE

SOME YEARS AGO, DURING my OE in England, I was standing in line waiting to buy Ranulph Fiennes' book *Mind Over Matter*, about his recent Antarctic expedition.

Soon it's my turn at the front of the table. Without looking up, he takes a fresh book from the pile, opens the cover and says gruffly, 'Any message?'

I hesitate, then say, *'Don't give up.'*

Now he looks up. 'And who's it for?'

'Me.'

He writes the line, snaps the book closed and hands it to me.

'You shouldn't. Good luck.'

ACKNOWLEDGEMENTS

To every single one of you, in New Zealand and around the world, who wrote in with messages of encouragement while we were down on the ice, thank you so much. They were much appreciated and they all helped.

To Lady June and the late Sir Ed Hillary: one way or another you have helped make happen the most incredible experiences of my life — first in Nepal, then the Atlantic, and now Antarctica. Thank you again for being so generous with your time, energy and support.

Kate, your unwavering support got me down to the ice. My family, especially you Bridget, gave me the belief I could get there, and your messages along the way made sure we did. To Rob and Isabel, you have become a huge part of my life, and the fact I got to the start line, the toughest part of any campaign, was only through your help.

— Jamie

To my wife Magda, the Hot Polish Girl. Thank you for being so patient with me, and for being the best wife in the world. For all my family and friends for being so enthusiastic and supportive, both in the proposing and the trekking, especially Mum — I appreciate your support and relentless cheerfulness far more than I ever can say.

— Kevin

To Rob Hamill, mate! You know we couldn't have done it without you.

To APL. Mitch, Craig and Shane, thank you so much for your financial commitment and your support. Working with you was a real pleasure. Let's do it again!

Rochelle, Annalise and Simon, thanks so much for all your marketing and behind-the-scenes efforts; your daily messages were always looked forward to.

Waikato University were once again fantastic supporters of our expedition, specifically Roy Crawford and Sarah Knox. It was great to have you on board for this second campaign, and we look forward to sharing ideas with you all in the future.

Brent Impey, Mark Jennings and Keith Slater from TV3 for once again being the financial engine room behind the scenes. Peter Everatt from the Radio Network for backing us without hesitation. Bernard Hickey from Xtra — quite simply there would have been no expedition without you. Scott Graham from Tactical Media, without your nous and commercial sense we would still be baking cakes. And Deb Fritz for being the glue behind the scenes and keeping all the stakeholders happy. Nigel Keats from Clemenger BBDO and Tom Osborne from Mediaonline for knowing an opportunity when they saw one and being able to think and work outside the box.

Getting the right clothing was always going to be one of the most essential aspects of this campaign. Jackie Murray and The North Face team's passion for our safety could only be rivalled by our mothers! During all of our preparation in New Zealand and Canada, and throughout the expedition in Antarctica, we were in the safe hands of, without doubt, the best outdoor clothing on the planet.

Sandy McLean and Matt from AMPRO in New Zealand. During

a time when we were unsure if we would even make it to the start line, you really believed in us and supported us so generously. The MSR stoves and tents, the Nalgene bottles, the Gerber tools, along with everything else you gave us, ROCKED!

A big thank you to François Smith from Dick Smith Electronics (this book was mostly written on your laptop). Rob McGregor and the Victoria Park New World team — I hate to think how much hungrier we would have been if we hadn't had your support. We spent a lot of time in Antarctica imagining that we were walking up and down your aisles! Anne Mellor from LAN Chile — without your flight deals we would still be rowing towards Antarctica. Thank you very much for your help.

Kelvin Ricketts and Craig McKay from The Nuance Group. Most of the pictures in this book were taken on your camera gear. You guys really are the unsung heroes behind so much of New Zealand sport and we are extremely grateful for your contribution.

Steve Blackwell and Alastair Noble from the TR Corporation for coming on board, backing the dream and providing your generous 'soup to nuts' communication solution. Thanks to you, we were the envy of other expeditions!

Shamus, your creativity, knowledge and inventing skills and attitude towards innovation never cease to amaze. If there is anyone who is going to come up with a jetpack it will be you. Gary from iMapping, I like to think that you recycled at least some of that code into the Virtual Gazza and so all your hard work wasn't wasted! Greig Brebner from Proline Plastics, thanks so much for the great work on the boot plates.

Jon Ackland for your wonderful advice — no one knows performance like you.

A big thank you to our very patient managers in the months leading up to the trek. Kevin would like to thank Pawel Grochowicz for being such an understanding and supportive boss at Telecom. Jamie would like to thank Wayne Besant, Glenys Powell, Graham Meecham, and the entire ANZ retail network, and also from ANZ, Mark Wood,

Dominique Crikemans, Greg Campbell, Jonathan Thompson, Chris Walker and Rebecca Hooper (now Rebecca Corbbett thanks to meeting Simon at Jamie's wedding!). Thanks ANZ for working with Cushla Baggott, Mitchell and Partners.

I (Kevin) was really touched that my old scout troop, the Captain Musick Air Scouts, ably led by Phil Barge, got in behind the expedition and did a fantastic job fundraising. It was great to talk to you from Antarctica.

A very big thank you to the Hon. Trevor Mallard (then Minister of Sport) for the investment and interest that you took in the campaign, and taking the time to come to our launch function.

Brent Palmer from Yacht Lifeline, a big thank you for the great stories and the medical advice — did you recognise your loo story? Chris Gebbie from Pukenui Lodge for being such a passionate kiting fanatic and for being so helpful sourcing our wonderful Ozone kites, and Dean Agnew of Trillian Trust for helping fund them. Gemma Ede from FCM Travel Solutions for the first feature on the campaign — we were committed after that! Gill Clarke from Adventure Travel for helping us get to the Arctic for our training, as well as Punta Arenas. Rob Barlow at Bendon Man for all the support 'down south'.

Lachie Johnstone and Murray Fox from Wholesale Frozen Foods. Your freezer was cool! Thanks so much for letting us hang out in it, we learnt a lot. Arthur Ballantyne and Back Country Foods — we still haven't tasted a roast lamb and vege meal that can compare with your freeze-dried meals. Bronwyn Jones and Michael and Edward Lodge from Inside Out for the simulated altitude training that helped prepare us for the rigours of the Plateau. Jeremy Werkhoven from Classic Embroidery Products in Wellington. Graeme Dingle for your advice and helping us launch the campaign. Hayden Lang from Spy Optics — best glasses of all those we tested! David Watt from Brandex for the Suunto watches. Nigel Cranston from 180 degrees biscuits — they brought us back to life each night in the tent. Lou Sanson from Antarctic New Zealand and Nigel Watson from the New Zealand Antarctic Heritage Trust for your enthusiastic support. Sean

Drinkwater from Fisher for accessing the cross-country skis for us. Riki Mitchell from the Snow Centre for helping fit the most comfortable ski boots we've ever worn in our lives. Martin Bolton from Nutralife for the protein powder that helped us put on weight before the trip. Tim Peters from Energizer NZ Ltd for providing the world's best batteries. Jim Cotter for his dietary and performance advice.

Kevin would like to thank the tremendously patient Zeph and his team at Café Jazz, Remuera; Maddy and Chris and the girls at the Lounge Café, Birkenhead; Kay and Rosa at The Woolloongabba Café, Brisbane. Close to 1500 coffees were consumed in the writing of this book.

And finally, in memory of Anton Wopereis, the kind and patient guide who taught us crevasse-rescue techniques on the Tasman Glacier and who died tragically in a climbing accident on Mount Cook on 1 January 2008.

ENDNOTES

CHAPTER 2

Page 23. *'Men wanted for hazardous journey'*. Unfortunately the original source for this ad has not been found.

Page 24. *'They are mostly just lucky guesses'*. For example the Piri Reis map of 1513, according to some, shows the coastline of parts of Antarctica in an ice-free state, implying either some highly advanced ancient civilisation or perhaps extraterrestrial technology. For this particular map another more plausible, if duller, explanation is that the part of the 'Antarctic coast' depicted is just the South American coastline bent to fit the shape of the parchment.

Page 24. *'Substitutes were being found for whale oil'*. JN Tønnessen and AO Johnsen, *The History of Modern Whaling*, C Hurst & Co, 1982, p. 53.

Page 25. *'In their haste'*. The incident described is the first undisputed landing on the Antarctic 'mainland'. Some historians argue that one or more American sealers might have landed earlier, but probably on the Antarctic Peninsula.

Page 26. *'A dozen yards behind the boat'*. Fredick A. Cook, *Through the First Antarctic Night, 1898–1899: A Narrative of the Voyage of the Belgica among Newly Discovered Lands and over an Unknown Sea about The South Pole*, Kessinger, 2007, p. 127.

Page 27. *'We become pale, with a kind of greenish hue'*. Cook, p. 254.

Page 29. *'Antarctica, as everyone knew'*. Markham was particularly outraged when the English newspaper magnate Sir George Newnes spent an enormous fortune backing what was passed off as a British expedition, but was in fact Norwegian in everything but name. In 1899 this expedition wintered over in Cape Adare, and it was only a small consolation to Markham that, as he would have put it, being foreigners and excitable, they had quickly succumbed to madness, near mutiny and the inevitable death of a minor character, and had achieved relatively little.

Page 29. *'Although senior officers described Scott'*. Diana Preston, *A First Rate Tragedy: Robert Falcon Scott and the Race to the South Pole*, Houghton Mifflin Harcourt, 1999, p. 23.

Page 29. *'laziness, untidiness, touchiness and tendency to gloom'*. Ranulph Fiennes, *Captain Scott*, Hodder & Stoughton, 2003, p. 150.

Page 30. *'a moral cowardice of which I am heartily ashamed'*. Captain Robert F. Scott, *The Voyage of the 'Discovery'*, Wordsworth Editions, 2009, p. 437.

Page 30. *'Athletic, brainy with a keen quick intelligence, great courage and charming manners'*. Albert Armitage in David Crane, *Scott of the Antarctic*, Harper Perennial, 2006, p. 198.

Page 30. *'I have never known anybody, man or woman'*. Apsley Cherry-Garrard, *The Worst Journey in the World*, Penguin, 1937, (3rd impression), p. 227.

Page 30. *'The barrier edge'*. Scott, *Voyage of the 'Discovery'*, p. 123.

Page 31. *'The cold white light falls'*. Scott, *Voyage of the 'Discovery'*, p. 255.

Scott goes on with his extraordinary world picture: 'And indeed it is not a spell that rests on man alone for it is on such nights that the dogs lift up their voices . . . If one is sentimentally inclined, as may be forgiven on such a night, this chorus almost seems to possess the woes of the ages; as an accompaniment to the vast desolation without, it touches the lowest depths of sadness.'

Page 31. *'With spring approaching . . . twenty thousand years'*. This is referring to the crossing of the Bering Strait and the inhabitation of the Americas.

Page 32. *'Those being in short supply when'*. Shackleton was rejected immediately. However, he had a Plan B. By a stroke of luck he had met the son of Llewellyn Longstaff, the man who had underwritten the expedition. When Shackleton was next back in England, he visited Mr Longstaff and, on the basis of his charm and personality, managed to get an interview and then a position on the *Discovery*.

Page 32. *'The UV rays seared their eyeballs'*. They had nothing effective to treat it with, although they tried a range of things. In particular, 'cocaine has only a very temporary effect', Scott complained. Scott, *Voyage of the 'Discovery'*, p. 425.

Page 32. *'On more than one instance two of the party'*. Fiennes, *Captain Scott*, p. 96.

Page 32. *'A fairer sight could scarcely meet'*. Scott, *Voyage of the 'Discovery'*, p. 458.

Page 33. *'I turned in at once when'*. Beau Riffenburgh, *Shackleton's Forgotten Expedition: The Voyage of the* Nimrod, Bloomsbury, 2005, p. 14.

Page 33. *'fifty thousand New Zealanders'*. Riffenburgh, p. 144.

Page 34. *'The only fact it had proven conclusively was that dogs don't work in the Antarctic'*. At least they don't when you aren't an experienced dog handler and the dogs aren't trained. As both Amundsen and Scott showed in their 1911–12 expeditions, dog teams can be very effective in Antartica.

Page 35. 'Shackleton was so enthusiastic'. Riffenburgh, p. 199.

Page 38. *'Had we lived'*. RF Scott, *Scott's Last Expedition,* vol 2, Macmillan, 1913, p. 473.

Page 38. *'I realised how lucky I had been'*. Ranulph Fiennes, *Mind Over Matter: The Epic Crossing of the Antarctic Continent*, Trafalgar, 1994, p. 169.

CHAPTER 3

Page 43. *'He radioed Scott Base'*. Geoffrey Lee Martin, *Hellbent for the Pole*, Random House, 2007, p. 112.

Page 46. *'You shall go to the Pole'*. Fiennes, *Captain Scott,* p. 176.

CHAPTER 4

Page 61. *'Presumably before the enraged doctor'*. When, some months later, the *Discovery* arrived in New Zealand and the crew received their mail, Shackleton found that Mr Dorman had consented and then, not long after, had died.

CHAPTER 5

Page 72. *'It doesn't do to dive straight in'*. Scott, *Voyage of the 'Discovery'*, p. 326.

Page 75. *'In the Second World War'*. Sara Wheeler, *Cherry: A Life of Apsley Cherry-Garrard*, Modern Library, 2001, p. 262.

CHAPTER 6

Page 79. *'To get the expedition rolling'*. And for this Beardmore got ownership of the *Nimrod* after the expedition! Riffenburgh, p. 106.

Page 86. *'Amundsen walked into the telegraph office of Eagle'*. Eagle, Canada, was an unusual place from which to receive a telegram from a sea captain — it is on the Yukon River, almost 1000 kilometres away from the coast. Amundsen had sledged down there.

Page 87. *'many of them ladies'*. Charles Morris, *Finding the North Pole: Dr Cook's Own Story of His Discovery*, Kindle edition, location 2043.

Page 87. *'On 6 September 1909 he telegraphed'*. Peary also engaged in this droll exchange with President Taft via telegram:

'To President of the United States. Have the honor place the North Pole at your disposal RE Peary, USN.'

'To Commander Peary. Thank you for your interesting and generous offer, I do not know exactly what I could do with it.' (Robert Silverberg, *Scientists and Scoundrels: A Book of Hoaxes,* Bison Books, 2007; p. 133.)

It is interesting to note that, even if Peary's expedition did make it to the North Pole, the first person there would not have been Peary himself but his African-American employee, Matt Henson, who had been in front scouting the route.

Page 87. *'He said that he would be delighted to'.* Cook's case wasn't helped by the fact that the photograph he claimed was him at the summit of Mount McKinley was now shown to have a remarkably similar backdrop to a much lower and altogether safer point, some 19 miles away. Then Cook's climbing partner, Edward Barrille, signed an affidavit stating that they had never got to the top of McKinley and he was only saying so now because Cook had promised money which hadn't been paid. Cook responded that the poor man was clearly being manipulated and coerced by the dark forces associated with Peary.

Page 88. *'The question used to be what lies about the North Pole, now it is, who lies about it?'* Eventually public opinion turned against Cook and he became considered a fraud — even Amundsen described him as 'one of the greatest humbugs the world had ever seen'. (Roald Amundsen, *The South Pole: An Account of the Norwegian Antarctic Expedition in the 'Fram' 1910–1912,* Kindle edition, location 496.)

Yet he did, and still does, have strong supporters.

Cook eventually became involved in the oil industry. In 1923 his company was charged with making fraudulent claims about the size of their future production. While his confederates received light sentences he was given a very severe fourteen years and nine months in Leavenworth Prison. (Cook's supporters say that the judge was influenced by Peary.) The conman had at last been caught.

Or had he? There was one last twist. The oil wells went on to produce far more oil than Cook had claimed. In 1940, President Roosevelt gave Cook a full pardon. Maybe Cook had been telling the truth the whole time?

Page 90. *'The general kindness and hospitality of New Zealanders'*. Scott, *Voyage of the 'Discovery'*, p. 82.

CHAPTER 7

Page 109. *'Johansen was pulled from the Pole team'*. Amundsen never forgave him. As soon as the *Fram* arrived back in Tasmania, Johansen was dismissed and had to make his own way back to Norway. He never recovered from the disgrace, fell into depression and committed suicide a year later.

CHAPTER 9

Page 124. *'The heel of the advanced foot'*. Scott, *Voyage of the 'Discovery'*, p. 407.

Page 126. *'3.3 nautical miles'*. A nautical mile is conveniently defined as one-sixtieth of a degree of latitude, equivalent to 1.15 miles or 1.85 kilometres. All miles referred to in our trek to the Pole are nautical miles unless otherwise stated.

Page 129. *'the exceptional exercise gives bad attacks of cramp'*. Scott quoted in Cherry-Garrard, p. 369.

Page 135. *'We were flying over the ice as fast'*. Scott, *Voyage of the 'Discovery'*, p. 530.

Page 137. *'I should like to keep the track to the end'*. Scott, *Scott's Last Expedition*, vol 1, p. 458.

CHAPTER 10

Page 142. *'On long cold journeys one's fingers'*. Scott, *Voyage of the 'Discovery'*, p. 324.

Page 143. *'We stuck ten yards from the camp'*. Bowers quoted in

Cherry-Garrard, p. 369.

Page 156. *'Dealing with deviation (magnetic)'*. Strictly speaking, the change in angle of the field depending on where you are is more commonly referred to as declination.

Page 161. *'An occasional glass of wine'*. Roald Amundsen, *The South Pole*, Kindle edition, location 974.

CHAPTER 11

Page 168. *'We are lucky if our foot gets half way'*. Scott, *Voyage of the 'Discovery'*, p. 332.

Page 168. *'The time consumed in all these simple operations'*. Scott, *Voyage of the 'Discovery'*, p. 327.

Page 173. *'Sledging therefore is a sure test'*. Scott, *Voyage of the 'Discovery'*, p. 344.

Page 174. *'Since the mid-1970s, when scientists first started looking, more than twenty-five thousand asteroids have been found'*. Ralph Harvey, 'The Origin and Significance of Antarctic Meteorites', *Chemie der Erde — Geochemistry*, 63, no. 2 (2003): 93–147.

Page 177. *'The march has been arranged to absorb'*. Scott, *Voyage of the 'Discovery'*, p. 342.

Page 178. *'This is a moment to be lived for'*. Scott, *Voyage of the 'Discovery'*, p. 325.

CHAPTER 12

Page 184. *'Our earliest ancestors started using tools . . . the last Ice Age began'*. The one we're still in — as evidenced by the permanent ice caps on Greenland and Antarctica. Geologically speaking, a relatively rare event.

CHAPTER 13

Page 190. *'The Lord only knows how deep'*. Cherry-Garrard, p. 378.

Page 191. *'Little wonder he looked dazed'*. Cherry-Garrard, p. 392.

Page 191. *'We have today experienced'*. Lashly quoted in Cherry-Garrard, p. 399.

Page 192. *'Most of them could be seen by the strip'*. Cherry-Garrard, p. 378.

Page 199. *'Shackleton forced upon me'*. Riffenburgh, p. 257. This was on the *Nimrod* Expedition returning from the Pole.

Page 207. *'The largest recorded iceberg, B15'*. Jeff Rubin, *Lonely Planet: Antarctica*, Lonely Planet, 2005, p. 252.

Page 208. *'At least not most of it'*. Ice *is* expected to melt in the Antarctic Peninsula, particularly the northern part — there just isn't that much of it. If the West Antarctic Ice Sheet was to melt, and according to some scenarios it will, then it could raise the sea level 1.5 metres. The Scientific Committee on Antarctic Research, *Antarctic Climate Change and the Environment*, Victoire Press, 2009.

Page 208. *'What a splendid place for growing spuds!'* Scott, *Voyage of the 'Discovery'*, p. 565.

CHAPTER 14

Page 209. *'We are gradually passing from the hungry'*. Scott, *Voyage of the 'Discovery'*, p. 410.

Page 211. *'Lunch has become almost an insult in its insufficiency'*. Scott, *Voyage of the 'Discovery'*, p. 343.

Page 212. *'One remembers declining a particularly succulent dish'*. Scott, *Voyage of the 'Discovery'*, p. 421.

Page 215. *'More staring, until we are both satisfied'*. When we returned to Hotel Condor del Plata and checked our method with scales, we found that we were accurate to within 3 grams, the weight of a single nut.

Page 220. *'Scott came up to me'*. Cherry-Garrard, p. 377.

Page 221. *'Scott was fairly wound up'*. Cherry-Garrard, p. 378.

Page 223. *'We are struggling, on considering all things'*. Scott, *Scott's Last Expedition*, vol 1, p. 399.

CHAPTER 15

Page 224. *'All we have done is to show the immensity'*. Scott, *Voyage of the 'Discovery'*, p. 548.

Page 226. *'Thin air, low pressure and oxygen deficiency'*. Wilson quoted in Fiennes, *Captain Scott*, p. 323.

Page 226. *'the intense cold reduces the air pressure still further'*. A fuller explanation can be found at http://antarcticsun.usap.gov/pastIssues/2002-2003/2003_02_02.pdf

Page 227. *'Tonight Shackleton upset the hoosh pot'*. Scott, *Voyage of the 'Discovery'*, p. 432.

Page 231. *'untiring energy and the astonishing physique'*. Scott, *Scott's Last Expedition*, vol x, p. 284.

Page 231. *'a man of Herculean strength'*. Scott, *Voyage of the 'Discovery'*, p. 545.

Page 231. *'The next day, the B team — Lieutenant Teddy Evans'*. Confusingly there were two people on the *Terra Nova* Expedition called 'Evans'. Scott's second-in-command, Lieutenant Edward 'Teddy' Evans, and Petty Officer Edgar 'Taff' Evans.

Page 232. *'There was no more need for us'*. Lashly quoted in Cherry-Garrard, p. 394.

Page 232. *'A last note from a hopeful position'*. Scott, *Scott's Last Expedition*, vol 1, p. 412.

CHAPTER 16

Page 244. *'The worst has happened, or nearly the worst'*. Scott, *Scott's Last Expedition*, vol 1, p. 423.

Page 245. *'fairly slithered along before a fresh breeze'*. Bowers quoted in Cherry-Garrard, p. 501.

Page 245. *'There is no doubt Evans is'*. Scott, *Scott's Last Expedition*, vol 1, p. 430.

Page 245. *'Evans has nearly broken down in brain we think'*. Scott, *Scott's Last Expedition*, vol 1, p. 446.

Page 245. *'He has lost his guts'*. Oates quoted in Fiennes, *Captain Scott*, p. 331.

Page 245. *'He was on his knees'*. Scott, *Scott's Last Expedition*, vol 1, p. 446.

Page 246. *'Providence mercifully removed him'*. Scott, *Scott's Last Expedition*, vol 1, p. 462.

Page 246. *'He was the biggest, heaviest and most muscular'*. Cherry-Garrard, p. 516.

Page 247. *'The increase of ration has had'*. Scott, *Scott's Last Expedition*, vol 1, p. 454. They were clearly being affected by the shortage of food.

Page 247. *'Overnight it was as if the Antarctic winter'*. In the Arctic the coldest temperatures are experienced only for a few months around the middle of winter, while in the Antarctic temperatures quickly plunge after the brief summer. That said, March 1911 had unusually cold temperatures, possibly a one-in-thirty-years event. Given that it was these temperatures that led to Oates' and then Scott's frostbitten feet, one of the main causes of their deaths may simply have been that the expedition was very unlucky with the weather. See Susan Solomon, *The Coldest March: Scott's Fatal Antarctic Expedition*, Yale University Press, 2001.

Page 248. *'in a very queer street'*. Scott, *Scott's Last Expedition*, vol 1, p. 457.

Page 248. *'He is wonderfully plucky'*. Scott, *Scott's Last Expedition*, vol 1, p. 457.

Page 250. *'He did not — would not — give up hope'*. Scott, *Scott's Last Expedition*, vol 1, p. 461.

CHAPTER 17

Page 251. *'Our sledge weight was reduced'*. Scott, *Voyage of the 'Discovery'*, p. 664.

Page 255. *'Every day we have been ready to start'*. Scott, *Scott's Last Expedition*, vol 1, p. 464.

Page 257. *'Make the boy interested in natural history'*. Scott, *Scott's Last Expedition*, vol 1, p. 471. Peter Scott went on to win an Olympic medal, skipper an America's Cup Challenge, be decorated for bravery in the war, become one of the founders of the World Wildlife Fund and make dozens of wildlife documentaries, among many other things.

Page 257. *'When they returned to their tent that night'*. This was only a rough estimate as they had left their measuring instruments in the tent. Riffenburgh, p. 231.

Page 258. *'I thought you'd rather have a live donkey'*. Riffenburgh, p. 232.

Page 258. *'Instead he lived to outrageously cheat death'*. At least partly. Shackleton died of heart failure thirteen years later in 1922 on board the *Quest* bound for another expedition to Antarctica. He was only forty-seven.

Page 259. *'Whatever regrets we have done our best'*. Riffenburgh, p. 232.

Page 261. *'It might have made sense for Scott'*. In fairness to Scott, if he had thought that the rocks were holding them up there is no doubt he would have left them behind. It is more likely that Evans and then Oates were the limiting factors. It was only after Oates walked out, on or about 16 March, that the weight may have been an issue. By that point they didn't rate their chances very highly and had started to focus on their legacy.

Page 262. *'the only remaining officer, Edward Atkinson'*. Atkinson was the only remaining *functioning* officer. The second-in-command, Edward Evans, was invalided with scurvy.

Page 263. *'in my own mind I was morally certain'*. Atkinson in Cherry-Garrard, p. 430.

Page 263. *'They may even now be fighting'*. The men on Inexpressible Island astonishingly did survive the winter in a snow cave, and walked back to Hut Point themselves the following spring. See R Priestly, *Antarctic Adventure: Scott's Northern Party* for their story.

Page 263. *'It would be too terrible to find'*. Cherry-Garrard, p. 475.

Page 264. *'Bowers and Wilson were sleeping in their bags'*. Cherry-Garrard, p. 475.

Page 264. *'Captain Scott's face'*. Cherry-Garrard in Fiennes, *Captain Scott*, p. 380.

Page 264. *'It is all too horrible'*, Cherry-Garrard, p. 480.

Page 265. *'I do not know how long we were there'*, Cherry-Garrard, pp. 477, 479.

CHAPTER 18

Page 270. *'My greatest desire now'*. Frank Wild quoted in Riffenburgh, p.258.

CHAPTER 19

Page 271. *'It seemed as if our voyage and all its labours'*. James Clark Ross quoted in Riffenburgh, p. 236.

Page 274. *'The Pole. Yes, but under very different circumstances'*. Scott, *Scott's Last Expedition*, vol 1, p. 424.

Page 278. *'A few days later the Ilyushin'*. In those few days I went to get the first cache that we laid out. The first GPS led me to the wrong spot, so I was pretty excited when the second GPS got it right (see the front cover). I was able to snow-kite back, saving two days of walking. Our second cache, the one off Thiels, was picked up by ALE at the end of the season.

CHAPTER 20

Page 279. *'I have had the world lie beneath'*. Sir Edmund Hillary, *Nothing Venture, Nothing Win*, Hodder & Stoughton, 1975, foreword.

If you enjoyed this book, and would like
to see more content, including videos and
pictures, or leave feedback, please go to
www.EscapeToThe Pole.com